'With lucid precision Jo Case uncovers the hidden identity of a boy and his mother. Like Helen Garner, she has a steady, careful eye, and uses it to bring back news of glorious, rackety life. A work of love and beauty.'
Susan Johnson

'Gutsy and heartfelt, *Boomer & Me* not only relays the rhythms of what it's like to raise a child with Asperger's, but illuminates the fundamental challenges of being any parent. Jo Case has written a wonderful, honest and deeply affecting account of motherhood, with all its contradictions, anxieties and joys intact. A stunning memoir.'
Benjamin Law

'Jo Case doesn't milk, or mine, or plunder her experiences of motherhood; she lays them out with dignity and humour. You trust her. You are with her every step. This book will do a lot of good in the world.'
Maria Tumarkin

'Jo Case's memoir is a deft and graceful piece of story telling, providing a moving insight into what it is to be the mother of a child with Asperger's. But her book is also far more than that. In telling her own story she manages to illuminate the deeper, universal truths that underpin the experience of motherhood. Courageous, compelling and shot through with gentle humour, this is a book that all parents should read.'
Monica Dux

'A moving, informative, and at times downright hilarious memoir about Jo's experiences raising her son.'
Kill Your Darlings

'In this brutally honest account, Case doesn't hold back in revealing her innermost emotions …'
books+publishing

Jo Case is senior writer/editor at The Wheeler Centre in Melbourne. She has been books editor of *The Big Issue*, associate editor of *Kill Your Darlings*, and deputy editor of *Australian Book Review*. Her reviews, essays and opinion pieces have appeared in the *Age*, *Australian*, *Sydney Morning Herald* and *Monthly*, and have been broadcast on ABC Radio National's 'The Book Show' and Triple R's 'Breakfasters'. She has also been published in *The Sleepers Almanac* and *Best Australian Stories*.

BOOMER & ME

BOOMER & ME

JO CASE

hardie grant books
MELBOURNE · LONDON

Published in 2013 by Hardie Grant Books

Hardie Grant Books (Australia)
Ground Floor, Building 1
658 Church Street
Richmond, Victoria 3121
www.hardiegrant.com.au

Hardie Grant Books (UK)
Dudley House, North Suite
34–35 Southampton Street
London WC2E 7HF
www.hardiegrant.co.uk

Cataloguing in publications data available from the National Library of Australia

Boomer & Me: A memoir of motherhood, and Asperger's
ISBN 978 1 7427 0258 2

Illustrations by Oslo Davis
Cover photograph by Tony O'Loughlin
Cover and text design by Peter Daniel
Typesetting by Kirby Jones
Typeset in 9/13pt ITC New Baskerville Std
Printed and bound in Australia by Griffin Press

To my family:

'Leo' and Tony
Mum and Dad
Simon, Nick, Liz and Sarah

CONTENTS

PROLOGUE

My new dog scratches at the back door. Deep claw marks form grooves in the wood, flaking paint onto the back verandah. Similar scratches mark my legs, fine cobwebs of broken skin. She leaps at me when I return from even the shortest of absences, like when I emerge from inside the supermarket while she's tied up on the footpath. She barks when she's left alone: short, sharp blasts that burrow into my skull and pierce my ears. She keens as if my every absence might be the final one. As if she will be alone forever.

I don't like dogs. This one bewilders me, with her assault of belonging and her naked need. I can't believe she is mine.

Leo can't believe it either; he can't believe his luck. He buries his face in her pillowy fur, puts his small arms around her neck, croons into her cottonwool ear. He connects with dogs in a way he doesn't with the kids at kindergarten. With dogs, intimacy is easy. All they want is affection and attention.

I watched Leo with a dog at the playground a few weeks ago; he took it on the slide and the seesaw while I spun out an awkward conversation with its owner. I watched Leo glow as he lavished the dog with love, and wondered if he was lonely. When he saw a dog's picture in the pet-shop window a few days later, its pointed ears cocked beseechingly at the camera, I said yes, we could have it, without really thinking.

Leo has named the dog Snuffy, after the dog I had as a little girl, whom I named after a favourite children's book. My copy is now on Leo's bookshelf, his name written under mine on the inside cover. Now, he reads the book aloud to the dog; she jumps at his shoulders and knocks it to the floor.

'*You've* got a dog?' laughs Mark, Leo's dad, when he comes to pick him up. 'I just can't see it.'

That night, the dog sits beside me on the couch, shedding white hair on the cushions and laying the weight of her head against my leg. I let her climb onto my lap, her claws pricking my legs, as I sit and cry, at everything and nothing. Her pulsing heart and warm body are strangely welcome. This suggests how low I have sunk, how lonely I am. I feel I will be alone forever, though this is obviously not true: Leo will be back in a week. I look at her with bemusement.

'How did you get here?' I say, my voice loud in the semi-dark, even with the sitcom laughter of the television across the room.

I quit my job recently because the fog engulfing my brain made it impossible to work; I was making simple, humiliating mistakes every day. My former boyfriend, the one I thought I would spend my life with—the one Leo still asks for—wants to get back together for the millionth time. I am trying to resist what seems like a step back onto a treadmill of getting together and breaking up. I put my face in the dog's fur, her smelly, sticky fur, and try to concentrate on getting through the next minute, the next ten minutes, through the night.

'Why do you have a dog?' asks the former boyfriend, Tony, when he comes over to talk about how his life is not working. 'You hate dogs.'

Tony loves dogs. He pats Snuffy, digging his fingers into her fur so that her back arches in delight. She twists to lick his hand.

Soon, we will get back together. Tony will go out one day and come back with his own dog, Doug, as wary and snappish as Snuffy is heedless and affectionate.

We will be a family.

PART ONE

1. A GOOD-ENOUGH MUM

I was sick in bed when I got the phone call offering me my dream job. I said all the right things about how happy I was, but when I hung up, I turned into my pillow and sobbed until my eyes and throat were raw. Lying in the daylight gloom of my bedroom, surrounded by sodden tissues and half-empty water glasses, the television flickering mutely at the foot of the bed, I knew I had abandoned my child.

'What is *wrong* with you?' asked Tony, when he got home from uni and saw my ravaged face.

'I got the job.'

'Congratulations!' he said, dropping his satchel and sitting beside me on the bed. 'Isn't that good news?'

'I guess,' I said, and erupted again.

Tony hugged me to his chest and stroked my hair.

'Hey,' he said, 'it's okay.' He sounded as if he wasn't sure at all—of why I was crying or whether everything would, in fact, be okay.

The job, as deputy editor of a literary magazine, had been advertised during our recent honeymoon. It lobbed innocuously into my inbox as we sat on the balcony of my mother-in-law's beach house: me dressed hopefully in my swimsuit, Tony in basketball shorts and a Corona T-shirt. Between bites of Vegemite toast, I'd wondered if I should apply. It seemed a long shot: a big step up from editing a bookshop newsletter.

A yellow-crested cockatoo landed nearby; I stood to crumble a fragment of toast onto the balcony rail. As the bird hopped closer, I decided I would give it a try.

'What have you got to lose?' said Tony.

* * * *

Six months later, I've swapped working from home for travelling to an inner-city office five days a week. Tony takes Leo to his classroom in the mornings while I start work early so I can pick him up from After School Care at 5 pm. The hour between then and starting dinner at six is dedicated to spending time together, usually walking in the park behind our house, climbing trees, swinging on ropes and walking the dogs. One day a week, I finish early so that I can pick up Leo from school and talk to his teacher.

'What's wrong with all that?' asks Mum, when I confide my neglect. 'You can't give up your whole life for your child. I'm sure Leo is fine.'

'Yeah,' I say, holding the phone between my chin and my shoulder so I can use two hands to cut the pumpkin. 'But *we* never went to After School Care. Especially not in Year One.'

'You had a babysitter.'

'That was different. She was our neighbour. We were in our own house. I don't think Leo likes After School Care.'

'Doesn't he get to play with his friends there? Surely he likes that.'

'Sort of.' Leo is friendly with most of the kids in his class, but the closest thing he has to a specific friend is Conor, who doesn't go to After Care; they often play together by doing their own thing in the same space, anyway. 'He just always looks so happy to see me.' I sweep the orange curves of pumpkin into the oven tray.

'Oh, Jo-*anne*,' says Mum. 'You should be glad that he's happy to see you. That won't last forever, you know.'

But I can't shake the feeling that I'm doing things wrong.

Maybe it has something to do with the Communication Book.

* * * *

At home, we have no significant problems with Leo's behaviour. He does what he's told, mostly. He accepts punishments with reasonable grace, even when we're out in public and I make him put his hands on his head and stand still, as a substitute for his standard punishment of being sent to the laundry. When, channelling my schoolteacher parents, I make him write out lines or write letters of apology for bad behaviour, he does it with very little grumbling. (Though when my cousin visited from Adelaide recently and saw me handing out such a punishment, he laughed so hard he had to go inside and sit down.)

The reports from school seem to describe a different child. At the beginning of the year, he would walk out of the classroom to rummage in his schoolbag during lessons or wander in late from lunch breaks— long after the bell had rung. When the class was being spoken to, he would be reading a book under the table or drawing a picture. When they were gathered together on the mat, he'd be restless and inattentive, sometimes facing away from the teacher.

We didn't get those complaints from his Prep teacher last year, when I'd been at the school every day. But then again, she'd often allowed him to do his own thing. He'd arrived at school knowing how to read chapter books; she encouraged his individualism as a quirk of his intelligence.

One day, waiting for my weekly shift as classroom helper to start, I'd been embarrassed to see Leo turning the pages of a Horrid Henry novel as the rest of the class pointed to letters of the alphabet and chanted 'A, A, A ... B, B, B ...' I hissed at him ineffectually to *put that book down!* His teacher paused in her chanting to wave me off. 'It's okay!' she called. 'He's allowed to do that.'

Later, she showed me the magazines and workbook she'd placed in a cardboard box on his desk, for when Leo finished his work early, or when he was far beyond it, as in the case of the alphabet chanting. Then she told me what every middle-class parent secretly longs to hear. 'I think he's gifted,' she said. 'I'd like to have him tested. Is that alright with you?' It was fine with me and Mark, though the deputy principal told us he was too young for that sort of thing. She told us we should be focusing on his behaviour instead.

This year, Mark and I have been consulting with his teacher every week. We reinforce the rules of school with corresponding punishments at home; it's slowly working. A daily Communication Book travels in his schoolbag, between school and both his homes. Leo hates it. It makes him feel different from the other kids.

* * * *

'Can you make birthday cupcakes for my class?' asks Leo.

We are eating fish and chips from a paper parcel on the coffee table, dipping deep-fried fragments into a puddle of sauce ringed in grease. Leo, Tony and I are wearing striped flannelette pyjama pants, though Leo is the only one in a matching shirt.

'Absolutely,' I say, feeling smug about being the kind of mother who does such a thing. Here is my chance to make up for the time in After Care, the Communication Book, the breakfasts he eats without me. Here is a chance to prove that I have not, in fact, chosen my job over my child. Maybe I can do it all?

Leo will be at Mark's house on the morning of his birthday. I call to ask Mark if he'll pick up the cakes and deliver them to school.

'Of course,' he says. 'Leo told me he was going to ask you to do that.'

'That's what mums do, isn't it?' I say.

'Well, he's very excited.'

Leo is in bed, reading by the light of his bedside lamp. I am picking at the cold chips, watching a re-run of *The Fresh Prince of Bel Air*. There are four episodes in a row tonight. Every time Will Smith starts singing the theme tune, Tony and I look at each other and join in. We both grew up watching this after school, with our brothers and sisters.

'CAN YOU TWO SHUT UP?' calls Leo from his room. 'I'm trying to get to sleep.'

'Don't say *shut up*!' says Tony. The next time the theme tune starts, we whisper it.

* * * *

I spend much of the day groaning about having to bake cakes this evening, shouting over the cubicle that divides my small office from our business manager. She is an impeccable homemaker who cooks dinner for her husband and son every night, and makes them breakfast and a packed lunch every morning. She kindly empathises about the enormous cake-baking task ahead of me.

After dinner, I realise I should've shopped for ingredients when Leo first asked me to make the cakes—or even during my lunch break, instead of humble-bragging. Tony takes my hastily scrawled shopping list to the supermarket while I settle on the couch under a blanket.

By the time I notice the gaps in my list, it's too late to do anything about it. Tony has changed into his pyjamas and it's too dark to walk or ride through the park back to the supermarket.

The biggest problem is the near-empty sugar container. Last weekend, Leo shook it over his head like a lone maraca and the lid fell off, spilling sugar over his head and shoulders like a nasty case of dandruff. I remember laughing uncontrollably at the sight, but somehow *not* taking this as a sign that I needed to restock the sugar.

'Why don't you use icing sugar as a substitute?' suggests Tony.

The last time I followed advice like this was Leo's fourth birthday, when I made the chocolate cake on the morning of the party. We'd run out of cocoa and my then-flatmate Jason, a chef, suggested I use chocolate essence instead. I thought it sounded weird, but because he was a chef, I trusted him. When the cake came out of the oven, it was as sunk as the *Titanic*.

'Fill the hole with icing,' Jason suggested, in the same confident tone he'd used to suggest the chocolate essence. I tried, but it still looked like a car had run over it. I'd ended up running past the arriving party guests to the Greek bakery down the road, returning with an immaculate layered sponge cake.

There is no such option tonight.

'Why don't you use one of the packet mixes in the cupboard?' asks Tony. It's not the first time he's suggested this. I'm not a great cook, but I can bake, if I have the proper ingredients.

'No,' I say. 'You can't use a packet mix for *birthday* cakes.'

Tony picks up a frilled patty pan and turns it sceptically. It is unfortunately large: the size of a muffin rather than a dainty cupcake. This is the other problem.

'Aren't these a bit big?' he says.

'*You* bought them.'

'Well, you didn't tell me what size to buy!'

'I didn't realise they came in sizes.'

'Maybe you should call your mum,' he says. 'Ask her how to make the cakes fluffier.'

It's not uncommon for me to call Mum for advice when I'm cooking— even for questions like, *How long should you hardboil an egg?*—but I glare at him. He explains that, maybe, if I can make the cakes *extra fluffy*, they'll rise higher and fill the enormous patty pans.

'Get out,' I say. 'Please.'

Once he's settled in front of the television, I beat the batter extra hard, just in case. Then I add a pinch of icing sugar.

Half an hour later, I carry a plate of cakes, iced in the colours of Leo's favourite football team, into the lounge room. They have only risen to the halfway line of the patty pans, but I'm hoping the icing will distract from their stunted growth.

'Ta-da!' I say, standing in front of the television.

Tony looks at the plate in silence. He frowns. He is working up to something.

'They're a bit small,' he says at last. 'Maybe you could take them out of the patty pans?'

'I can't. They're important.' I'm now dismissing Tony's suggestions out of principle.

'Oh. Okay.'

'Do they look like West Coast Eagles cakes?' I ask.

'Not really.'

I look at them sadly. I don't really know what shade of blue and yellow the West Coast colours are, but if I had to hazard a guess, I suppose the blue wouldn't be a pastel sea-green.

'Can't you make the blue a bit darker?'

'No. I can't. If it's darker … it won't taste any good.'

'Really?' Not really, but I can't fix it now. It's nearly midnight.

'Yes. We will tell him that these are West Coast colours and he'll believe it. And he'll love them, I'm sure.'

'Sure,' says Tony, angling his head to see behind me to the television screen. 'They'll be fine.'

I don't believe him, but I photograph the cakes anyway.

I've been researching blogs at work recently, preparing to create one for the magazine. I started off reading literary blogs, but soon found myself taking a side journey into blogs by people who write passionately about books, but also about their lives. Snooping into these strangers' worlds, their conversations and their networks via the blog comments,

I'm building up a database of contacts for promoting the magazine. But it's more than that.

On one blog, I'm quickly absorbed in the minutiae of life in Alice Springs, as experienced by a scriptwriter who makes her living as a creative writing teacher. On another blog in the same circle, an Adelaide writer and mother of two shares snatches of life with young children, in a voice so funny and poignant that I soon find myself following it like a novel.

I want to do this, too. To join in the conversations that bounce between blogs—on writing and motherhood, sexist ads, freelance writing. It's like happening on a really good party and longing to crash it. Most of all, I'm excited to find other mums who confess to not enjoying schoolyard socialising, who talk about books and have children whose eccentricities they relish. I don't meet people like this in real life.

And, secretly, I want to craft my experiences into stories, like I did when I was creating stapled-together picture books as a kid, or when I was writing comic books with my friends about our high school crushes. Like the exercise books where I wrote unfinished novels about a fantasy version of myself. Or the stories I write and illustrate with Leo, on scrap paper, about the two of us.

My own anonymous blog has been sitting there, prettily empty, for the past fortnight, daring me to begin it. I upload my photographs of the imperfect cakes. Then I write about my night, under the title 'Supermum goes awry'. When I read it back, I'm pleasantly surprised. It's not awful. I email it to Mum and my sisters.

Then I finally go to bed.

It is 1 am. I have five hours of sleep ahead of me. But I'm feeling calmer than I have all night.

* * * *

I'm at work when Mark picks up the cupcakes. He rings me from the driveway so Leo can deliver his feedback.

'Happy birthday darling!' I say. 'Have you had a good day so far?'

Leo tells me about his presents and his pancake breakfast. I try to ignore the chasm in my chest, despite six and a half years now of sharing birthdays, Christmas, Easter with his dad.

'The West Coast cakes are awesome, Mum!' he says. 'So cool! All the kids will love them. Even the ones who don't go for the Eagles.'

I laugh. 'Did Tony tell you they were West Coast?'

'Yeah,' he says. 'But I would have known anyway.'

2. (NOT) MOVING HOUSE

'Can I help?' asks Leo.

'With what?'

'Looking for a house,' he says. 'I can help you find something the *whole family* will enjoy!'

Unfortunately, this family has different ideas about what we want right now.

I'm longing for a house near a train station, a short walk to somewhere I can get a decent coffee. Tony wants to move back to the inner-northern suburbs where we used to live (where our friends still live). Leo wants to stay near the park two houses away.

And of course, there's the matter of our dogs. We need a landlord who'll allow two excitable terriers. Even in an easy rental market, it would be a tall order. But most of the open inspections we visit attract crowds of hopefuls. Some renters are even bidding for houses, especially in the inner-north.

Leo sits on my lap and we browse the offerings on Domain.com together. I sigh as he points to a 'large family home backing Cruikshank Park', a couple of streets away from where we sit. I chose this place because I'd grown up living across the road from a park very like this one: a reclaimed patch of tamed scrub with bike paths, grass kept low by the council, and a creek bordered with eucalypts and the occasional weeping willow. For the past two years, we've done the things I remember from childhood: climbed the trees, jumped the creek on our way to school or slid down cement drains.

At our last house, a suburb away, we lived just off the main shopping strip, within a short walk of two train stations. We were less than five minutes from a supermarket, three kinds of take-away and three cafes. Leo and I moved there together on our own; Tony moved in with us later.

Here, it's a twenty-minute walk to the nearest train station and I don't drive. The bus that stops outside our house is erratic and only runs one way. The buses are old and so are the drivers, who are known for stopping so abruptly that passengers standing for their stop fall backwards onto their seats. Once, a driver mounted the kerb and clipped a gum tree, snapping off a lower branch. Too often, I can't be bothered going out and sit brooding instead. Tony had warned me this might happen, but I was entranced by the creek and refused to listen.

There's an inspection late this afternoon; a house near the shops and train station. Leo and I arrive on my bike, which I chain to a tree as a woman steps out of her car to greet the real estate agent. She has a blonde ponytail and wears a powder-blue tracksuit: casual but polished. I imagine her as a doctor or lawyer, or perhaps married to one. I'm wearing tracksuit pants too, but mine are matched with a fur-lined parka and pink Converse sneakers. Leo's face is painted in the West Coast Eagles colours: warrior stripes of blue and yellow mark his cheeks. When I left the house, I didn't see these things as a problem. Now, I remember wearing suits to impress real estate agents when I was a teenager.

We trail the blonde woman and the real estate agent through the house and into the small backyard. There are polished boards and muted brown carpets. The kitchen and bathroom are clean and modern. A park with a playground and a vast carpet of clipped green lawn perfect for kicking a ball, or running, is across the road. It's not a canvas for the imagination in the way that Cruikshank Park is, but it's a good place to play. Leo sings to himself as he wanders through the rooms and down the hallway. At the front door, the real estate agent asks the blonde woman if she wants two application forms. He hands me one. From behind a forced smile, I tell him I'll need two; that my husband is at work.

Across the road, in the park, I sit on a bench while Leo climbs a metal grid and makes his way across a rope bridge.

'Look at me!' he calls.

Leo and I agree: we like this house.

Two days later, the real estate agent calls me at work to offer us the property. But when I ring Tony to share the good news, he has decided we can't afford the extra sixty dollars a week in rent.

He doesn't want to be paying extra money while he's on student exchange in Mexico next year. On the other hand, I don't want to be living here, with no transport, during the six months when he's away. Tony wouldn't mind paying the extra money if we were living somewhere like Brunswick, his ideal suburb, but resents paying money he can't afford for a place he doesn't want to live in. I don't want Leo to have to move schools. Tony thinks a change of schools wouldn't be so bad, seeing as how Leo doesn't have many friends at his current school. I don't want to take him away from the friends he does have. And if he changes schools, Leo's dad will argue that he should go to school near him.

We talk in circles for hours.

I want Leo to go to school in my neighbourhood.

I want to move house as soon as I can.

I want to live near public transport.

I want Leo to be as happy and as little disrupted as possible.

I want to agree with my husband.

I want to work from home again.

I want more time with my son.

I want to go to Mexico too.

I call the real estate agent back and tell him we can't take the house after all.

The next night, we stay up late talking about where to live, arguing the options. Eventually, we agree on a compromise: that we'll move north, but on the promise that we get a backyard for Leo—with room for his swing-set—and a study of sorts for me.

On the way to bed, Tony makes an internet pit stop. He's excited, but even with the extra rent we're prepared to pay, it seems impossible to get a place with a backyard bigger than a courtyard, or a room that could serve as a study.

Instead of following Tony to bed, I stay on the couch. Wrapped in a blanket, I sob quietly into the cushions, feeling alternately sorry for myself and aware that I have had worse problems in my life.

I wake with a stiff neck and cramped legs. The heater glows artificially red; it's been left on all night. Under my blanket, yesterday's clothes are damp on my skin. Sweat pools at the nape of my neck, my hair is sticky with it. I can't stop yawning as I limp to the shower.

Tony laughs when he comes into the bedroom to find me sprawled across the quilt, wrapped in a towel, doing nothing. Staring at the ceiling, listening to Leo move around the kitchen. I'm focusing on my breathing. He kisses me lightly on the forehead, envelops me in a hug, then drops to lie beside me on the bed. I turn to face him.

'So, what are we going to do?' he says.

We decide to stay where we are.

I drag myself out of bed just before eight-thirty. Normally I sleep in on weekends, making up for the 6 am starts I've never got used to, but today is Leo's official birthday party. It's Mark's year to host it. He's chosen a local YMCA as the venue for a dress-up party with gymnastics activities. I'm doing the birthday cake, cupcakes, chocolate-chip cookies and assembling fourteen lolly bags, with variations for girls and boys. Girls get pink and purple glitter pens with feathered plumes. Boys get superhero pens: Batman or Superman.

I wash a week's worth of saucepans, sharp knives, colanders and microwave dishes, stacking them in a precarious tower on a drying rack probably designed to hold a night's worth of dishes. I wipe the table, pretending not to notice the crumbs that fall to the linoleum floor below. After I collect an armful of clothes from the overflowing basket in Leo's room and stuff them in the washing machine, I distribute the piles of roughly folded clean clothes stacked on the couch to their rightful bedroom drawers and wardrobes.

'Hey,' I say as I drop Tony's T-shirts on his dresser. He grunts and buries his face deeper into his pillow. I have a shower. When I come out, Tony's head is no longer visible above the quilt. 'I'm going to Coles now,' I say, apparently to myself, as I pull a jumper over my head. 'Uh,' comes the reply.

As I move towards the front door, trying not to look at the piles of books and papers and discarded jumpers that still litter the house, a moan emits from the bedroom. 'Are you going to help me?' He is half joking, half letting me know, in coded terms, that he feels rotten.

'WHAT?' I yell. 'Me help *you*? I'm going to Coles for cooking supplies or I'll be behind. And I'm about to go by myself, on my bike.'

'I'm sick,' comes the voice again, quieter and less guttural. I shut the door behind me.

Tony is sick. Not this morning, not this week. He is sick in that other way. Not a cold or a flu that engulfs you and then disappears, leaving you to ease back into your everyday life. Tony has Crohn's, a digestive problem of the intestines that requires him to take the quantities of daily medication you might expect of a cancer patient. The medication—steroids—affects his moods, just as his Crohn's drains his energy levels. It thins the hair on his head and makes the hair on his arms grow thick. It leaves him with a diet of meals that leave me tired and hungry when they synch with mine (dinner, mostly), but must do so times-ten for him. He doesn't have the escape clause of carbohydrate-heavy breakfast, lunch and snacks that I do. He can't eat bread or pasta, he can't eat sugar, he can't eat tomatoes, he can't eat potatoes. This is just the beginning of a long list.

It can be hard to remember to be sympathetic when the person you live with is sick in that ongoing, fairly unchanging way. Sometimes there are stomach cramps frightening in their intensity. Sometimes he is too drained of energy to fulfil social commitments. Occasionally he needs a slab of days off work. But most of the time, it is a variation on the same undercurrent of feeling worse than he should, worse than other people do. It can be hard to remind yourself that a person might be staying in bed while you clean the house and prepare for a party because they are sick. Because, you see—then again, they might *not* be. Or so you tell yourself.

I try, but I am not a patient person. I am not good with illness. I often cook two meals at night—for instance, one version of spaghetti bolognaise with tomato sauce and pasta; one with mince meat and rice pasta. But afterwards I eat a bowl of ice-cream, perhaps pick at half a block of chocolate, while Tony sits beside me eating another bowl of rice porridge, or a kiwifruit. I adapt, but only so much. Tony has a friend with similar health problems; her husband has changed his diet to match hers—'out of solidarity,' Tony tells me. 'It makes everything— shopping, cooking, self-discipline—a lot easier.' Their diet is especially extreme: they can only eat raw foods. I know I should do the same, but I just can't. I don't want to.

When I broke up with Leo's dad, when Leo was nine months old, it was not long after Mark had been hospitalised with a punctured lung. There were other things at play, but I know that it didn't help. I was not equipped to look after a new baby *and* a grown man. I was not prepared to make sure he had clean underwear.

I'm not a good sick person either.

My first months of my job at the magazine were fantastic. I felt guilty about losing time with Leo, but being able to start early and pick him up at five each afternoon meant I wasn't losing much more than an hour each day. On weeks I didn't have Leo, I worked late. I decided to overhaul the magazine's website and taught myself web software from a textbook. I created marketing materials to lure new advertisers. I organised a regular spot with a local public radio station. I felt like I was achieving things.

But then I got sick; a lingering complication from a childhood surgery that resurfaces every five years or so. I stayed home for a few days, then a week, then longer. I came back to work because it didn't seem like I was getting better and I couldn't stay home forever. I couldn't ride to the train station anymore, so I caught buses instead, adding to my travel time. I was leaving home in the dark; as I crossed the park to the bus-stop on the other side, I could see my breath crystallise, glowing in the light of the street lamps. By the time I got better, six weeks later, the magic of the job was over. Leo was getting into trouble at school more often; it was hard to find the opportunity to talk to his teacher about it.

When everything is going right, combining full-time work and a young child seems doable. But when things go wrong, the system collapses.

* * * *

When I return from the supermarket, Tony is up and dressed, his hair shower-damp. He hunches over a bowl of rice porridge at the kitchen table, reading *The Age* on his laptop between mouthfuls.

'How are you?' I ask. He shrugs. I pat his shoulder—a gesture he hates, but I do instinctively—and busy myself emptying the shopping bag.

We agree that this batch of cupcakes is much better than the one Leo took to class. The cakes are golden-brown on top, spring back when prodded with a finger and rise a respectable few centimetres above the patty pan. I've decided to decorate them with superhero type slogans—'SPY' and 'CODE'—but realise I don't have, and have never owned, an icing piper. I send Tony to get one, along with cocoa for the chocolate cake.

'Shall I get a packet mix for chocolate cake, too?' he asks.

I frown at him. 'My *grandmother* gave me this recipe,' I say. 'I told Mum I wished I had the recipe from her old Women's Weekly cookbook for Leo's birthday cake and Nana copied it out for me, *by hand*, then sent it to me in the mail.'

'Then you should definitely use it,' agrees Tony. 'Of course.'

'Thank you.'

'But should I get you a packet mix as backup? Just in case?'

'Okay.'

It's odd, but I feel like a proper mother when I bake, which isn't often. Or when I cook a meal that consists of more than a combination of sausages and vegetables, or fish and vegetables. I think it's because I have fond memories of coming home to my mother's baked goods when I was young. Being one of five children, in a family where often one of my parents wasn't working (due to either pregnancy or illness), sanctioned after-school snacks were usually piles of Vegemite toast. For a few days after the fortnightly Thursday night shopping trip to Bi-Lo, it might be muesli bars or small packets of chips. So the smell of biscuits or a microwave cake (which we thought miraculous and exotic) was exciting. I've never forgotten coming home from school one day to find warm banana bread on the kitchen counter *and* chocolate-chip biscuits in the oven—and feeling luxuriously happy and cared for.

Tony can't find an icing piper, but he comes back with tubes of coloured gel—red, yellow and electric blue—for cake-decorating. The packet of cake mix goes straight into the cupboard and stays there.

At the Footscray YMCA, we need to make two trips from the car with all the food. We take the cupcakes and chocolate cake first. Leo spots me from the doorway of the gymnasium. He is wearing his navy school trackpants, a smudge of dirt at one knee, with a striped Bart Simpson T-shirt and a leather jacket that is a miniature version of the one Mark is wearing. He comes running across the carpark at full speed, stopping just short of knocking me and my cakes flying across the bitumen. The large cake is unremarkable: a symmetrical iced chocolate circle. Some of the cupcakes are jewelled with sprinkles and lollies, others iced with words.

'WOW!' says Leo. 'Cool cakes Mum! Can I have one now?'

Smug with success, I slip one out from under its cling-wrap cover and surreptitiously hand it to him while Mark and his wife Rachel cross the carpark to catch up to us.

'What are you dressed up as Leo?' I ask. He answers through a mouthful of cake, crumbs spraying down his chin.

'Oh, I'm a rock star.'

'Hmmmm.'

'Do you like his jacket?' asks Mark, kissing me hello on the cheek. 'Pretty cool, isn't he?'

'Hmmm,' I say. 'Yes.'

The staff at the gym run activities for the kids, leaving the adults with nothing to do. Tony, Mark, Rachel and I sit in the room with the long table set up for birthday lunch. I pour lemonade into a clear plastic cup and hand the bottle to Rachel. She is telling us about the renovations they've been doing on the cottage they recently bought in South Melbourne.

'It's hard work, but it's so rewarding when you finish,' she says. 'Your house is transformed and you look at it and think: *I did that.*'

'I know what you mean,' I say. 'I feel the same way when I do the housework.'

Rachel gives me a disgusted look.

'You know,' I continue, 'I really don't want to do it, and I'm tired, but if I get off my arse and do the work, I feel so much better. I look at the end result and I feel satisfied.'

'Oh yes.'

'It's a similar feeling, really.'

Tony changes the subject.

I follow Mark out to the hallway where he stands behind a glass wall, watching the kids. The floor is painted with the coloured lines of a basketball court. Ropes hang from the ceiling. Small trampolines are scattered around the room. Royal-blue gym mats, the kind I remember from high school PE classes, are spread in careful rectangles in all the areas where the kids are expected to crash, or are likely to fall. The hall echoes with squeals and shouts. Leo is running beside the rest, whooping with joy, following a circuit from rope to trampoline and back again.

'Look at our boy,' says Mark, putting an arm around my shoulder. He gives a satisfied sigh.

'I know.' While I share his wistful admiration, I can't help but notice that Leo is with the crowd, but not quite of it.

The kids gather to pile their plastic plates with sausage rolls and cupcakes, to drink brightly coloured fizzy drinks. They shout a lot, especially the boys. At one point, before 'Happy Birthday' is sung, the boys spontaneously start to scream, just for the joy of hearing their voices fill the room. They jam their hands over their ears and stretch their mouths wide. The few girls in attendance look on in mature bewilderment from across the table. We parents watch, laughing, letting the boys go on until it becomes clear that they need us to stop them. The mania doesn't entirely ebb; their eyes remain bright with the rush of it. Leo is one of the last to stop.

The kids are mostly drawn from Leo's class: insecure Seth, the friend he's made this year; tiny red-haired Mia, the only other one from his kindergarten to go to this school; boisterous Mitchell and athletic Jack. Leo hasn't been invited to any birthday parties this year. It's September.

Conor was in his class last year; he's been his most consistent friend. Leo went to his birthday party last December. They're occasionally, if not often, at each other's houses after school. His mother, Lucy, will usually offer me a coffee, tea, or even a glass of wine when I pick up Leo. Her house is routinely messy—dishes scattered on the counter and by the sink, discarded jumpers balled up on the couch, newsletters and half-opened mail fanned across the coffee table. I feel easy about inviting her into my house, which is similarly dishevelled, though I'm less confident about exactly what to do once she comes in. I know I should offer coffee, tea and food, but I don't drink tea and have often run out of milk. Our biscuit supply is uneven. And how long should we sit and make conversation? Lucy is the only person I have these interactions with; I have no other friends with kids except Linda, a former work colleague who's now moved to the country. And with Linda it's different: we were friends before our kids were.

I know that Leo suffers from my inability to befriend other mums. He rarely has play-dates (which surely lead to party invitations). At his age, play-dates are extensions of the mothers' friendships: afternoon coffees and weekend film outings. I'm about ten years younger than the other mums; I don't own a house and I can't feign an interest in choosing kitchen tiles or negotiating with tradesmen. I have no recipes to swap and no interest in gourmet ingredients. I know nothing about traffic problems, given that I don't drive a car. I'm not a proper grown-up.

I met Lucy in the school playground, before our boys started school, on the day we took them in to buy their school uniforms.

Leo wanted to try out the playground behind the transportable classrooms. I stood and watched as he swung his way along the red-painted rungs of the monkey bars, shouting a monologue on his mastery of monkey-bar tricks.

'Look, Mum, LOOK! I skipped THREE BARS!'

At the other end of the playground, a small blond boy picked his careful way up the boxy climbing frame, his gaze focused on his summit. His hair curled at his neck. A woman in a loose shirt and jeans watched his progress and called encouragement. We stood like that for a while, two mother-and-child pairings, alone together in the quiet of the near-empty school grounds. Our eyes collided across the tanbark, then skimmed away. She was the first to break the awkwardness, calling out a greeting, then coming to stand beside me. She introduced herself and her son. The boys continued their separate, absorbed play as we talked—each of them occasionally interrupting our conversation to call attention to what he was doing. ('Mum! Look at me!') We discovered that we had both separated from our children's fathers and shared custody; we bonded over feeling like outsiders as a result.

Lucy's not an outsider though, not really. She has been a member of the same mothers' group since Conor was born; they still meet regularly and their kids are all friends. And she talks to the other mums in the schoolyard with an ease I could never imitate, let alone feel. She remembers their kids' names, their husbands, the details of their house renovations. Her conversations go somewhere, they flow. I never know what to say.

* * * *

We stop to get Vietnamese take-away on the way home from the party, after kissing Leo goodbye in the carpark. I wait in the front seat, too tired to move, watching the treeless streets and peeling shopfronts of Footscray. Snot thickens in my nose, my ears throb. The cold that began as a persistent sniff last night is threatening to take me over.

'Did you see Rachel's reaction when she was talking about renovations and I compared it to cleaning the house?' I laugh, as Tony slides into the front seat beside me. He passes me the plastic bag, fragrant with chicken vermicelli. The damp warmth soaks into my jeans.

'Yeah. I was so embarrassed,' he says.

'What?'

'I couldn't believe you said that. Renovating and cleaning aren't the same thing at all.'

'Yes they are, kind of. I mean, they're both about doing work you don't want to do to make your house look better.'

'Renovations are a big project. Cleaning is just what you're *supposed* to do.'

I look out the window and think about lying on the couch for the rest of the afternoon. All I will do is eat and watch television.

3. SUBURBAN REVOLUTIONARIES

We wake to the shrill of the phone. It's Vanessa, calling to announce that she'll be arriving early. She's decided to make a banner, and she needs my help.

Last night, after more drinks than usual, I'd already begun to regret my decision to go with Vanessa to the G20 protest. It's the end of a long working week and the last thing I want is to leave the house and walk around the city—for any reason. Let alone spend the morning knitting together a tentative new friendship. But I've made the commitment, and there's no turning back without seeming rude, not to mention shallow.

Besides, as I'd told my childless friends Nikki and Kabita last night, an invitation to an anti-globalisation protest is a novelty in the schoolyard. And, as I *didn't* tell my friends, Vanessa seems oblivious to the fact that I somehow don't fit in there. Unlike most other mothers, who make conversation about the weather and the teacher but never cross the line into intimacy, she doesn't seem to mind that I'm so much younger than them, that I share custody of my son with his father, that I don't own a house or belong to a playgroup. When, a few weeks ago, I tentatively approached her on the bitumen beside the school's community garden as our sons giggled and whispered to each other, she accepted my invitation for Angus to come and play at our house—

and what's more, she returned the invitation a week later. The few other times I've approached mothers to extend a play-date invitation, they've come up with reasons why it won't work, *not today*. Only Conor and Seth (whose down-to-earth dad picks him up) have been over to play, or had Leo over.

When I arrived to pick up Leo, Vanessa invited me into the hallway, sat me on the couch in her gleaming display-home family room, and confided her issues with her mother and her passion for the writings of George Monbiot as she filled two latte glasses at her bench-top espresso machine.

At last, I'd thought as I left the house an hour later, having accepted the invitation to today's protest, *I think I've found a friend with kids!* Conveniently forgetting that I do have two whole friends with kids: Lucy and Linda. But Lucy is from the world of the schoolyard, while Linda is from the world of work, of books. Vanessa seems like she might be a border-crosser.

When Vanessa rings the doorbell, I'm standing barefoot on the bathroom tiles, shrugging my hips into jeans. Remnants of last night's mascara is—I will later discover—smudged from my eyelashes in a charcoal bruise halfway down my cheek. Vanessa is dressed for the protest in T-shirt, jeans and sneakers, sensibly armed with a backpack and water bottle, her medium-brown hair scraped back in a no-fuss ponytail. She edges uncomfortably through the doorway, three rolls of packing tape under one arm, two enormous slabs of white card under the other. After the obligatory exchange of cheek-pecks, I lead her down the hallway, wrestling the placards—almost as tall as I am—out the back door and onto the back deck, where I perch on the arm of our outdoor couch and continue the work of waking up.

After telling me how the nice lady at Mitre Ten had given her these discarded cardboard advertisements for free and confirmed they were just right for a protest banner, Vanessa springs into action. Do I have scissors? String? A lead pencil? I obediently fetch the requisite tools, then shuffle back to my position on the couch, angling my damp hair towards the sun. I've been to protests before, but never prepared to this level. I think I'd kind of shambolically grabbed supplies for the day (water, camera, purse—and if with Leo, books and food for him) and lurched out the door.

'What do you think we should write?' asks Vanessa, her sneakers flexed beneath her as if for take-off, knees bent purposefully forward.

'I don't know,' I say dumbly, wishing we could forgo the banner in favour of breakfast along the way. Perhaps at a cafe in the city. Degraves? Poached eggs on toast, a latte …

Vanessa has a few ideas, she says. Her first one seems fine: *Free Trade Makes Third World into Fourth World*. I don't have anything better in mind. In fact, I'm still preoccupied with food fantasies, interspersed with pondering whether I said anything stupid over last night's drinks. And whether—as I watch across the straggled lawn through the shield of my sunglasses—my husband is planning to strip our lemon tree in its entirety. He's on his way to visit the anti-whaling activists from Sea Shepherd, with his best friend Carlo and his wife Jane. He is systematically filling large green shopping bags with donations for the cause.

Vanessa traces out her slogan in careful block letters on the cardboard, having first wiped it clean and dried it in the sun for five minutes, the end signalled by her wristwatch alarm.

'I don't mean to be rude,' she says. 'But do you think you could help?'

'Oh. Sure.' I join her kneeling on the deck. We chat idly about school as we form letters using strips of packing tape. I begin to enjoy myself. It's a bit like school art class, or playing 'making things' with Leo, who's at his dad's this weekend. I wish he were coming with us—he'd be having a wonderful time right now.

'Don't you think,' says Vanessa, leaning back on her heels and frowning critically at my handiwork, 'that you should be using *three* strips of tape for each stroke of the letters?'

I meekly add extra strips to my undernourished half of the sign.

Tony brushes my cheek goodbye as he leaves for Port Melbourne with his three bags of lemons. The tree seems unmarked by the raid, its branches still heavy with the remaining fruit. Vanessa glances at her watch. 'Shit,' she says. 'We'd better hurry.'

As we drive through Footscray, ABC radio commentators talk about the crowd gathering in front of the State Library. It's 12.10 pm. We're running late, but we have a beautifully executed banner in the back seat.

'I'm sorry,' says Vanessa. 'I got up early but I just got sidetracked. I should have been at your house earlier.'

'That's fine.' I don't mention that I wouldn't have been up—or have answered the phone—earlier.

We park in North Melbourne and take the tram to the city. Passengers struggle to manoeuvre past our banner, folded in half where the tape joins the two placards. We step off at Bourke Street Mall and Vanessa prepares to unfurl her work.

'Let's wait until we get there,' I say quickly, self-conscious in the crowd of shoppers milling in the sunshine. We pass the queue in front of the Myer Christmas windows: children in strollers, families with fistfuls of shopping bags.

'We should open the banner now,' says Vanessa. 'We've got a captive crowd!'

'Let's not,' I say. 'We'll get in people's way.'

We talk about the idea of bringing the kids as we turn into the river of people on Swanston Street.

'Miles was shocked when I told him I wanted to bring Angus,' she says. 'I told him what you told me—that you took Leo to the S11 protests in his stroller and he was fine.'

'What did he say?'

'Oh …' she pauses, a reel of expressions flickering in her eyes. 'Nothing.'

I read stern words, or at least thoughts, about me being an irresponsible mother.

Leo had passed a blissful day back then, when S11 meant a globalisation conference, not the demolition of the World Trade Center in New York. I recall him cradled in the lining of an open parka, laid over the tiles of a Southbank cafe, inhaling milk from a bottle as friends and I ate lunch. A friend of his dad's—a journalist—holding Leo before a blank-faced police line, both of them smiling for the camera. He'd been passed around for hugs and photo opportunities, entertained by parades of shouting clowns, tulle-skirted hippies and amped-up bongo drummers.

When we get to the State Library, the crowd is underwhelming. Less than the five thousand estimated on the radio this morning, which Vanessa and I had scoffed at as inadequate on the way here.

'Oh,' she says, standing deflated behind her banner. 'I thought there'd be about ten thousand.'

'Yeah.' A wave of exhaustion crashes over me. Light-headed, I glance hungrily across the road at Melbourne Central shopping centre, where there's a food court. Vanessa unzips a lunchbox from her backpack and offers a shortbread biscuit—a practice run, she says, for baking with the kids at school next week. Accepting with more enthusiasm than I've mustered all morning, I wonder where all her energy comes from.

Vanessa talks animatedly, between shortbread bites, about George Monbiot's *The Age of Consent* and the notion that third-world nations should withdraw from dealing with first-world governments; have their own treaties. *If only more stay-at-home mums spent their free time reading Monbiot and forming theories about global justice*, I think admiringly. After all, it's the middle-class, home-owning, interest-rate-fearing mums and dads who drive politicians' actions.

I see myself as socially aware, politically informed. But somewhere along the way, thinking about jobs and overseas trips—and before that, impending marriage—I've lost touch. I skim the right newspapers and websites, watch *Four Corners* while I eat my post-dinner chocolate ice-cream, and occasionally fall asleep with *Lateline* on the television at the end of the bed. But I haven't been engaging with the ideas I find—rather, I observe them as part of the rolling backdrop to daily life, like the weather reports.

The last protests I attended were against the 2003 war in Iraq, as we were poised on the brink of invasion. I read books on the situation and interviewed the authors. I organised political events at the bookshop I worked at. On the night of one major anti-war protest, I was among a crowd in our basement bookshop as protestors marched and chanted overhead. My colleagues and I took time off to march in another protest, joining it as it passed the shop, marching under a lovingly prepared banner emblazoned with our shop's logo. That was four years ago.

Standing at the State Library in my sensible sandals and cheesecloth embroidered shirt, outwardly the stereotype of a right-on protestor, I know that Vanessa is the one actively surfing this particular zeitgeist. I'm just paddling in the shallows behind her.

A dreadlocked twentysomething slouches by in torn cargo pants, flashing us the thumbs up. 'Nice poster!' A black-clad hipster with a white card at his belt reading MEDIA snaps a photo from behind an enormous lens, followed by another passer-by, grinning in solidarity from behind a camera phone.

'She did most of it,' I admit.

A diverse crowd lolls on the library lawns. Some listen intently to the speakers, who pour words into megaphones from the back of a ute parked by the kerb. Others talk and laugh among themselves, sharing food and snapping photos. Men with bandanas tied over their noses, Zapatista-style, amble past others with slogans across their chests ('Capitalism makes me see red'). Others seem to be making their political statements in a more abstract manner. As always, there's a cluster of girls in pink tulle fairy skirts. On the other side of the lawn is a bearded man in an identical skirt, worn over jeans. But there are also middle-aged mum-and-dad types—like us—some of them with kids in tow. Drummers and clowns dart in and out of the crowd. It's like a street fair. But that's how I remember the S11 protests, too.

The carnival atmosphere is marred only by the flanks of police, many of them in riot gear: plastic face masks, batons. A row of stone-faced officers in reflective yellow vests lines the kerb of Swanston Street. Watching them, my confidence erodes at the edges, just a little. I remember arriving home from S11 flushed with the satisfaction of a good day out, then fielding calls from my family and friends, all of them breathless with sensational news reports and fears for our safety. I'd reassured them we were fine, as Leo pawed through a brightly coloured board book on the couch.

As the march finally begins, half an hour after our late arrival, I make sure we aren't in the first few rows, just in case there *is* trouble. Our banner stretches across one lane of Swanston Street. My shoulders ache almost immediately as I hold my end high. A megaphone leads a chant at my back: 'Whose streets?' / 'Our streets!' / 'Whose war?'

I look over at Vanessa as she yells, 'THEIR WAR!' I feel like I do at birthday parties and school assemblies where they sing 'Happy Birthday': too self-conscious to join in; too self-conscious not to.

Saturday shoppers line the streets, watching amiably. Many of them have brought out their phones and are snapping photos: amateur journalists enjoying their sneak preview of tonight's news bulletin.

'See, these people are on side,' I shout across the banner. 'That counts for something.'

'Why don't they join in?' frowns Vanessa.

We round the corner and turn past the Nike store as we make our way up Bourke Street.

'I've got a Nike bag, look,' says Vanessa in a furtive stage whisper. 'And shoes.' She waggles a foot, pausing momentarily in her marching.

'No one will notice,' I assure her.

'I thought about covering them with paper,' she continues. 'But I decided that was silly. They're old. I'm not going to throw them out.'

'No,' I joke. 'You don't want to waste the labour of those *tiny hands* that made them.'

She doesn't reply.

The crowd comes to a halt at the corner of Russell and Collins Streets. The Socialist Alliance hands out red flags as if dispensing lollipops; a red-shirted student leads another round of chants through his megaphone. Exotic birds perch in trees, wielding expensive-looking cameras. Policemen sit on horses in a distant line. I swing my camera towards them; one of the policemen has his own camera directed back at the crowd. Helicopters circle overhead. In an office building across the road, more photographers lean out a window. Everyone is watching everyone else. Nothing is happening.

Back at street level, we stand still, anchored by our banner. I wander aside to buy a magazine from a *Big Issue* vendor, pushing past a Superman in drag, inexplicably slathered in blue body paint. As I return to Vanessa, she makes a face at my magazine, saying something about wanting to support *The Big Issue*, but deciding not to because only half the money goes to the vendors.

'I write for *The Big Issue*,' I remind her. She half shrugs, as if to forgive me.

At this point, two friends arrive—coincidentally, former *Big Issue* colleagues.

'It's not like S11,' observes one of them, as the crowd cheers a protestor brandishing a fire hose from a roof. Bodies lurch towards the spray, seeking relief from the afternoon sun.

'I think people have lost their taste for violence, after *the other* September 11.'

'It'd be good to see a bit of a scuffle though,' sighs my other friend, looking out at the beatific fairies and painted toddlers waving red flags. 'It's always nice to see a *bit* of passion.'

It's time to go. My friends suggest we leave our banner behind.

'Yes!' I agree, too eagerly. My arms need a rest. And I haven't abandoned hope of detouring for food and coffee on the way home. 'We'll be gone,' I say, trying to sound persuasive, 'but *our message* will remain.'

'Wouldn't it be better to take our message out there, to the streets?' asks Vanessa.

'No!'

I photograph her with the banner before we leave, promising to email her the image.

'Maybe we'll get home and find out that it's all happened after we left, or when we weren't looking,' I say, and we all laugh.

We farewell my friends and—*at last*—Vanessa and I decamp for coffee and cake.

When I get home, I check *The Age* website. Plastic-clad protestors have splashed urine and hurled safety barriers at police. There are photos of faceless bodies in anti-contamination suits; I remember seeing them dancing in the street.

Later, Tony arrives home from his Sea Shepherd pilgrimage, euphoric. He's met the crew, including the founder of Greenpeace. They loved the lemons.

'And look!' he says, reaching into his backpack.

'*Oh,*' I drawl. 'So you've been to the revolution and bought the T-shirt?'

His grin collapses, and I apologise.

* * * *

'Why don't you come to Mexico?' says Tony. We are doing a circuit of the park, walking in the gold-lace light of the early evening, dappled sunlight over a fading sky. The dogs run circles by our feet—away and along the creek, then back again, as if to check we are still here. I wind an empty lead around my wrist, considering.

'I'd love to come to Mexico. But what about my job?'

'Leave it,' says Tony. 'You hate it anyway.'

'I don't hate it. Not the *job*. I just hate working full-time, in an office.'

'Then you should leave.'

'It's not that simple.' To abandon the job would be to abandon my ambitions, such as they are. I'd thought this would be my dream job, working as an editor on a literary magazine. If it isn't, what is? I have no idea. I suspect I don't have any ambitions after all. I suspect I just want to manage my own time again. To have my autonomy back. That doesn't seem like a good enough reason to quit a job. I also suspect I'm not as good at my job as I was before I got sick; I've lost momentum. I don't work late or come up with new schemes anymore. I spend too much time shouting over the partition that divides my desk from our business manager, about films or our husbands. That doesn't seem like a good enough reason to quit either.

'What would we do for money?' I say. 'How would we pay the rent?'

'You'll get another job.'

I marvel at Tony's confidence. Then again, it's not like I've never left a job with nowhere to go. I've done it twice in the past five years. But both times, I was on the edge of a breakdown. I quit those jobs because I was no longer in a fit state to work and I didn't want the pressure of a deadline urging me back before I was ready. I quit because I didn't think I was good at them anymore. Both times, I found new jobs without much trouble, when I was ready. But the last time, I touched the edges of real poverty before I was hired by one of my freelance clients. I had to line up at a charity in Footscray and present a case for getting a cheque to cover my rent. I waited for over an hour in a small, crowded room. A skinny man with sunken cheeks and grey skin dozed in a corner. An African woman cradled a baby while two toddlers played at her feet. A hard-faced woman with a sluggish voice and pinned pupils talked to no-one—or everyone—from her chair. When I got the cheque, I realised with a shock that my circumstances had been judged as desperate as those of my companions.

'I'll have an apartment,' says Tony. 'It won't cost you any accommodation money. And you'd be paying rent at home anyway! Or we could leave the house and put everything in storage.'

'True.'

He slips his hand into mine. I squeeze it, then let it go to cross the creek. My sneakers squelch in the mud on the other side. Tony follows, his long legs carrying him over to land cleanly on the grass where I am wiping my shoes.

'You always find work,' he says.

In my last job, editing a monthly newsletter for a bookshop, I worked part-time from home. It wasn't a career job, but it was fun, and it fit perfectly with looking after Leo. I could work in the tracksuit pants I wore to bed (and walked Leo to school in), then shower and change before lunch. If I had finished my work, I could sit on the couch with a book or cycle to the shops for a coffee, rather than keep busy by filing my inbox or tidying my desk until four o'clock. I nearly got the job back recently, after my old boss heard a rumour that I was unhappy and thought my replacement was likely to quit. But she didn't quit, after all.

'What about Leo?' I say. 'I can't leave Leo for six months.'

'We'll bring him with us!'

'Can we afford to fly Leo to Mexico, too?'

'Probably not.'

'Well, then.'

'What if you come for a shorter time?' asks Tony. 'Say, two months?'

'I don't know. It's still a long time.'

I am thirty years old and I've never left the country. Tony and I got married in February this year; our wedding registry was a travel agency account where we've accrued enough money to pay for one return flight to Mexico. Tony is about to embark on a stint as an exchange student in Guadalajara, Mexico's second-biggest city. He's being funded by a grant from the university where he's studying politics and Spanish. The wedding money was to pay for me to visit him for a couple of weeks, on a delayed honeymoon of sorts. But the idea of a longer stint in Mexico—and maybe a detour to the US, where my mum grew up—is tempting.

'I'll think about it,' I say.

4. HELL IS OTHER PARENTS

Vanessa and I collide at the school gate, in a tangle of dog leads and frantic barking. Her dog is a waist-high German Shepherd with a glossy coat and a fractious nature. Privately, I nickname him Cujo. Our small dogs bounce and bark below him, like mice agitating a cat.

'Um, I saw Leo baring his bottom by the monkey bars just then,' she says. 'I told him that it was dirty and to pull his pants up, but I thought I should let you know.'

'Thanks,' I mumble, quickly changing the subject. 'So, I'm still picking up Angus tonight?'

'That'd be great. I've got a big essay to write and I've hardly done *anything*. See you at six?'

I'll need to tell Santa that there are no Bionicles for Christmas.

* * * *

Again and again, the note comes back to us in Leo's Communication Book: *Sorry to say, but Leo pulled his pants down at lunchtime again.* He seems to be imitating Bart Simpson. Unfortunately, it has the desired effect of making the other kids laugh.

We've banned *The Simpsons* until further notice. (A pity: it was so much fun to watch it together.) Then we banned him from Lego Bionicles—his favourite toy—for a week, then a fortnight. The current threat for a repeat of this behaviour is 'no Bionicles for Christmas'. I have no idea what to do next. Take away all his Bionicles? All his toys?

While Leo has largely learned how to behave in class, he's still getting into trouble in the playground, where there are no rules and no teacher regularly watches over him.

He loses his temper, he strays into out-of-bounds areas. And he pulls down his pants.

Angus pounces joyfully as I approach his classroom. He is bouncing on the spot with excitement, clouds of blue dust billowing at his feet and settling on his black lace-up school shoes.

'My mum said I have to tell you every time Leo says something rude!' he announces.

Rewind to two days ago. 'You're early,' Vanessa greeted me. 'Are you okay? You look terrible.' She pulled me into the 'good' sitting room—the one they don't actually use—to tell me about her afternoon. Apparently, she overheard Leo saying something about sucking a woman's breast on the way home and told him that if she ever hears anything like that again, he is *no longer welcome* at their house.

'I *like* Leo,' she said, in a tone that screamed the opposite. 'But Angus is innocent, and Miles and I would like to keep him that way. I don't mean to judge, but I don't know where Leo has picked that up from. Do you? He's a very advanced reader, so maybe he read it somewhere?'

Yeah, I thought sourly, *like all those Playboy magazines I keep in my bottom drawer.* I apologised and assured her I would investigate and give my son a thorough talking-to.

'I mean, it was one thing when he told Angus how babies are made,' she continued. 'I didn't really mind that. I mean, I didn't really want him to know about it yet, but what can you do? I *did* have to put up with him saying *penis* and *vagina* all weekend, but … but that was okay, I guess.'

'What exactly did you say?' I growled, as soon as we were out of the house.

'I said that *Supergirl* was the stupidest movie I'd ever seen and Angus said Supergirl was beautiful. So I asked him if he wanted to suck Supergirl's breast.'

'Where did you get that from?'

'From when you get born. You know, breastfeeding!'

Rachel is breastfeeding Leo's baby brother Quentin. I breathed a sigh of relief and told him never to say anything like that again.

Seven-year-old boys love to dob on each other. I have a magic formula that I recite to all visiting children. I don't want to hear about it unless someone is hurt, someone is in danger or about to get hurt, or something is being wrecked. I fill the gaps by keeping my ears tuned while they play, pouncing on bad words when they least expect it.

Vanessa has overridden my formula.

'He keeps doing it because it makes the other kids laugh,' says the deputy principal, Eliza. 'But they don't laugh so much anymore. They think it's weird.'

We're sitting in her office with the door shut, discussing the pants-pulling-down behaviour that has become Leo's speciality. Outside, in the corridor, Leo and Angus are providing a thudding, squealing soundtrack to our conversation. It's an effort to keep in the tears. I nod and agree, apologising for what seems like the thousandth time.

'Leo is a great kid,' she says. 'He's come so far this year. We've told him we're really proud of him. He's incredibly smart. Sometimes, perhaps, that causes problems. But we love having him around.'

'*Really*? You *do*?'

Eliza hands me a tissue. 'Of *course* we do.'

As we walk home through the park, I remind Leo about the message to Santa. And if he pulls down his pants in the schoolyard again, I warn, I will give all his Bionicles to his cousin, Jordan. The sky is dark with smoke from distant bushfires. I push through the heat and smog towards our street. Leo points to the wall of a nearby power station as we pass.

'That's graffiti,' he says. 'Seth says that when he grows up, he wants to write graffiti.'

The boys lean in to each other, giggling. Leo whispers something.

'Excuse me,' says Angus. 'Leo says that when he grows up, he wants to sniff vaginas.'

'WHAT?' I interrogate the boys. It turns out that Leo said he wants to sniff bums. Which is bad, but Andy Griffiths rather than Hugh Hefner territory. Angus just wanted to say *vagina*. I growl at them both. My throat hurts, my eyes sting, the backs of my knees are sticky with sweat.

As I unhook the picket fence and push open the gate, Angus taps my arm.

'Excuse me. Leo said that daisy is stupid.' He points into the garden. I look at him. 'And *stupid* is a bad word?'

He nods.

'Okay,' I say, and determinedly busy myself with locking my bike to the verandah post. Head down, I fantasise about killing Vanessa, who has clearly condemned me to a long and painful afternoon.

I am cutting up honey toast and Granny Smith apples at the kitchen table. Angus wanders in to fetch his carton of Ribena, and stays to watch.

'So, if Leo is rude again, his cousin will get all his Bionicles?'

'Yes.'

'Oh. You know, you could give them to me.'

'That's an interesting idea, but I don't think so.'

'Oh.' He takes a slice of apple from one of the plates. 'You could give half to me, half to his cousin?'

'No.'

'Maybe I could have just *one*?'

I snap. 'Angus, if I were to give you Leo's Bionicles if he was rude, you'd tell me he was rude, wouldn't you? So I don't think it's a good idea. They'll go to his cousin.' Pause. 'And hopefully, Leo will be good.'

'I won't say he's rude—'

'No.'

By 6.10 pm, I have a headache with trying to work out who is really being rude, who is making up stories, who actually deserves to be told off, and how to explain that I don't really care if someone said *bloody*. There are just as many complaints and rude words from 'innocent' Angus as Leo. Next week, I plan to revert to my dobbing guidelines.

Vanessa arrives at 6.30 pm, breezily. She has, as usual, brought Angus's brother, Tom, with her. The three boys dash out into the backyard for a lightsabre duel. Tony shoots her a look and disappears. He is furious, as is Leo's father, about all her fussing. They think she is a prude. Mark actually came out with a killer line when I told him how upset she was about the 'where babies come from' chat. 'What would she prefer?' he said icily. 'That Angus goes around saying *prick* and *cunt?*'

Vanessa deals with the frosty atmosphere by settling in for the long haul, to show that we are friends and everything is okay. She talks and talks. She follows the boys out the back and comments on the progress of the lightsabre duels. She tells me about a meal she made recently and gives me the recipe. She tells me how nice the lemon tree is, and about her lemon tree, and about her friend's lemon tree, and what her friend does with lemons, and how her mother propagates fruit trees, and how she herself does it. It is 7 pm. She asks me, finally, about the sucking breasts thing. I tell her about the breastfeeding and she is surprised and relieved. She tells me—again—that she wishes Angus hadn't been told the facts of life. She tells me—again—that he's been saying *vagina*. That she was doing the ironing and he said, 'Mum, you have a vagina, don't you?'

At 7.30 pm, she finally leaves, with a green shopping bag full of lemons. At the door, she grabs my arm and asks, 'Are you doing anything right now?'

I need to cook dinner, serve dinner, bath Leo, get him into his pyjamas, put him to bed and read him three stories. All within the next hour. And then I need to research and write an article.

'Why?'

'Angus is missing his bike,' she says. He'd left it at our place last week. 'Can you walk him to the park so he can ride it through to our street? I'll drive the car around and meet him on the other side of the park.'

'Okay.'

As we trudge to the edge of the driveway, Vanessa grabs my arm again. 'Hey!' she says. 'Come *here*!' And she grabs me in a hug. I smile weakly and wave goodbye as she and Tom get into the car and prepare to drive home.

'Why does Leo like Bionicles so much?' asks Angus.

'I don't know.' I try to be upbeat and friendly, overcompensating. 'I guess he just does!'

'I don't,' says Angus. 'I like superheroes.' And with that, he climbs onto his bike and pedals off down the hill towards the park, me jogging behind.

* * * *

Late at night, after Leo and Tony are both in bed, I get my terrible-no-good-day out of my system by writing a blog about it. Recently, I've begun to attract comments on my blog, even though all I write about is life with Leo. Some are from those other mums I longed to connect with; others are freelance writers who find that blogging is an invitation to write about whatever they like, and a way of socialising from their separate home offices. This suits me; if I have something to add to a conversation, I say it. If I don't, I don't. No small-talk required, unless you feel like it.

Doesn't this woman know that lemons are best used for gin and tonic? Tell her that next time she tries to give you recipes, says one commenter, Georgia.

At least your son knows what a penis and a vagina are.

I quit my job. I tell my boss that I plan to go to Mexico for a couple of months now, not a couple of weeks. He offers to give me leave without pay for as long as I need it. I tell him that I need to spend more time with Leo; that the full-time job is not working out. He says I can cut back to three days a week. But my mind is made up; I see that blank slate of freedom ahead. And whatever my working future, I'm keen to be more available as a mum again.

We have a few smart young interns working at the magazine. One of them has just finished her creative arts degree and is looking for a job. I agree to stay on until the end of January next year, so I can train her to replace me.

Mark is more than happy to take Leo while I'm gone; I work out a complicated arrangement for how I can pay him back for all seven weeks.

'You don't have to be so precise about it,' says Mark. He has always travelled overseas a few times a year; I have always taken Leo during his absence. 'It doesn't matter if we're a bit uneven in the end.' But I don't want us to be uneven. Finding a way that I won't lose any time with Leo—not really, not *overall*—goes some way towards alleviating my guilt about leaving him.

The bookshop where I used to work holds its Christmas party at a bowling green in Fitzroy. Lawn bowls is a new trend; one of the local publishers held its party at the same place a week earlier. Somehow, I cadge an invite to the bookshop party. It kicks off in the late afternoon;

people take off their shoes and walk barefoot on the lawn, suspiciously green in a year of strict water restrictions. The inner-city bowling club is on the tramline, opposite a row of restored Victorian terraces and a vegetarian pizza place. Speakers are set up at the back of the club, blaring pop music over the street.

My brother-in-law Jamie is here; he's an assistant manager. Kabita, one of my best friends, works in the shop on Saturdays, so she's here too. My old boss Emily, who managed the bookshop where Tony and I met, is now a sales rep for Random House. She comes out of the clubhouse carrying a plastic flute of champagne.

'Hey!' she says. 'I can't believe you quit the magazine. And I gave you such a good reference when you applied! I thought you said it was your dream job? What happened?'

I shrug. 'It was too much, with Leo. Working full-time.' I don't tell her that I didn't feel like I was doing a good job anymore, that I was uninspired.

'Fair enough. How is he?'

'Getting into a bit of trouble,' I admit. 'But he's mostly great.'

I drink a lot of champagne, more than I have in years. I talk to my old colleagues, my relatives, my friends. I explain, over and over, why I am quitting my job. It's a bit embarrassing, given the fanfare with which I left this place. I'm haunted by my excitement, back then, about mounting the next rung on my career ladder—a ladder I'm now descending. The managing director calls everyone together in the clubroom and gives a speech about the terrific year the company has had, exuberantly thanking all his employees. The music is turned up to full volume and coloured lights flash over a stage at the end of the room. Kabita pulls me over to dance; I've drunk enough that I give in to it. I feel like I've made a terrible mistake. Why did I leave here in the first place? What am I going to do next?

I leave the party and hide behind a tree near the clubhouse to cry. Emily follows me outside. 'What's wrong?' she asks.

'I want my old job back. What have I done?'

'You'll find another job,' she says. 'Don't worry about it. You're great.' Then she attempts a joke. 'I'll give you another reference!'

I cry harder.

'You're just emotional because it's the end of the year,' she says, a little uncertainly. I nod. 'And because you're drunk. And it's 1 am. Why don't we catch a cab home now?'

Emily lives in the western suburbs too. We sit on the kerb, under the cover of darkness, as we wait to be picked up. I lick my finger and wipe it under my eyes to remove the mascara I know is smudged there.

The next morning, I reach into my bag for my purse and pull out a plastic wineglass.

5. CAROLS IN THE PARK

I don't expect Carols in the Park to be fun. I'd much rather take the dog for a walk, or read a book on the couch, or even cook dinner. But taking your child to a school Christmas event is surely on the list of things a mother has no choice about.

And so Leo and I are riding through Cruikshank Park and across Somerville Road, my basket stuffed with a picnic blanket and backpack. Leo sits on a cushion strapped to the back of my bike, his arms around my waist.

'Wow!' he breathes, as we stop outside the park. 'This looks great!'

The browning grass is lined with card tables stacked with plates of home-made cakes and biscuits; with glitter glue, stickers and Christmas baubles. A loudspeaker blares eighties pop from a stage in the centre of the park, synthesiser beats filling the cooling evening air. A caravan sells Mars Bars beside the sausage sizzle. And behind the playground, a baby animal farm stocked with lambs, guinea pigs, goats and puppies is fenced into the corner of the park.

Leo jumps off his cushion and runs to the playground and back, while I wheel the bike up and down the street, looking for somewhere to chain it up. I pause at several likely-looking wooden posts, but they all prove too thick.

'Mum! Mum! What are you doing?'

'Wait here,' I tell him through gritted teeth, as I head further down the footpath to where an olive sapling is tethered to a wooden stake.

A patchwork of families is spread across the grass between the stage and the cake tables, while others border the primary-coloured play equipment. Grown-ups sit on rugs and deckchairs, brandishing plastic wineglasses or stubbies. Some of them bend to small children, but most are caught up in each other.

I spread our rug—actually one of Leo's old baby quilts—in a space by the stage.

'Can I have a sausage? A cupcake? I want to play!'

We go to the sausage van, where we eat what will pass as dinner on the way back to the rug. Sauce bleeds down Leo's arm. When I point it out, he licks it off like a puppy before tearing off to play.

Children are everywhere: scrambling on the monkey bars, banging elbows at the stalls, running from one activity to the next. They are variously smeared with dirt, sauce, icing and glitter, hats and ponytails askew. One small boy wears a belled Santa hat. Sisters stroll by wearing matching Christmas dresses, red and green and gold, teamed with Blundstones. Tinsel glints in their hair. Leo lines up for the monkey bars; he is momentarily still amid the chaos. The other children talk around him and over him, but not to him. He doesn't seem to notice, or to care. My stomach clenches in sympathy—I'm not sure if it's for him or for myself.

I sprawl on my stomach on the quilt, facing towards the stage and away from my neighbours on the other rugs. Directly behind me is a mother from Leo's class. She often stops me in the schoolyard to say, 'We must catch up! We will!' We never do. The charade has lasted all year. Last week, her son stopped me at the school gate to ask, 'When can I play at your house?' 'Any time,' I said, but she pulled him away with apologies about shopping to do. I'm not in the mood for another meaningless conversation—and it seems that neither is she. She stood behind us in the line as Leo and I were applying sauce to our sausages, but somehow our eyes didn't meet.

I pull *The Monthly* out of my bag. Small feet run across the edge of the quilt, kicking dirt over the pages. I brush it off without taking my eyes from the page. *Now is the time*, I tell myself, *to catch up on those articles I missed on the first read*. Leo's sneakers skid into view. I look up and shoulder my bag.

'Shall we look around?'

We visit the baby animals. Leo sits on a hay bale, hardly daring to breathe, as a guinea pig is placed in his lap. He strokes it tentatively at first, then with confidence. His face is intense with pleasure. He pats a sleeping dog, an indifferent lamb and a passing goat.

'You try,' he says as I watch him marvel at the lamb. 'Wouldn't you like a jumper like this?'

He sits with the dog, waiting for it to wake. It sleeps peacefully as the minutes pass, equally oblivious to the cacophony of picnic noise and the boy waiting to pat him. I take a photo and we move on. As we close the gate to the enclosure behind us, Leo taps a girl's shoulder. 'Excuse me,' he says. 'I recommend that you pat the lamb.'

After he's decorated his Christmas ornament and left it at the table to dry, he returns to the playground, I to my quilt and magazine. The wind is cold; I wrap myself in a gauzy scarf from the depths of my bag. The wind bites at the gap between my jeans and shirt. I tug my jacket down, but it rides up as soon as I relax. In the midst of this dance of tug and release, Leo lands hard beside my head. He pulls an Andy Griffiths book from his backpack and settles companionably by my feet.

'Don't you want to play?'

'Nah. Can you read to me?'

I wriggle to face him and we lie on our stomachs together, sucking on unsheathed candy canes. Raindrops fall on the page: light pricks at first, then steady, fat drops.

Leo has brought a smaller patchwork quilt with him, the size of a doormat. It's not useful for sitting on, but it's the perfect size to shelter under in the absence of umbrellas. He made it with my mum last Christmas; he picked out the material—glinting gold thread, white snowflakes on blue skies, smiling Santas on green backgrounds—and helped form it into a pattern. The bells sewn into the centre tinkle as we adjust it over our heads, just as the PA crackles, John Lennon stops mid-lyric and the mayor introduces himself.

'Wow,' breathes Leo. 'He's *famous*.'

The school choir is ranged along the stage. A teacher with a guitar starts the first song. On the rugs, no-one is singing. Leo scowls through the rain.

'I want to sing too.'

'You can.'

'Up there?'

'Here, you can.'

Under the quilt, I start to sing, hoping it's loud enough for him to hear but quiet enough that no-one else can. Leo continues to scowl out at the stage, but half joins in. My jeans cling wetly.

Santa is coming, with presents, in one hour.

I tug the quilt further over my head. Leo pulls it away. One of the few mothers who talks to me walks by, but I can't be bothered saying hello. I'm afraid of what else I might say, about how fed up I am with this whole school where nobody is anything like me, and this stupid night that only seems to get worse. And, of course, I'm fed up with myself. Even though I know tonight is not about me—it's about Leo—I'm more than ready to go home.

Leo sneezes.

'Okay, we need to go.' I jump to my feet.

'Noooo.'

'You're catching a cold.'

As I shake dirt from the large quilt and fold it under my arm, the mother sitting behind me looks over and smiles. She rolls her eyes conspiratorially. *Now that I'm leaving, she can see me.* I smile and wave goodbye.

Leo mumbles and moans all the way back to the bike. As I stuff the quilt into the basket, the PA dies. Two latecomers head our way, arms full of blankets and eskies.

'It's all off,' comes a voice from behind me. 'You're just in time to go home.'

'Jack arrived just as everyone was going home!' says Leo, too gleefully. 'He's too late, isn't he?'

I mount the bike and squint into the rain as we glide past the queue of reversing cars.

'When we get home,' I shout over the traffic, 'our Christmas tree will be waiting for us to decorate. I'll run you a hot bath and we can get the decorations out of the garage and then you can have hot Milo with marshmallows.'

Leo sighs contentedly. I feel him exhale against my back. 'Oh Mum,' he says, 'you've cheered me up by saying that.'

We cross the bridge over the creek. As I stand on my pedals to push us up the hill of our street, I do something I know I shouldn't.

'Leo,' I call over my shoulder, 'do you wish I was more like the other mums? That I hung out with the other mums?'

It's something I think about a lot. That if I hung out more with the other mums, he'd find it easier to make new friends. That his lack of play-dates is because we don't seem a suitable family to socialise with. If he socialised more often, and more widely, I'm sure he'd find it easier to slip into groups of unfamiliar (or vaguely familiar) children and pick up their rhythms.

'No, Mum,' he says. 'I like you the way you are.'

Pause.

'There is one thing I'd change ...'

Another pause.

'... but it's really something I'd have to change.'

'What's that?' I manage.

'Punishments.'

And then we're in our driveway, with Tony opening the front door to greet us. On the verandah, a pine tree lies patiently on its side.

6. NOT QUITE CHRISTMAS

Something's not quite right about Christmas this year. During the past few weeks, bushfires have shrouded the city in a days-long smoke haze and coloured the sun an eerie pale red. But Christmas Day dawns a different shade of grey, the clouds spitting silver needles of rain. We're spending Christmas in Melbourne, in an exhausting family relay: Tony and I moving between his divorced parents, Leo moving between his.

Leo is with us for Christmas Eve. He puts out a carrot for the reindeer and a cookie, a white wine and a candy cane for Santa. He writes a note across the back of two of my business cards, carefully lined up alongside each other. One says, 'Dear Santa, Have I been good?' The other card is a kind of form letter for Santa to fill out. It's headed with 'Dear Leo' and ends with 'Love Santa' at the bottom, with a blank space in the middle.

After bedtime, he gets up three times. His excuses: a drink of water, going to the toilet, having seen a reindeer outside his window. Eventually, we peek through his open doorway and confirm he is asleep. Tony messily eats the cookie and the carrot, taking care to spill large crumbs on the table. He writes Santa's answer in old-fashioned cursive, so Leo won't recognise our handwriting.

'He left crumbs!' shouts Leo in the early morning, running through the darkness to jump on our bed. 'He ate it! This *proves* Santa exists!'

Later, when he leads us to examine Santa's note, he tells us that Santa's handwriting is just like his teacher's.

Leo's dad picks him up for lunch and we drive to Tony's dad's house in Coburg, an hour away. There, we listen to carols on his new stereo and pull Christmas crackers at the lunch table. We eat a traditional Christmas roast—a turkey, a chicken, three kinds of salad, roast potatoes, prawns—wearing coloured paper crowns, before posing on the couch for a series of family photos. We're captured in winter clothes: I'm wearing a black cardigan and long black skirt, as if dressed for a funeral. Tony wears a Space Invaders windcheater. It's all very civilised and polite as we drink and discuss the selection of wine chosen by Tony's brother Jamie, who works part-time at an upmarket bottleshop.

We stop at South Melbourne and pick up Leo on our way to St Kilda (an hour's drive from both Coburg *and* our house), where we'll eat dinner with Tony's mother, Margaret, and her partner, Edwina. We arrive before Tony's brother and sister rejoin us from Coburg. There's another roast dinner, followed by ice-cream for dessert, and we keep eating even though we're full. Margaret and Edwina have a foster son, Jordan, who is three years younger than Leo. We call him Leo's cousin, to avoid long and complicated explanations. It's not precisely true, but it fits. That's the relationship. It feels a bit more like Christmas here, despite the rain—and now hail—hammering at the windows and the roof. Leo and Jordan shout with excitement as they unwrap their presents. Later, they upturn toyboxes full of Lego and trains in Jordan's bedroom. Edwina and I take turns getting up from the table to resolve squabbles.

I'm disappointed when it's time to leave for our last stop of the night. Tony has promised his best friend that we'll visit him for Christmas drinks after dinner. Margaret has agreed to keep Leo while we go; she now offers to keep him overnight. I'd rather take him home—or even stay here—but I go anyway, kissing him goodnight as Margaret settles him with a book on the fold-out couch in their lounge room. For me, Christmas is about family. Maybe because I've been living so far from my own family, who live in Adelaide, for so long. I don't want to be with Tony's friends; I want to be with my boy. But I don't tell Tony this.

The wind sucks my umbrella inside out as I step from the car outside Carlo's terrace house. We run to the shelter of the verandah without pausing to adjust it. Inside, Carlo, his wife Jane and another friend are half-heartedly nibbling from a plate of tiger prawns left over from lunch. Bowls of Christmas lollies are laid out on the lounge-room table: pink and orange marshmallow Santas, red and green sugared jubes, thumb-sized candy canes. We graze from the bowls as we play Trivial Pursuit by candlelight and trade stories about our Christmas Day. Carlo, Jane and Jon have spent the day at Jon's ex-boyfriend's house: no families. Tony tells them about driving all day between his parents' houses. Someone rolls a joint and passes it around.

The talk settles, as it inevitably does in this company, on the bookshop where most of them work. About a co-worker with bad shoes, a regular customer with an attitude, the way someone smells. It's after midnight when I close my eyes, *just to rest them*, and lie back on the embroidered cushions that cover the lounge-room floor. As I drift into sleep, I hear Jane telling Tony we should stay, that he's in no state to drive.

In the morning, we leave soon after we wake, to pick up Leo and drive home over the West Gate Bridge. The sun is filtering through the clouds.

* * * *

It's the day after Boxing Day, 8.45 am. Still dressed in my pyjamas, I open the door to Vanessa, Angus and Tom. The boys are dressed in matching outfits, with square vinyl backpacks. Vanessa is dressed for work. She tells me that she's packed lunches for the boys.

'It means they can just eat when they're hungry and they won't need to ask you for food,' she says.

After puzzling at this, I decide it might be because she's heard me tell Leo not to ask for food at their house. Tony says it's because she thinks we won't feed them properly. Leo and Tony are also still in their pyjamas. They sit forward on the couch, wrapped in dressing gowns, absorbed in Leo's favourite Christmas present: a Lego Star Wars PlayStation game. Tony downs his control as the boys enter and heads for the shower. Leo tosses a coin to see who should take over from Tony first. I set the timer for twelve minutes and tell the boys that I expect them to rotate when the timer goes off, before retreating to the kitchen to make pancakes. As I pull ingredients from the cupboards, I can hear the bickering start already.

'I want to be Luke.'

'No, I do!'

'Euwww! I'm Princess Leia. Help me change characters! I'm a girl!'

It is my policy not to know anything about working the PlayStation, which I loathe. Tony is summoned from the bathroom to fix the problem.

Soon, the boys are furnished with honey-smeared pancakes. When they finish, leaving a litter of plates and half-empty juice glasses, Tony takes their place at the table, damp-haired and fully dressed. He has things to do today, he informs me over his bowl. I eye him suspiciously.

'So you're leaving me alone with the kids?'

'I'll hurry back.'

I think about this and decide I'd rather cope on my own. They will drive him even crazier than they will me.

'Don't,' I say. 'Take as long as you like. As long as you *can*.'

The boys play a game they call 'Pooland', which revolves around building makeshift forts. They build a cubby under Leo's bed and another between the bedhead and the wall, draped with sheets. There is much shouting and squealing but I'm left alone until they move on to Lego half an hour later, when I'm summoned to hear the story of who got which piece first and who has stolen from whom. Leo is gripping the Lego Batmobile he got for Christmas and won't relinquish it.

'We share with him at *our* house!' exclaims Angus. I concur that it's polite to share. After a few rounds of Lego judge, between which I sit on the couch and try to read, the boys migrate to the study where they sprawl on the floor, drawing. They are relatively content.

On my way to refill my water glass, I pass Leo's bedroom and pause in the doorway to inspect the damage. The toyboxes are empty, their contents forming a second layer of carpet. The floor rug ripples like the aftermath of an earthquake, thick with Lego and other debris.

I order a clean-up and get a chorus of, 'Excuse me, but *I* didn't play with *that* one' and 'I didn't touch *those* toys'.

I channel my mother. 'I really don't care who made what mess. You all clean it up.'

'Excuse me,' calls Angus. 'Leo isn't really cleaning up. We're doing it all.'

Angus and Tom are mechanically piling toys into boxes. Leo is wandering across the room, singing to himself, fondling a brick of Lego.

'Okay,' I concede. 'You boys can go back to drawing.'

They disappear in an instant.

'But THAT'S NOT FAIR!'

So begins an argument that escalates to some smart-arse remark I don't even remember. I smack Leo's hand, not very hard. He glares at me defiantly. I'm not a hitter.

'Didn't hurt,' he says.

I smack him again, harder.

'Still didn't hurt.'

'*What*,' I wail, 'on *earth* are you doing? Why would you say something like that to me? Why Leo, do you *want* me to hurt you?'

'I'm trying to show you how tough I am,' he spits.

I am astounded by his honesty. And furious, of course.

I tell him that he is being ridiculous, that showing me how tough he is will not impress me and won't help him one little bit. At the same time, I'm aware that the 'tough' image is for the benefit of his friends on the other side of the door.

I tell him there will be no more Bionicles for the rest of the week. His entire body clenches with anger, concentrated in the fists bunched at his sides. He fixes his gaze on me and yells, at the top of his lungs: 'SHIT!'

His eyes both dare me to respond and recoil from the consequences he is inviting.

'That's your Lego and your Exo-Force and your Bionicles and your PlayStation gone for a week. Your friends can play with them, but not you.'

'SHIIIIIT!'

I am engulfed in the same pure anger he is burning with. The flames have leapt across the divide between us. I stand there and splutter, genuinely speechless. He has never done anything like this before, *never*. Well, not since he was a toddler anyway. And he didn't swear then.

I scoop up the toyboxes, now refilled with Lego, and take them to the study, one by one. Angus and Tom watch, wide-eyed, as I stack them neatly by Tony's desk. I manage a smile and a few reassuring words.

'I know what you should do!' shouts Angus. 'You should tell him Santa won't come to him next year! No Santa!'

I manage a 'Hmmm, maybe not' before I storm back into the bedroom, green garbage bag in hand.

'That's IT!' I shout. 'I'm taking some of your toys to give away to kids who deserve them. You're obviously *spoilt*. You've got *too many things*.'

And then Leo, a tiny, rage-fuelled powerhouse, is upon me. A punch lands in my chest, hard and deliberate. Another first. I look at my son and don't recognise what I see glaring back at me. I am appalled, at both of us. I grab him and try to smack his bottom. He ducks and weaves, twisting in my grasp, and manages to squirm away from me. His triumphant grin taunts me. There is no doubt about it. He is winning and I am losing control fast. Okay, I've already lost it.

'Go to the laundry,' I order.

'No.'

I try to bundle him up under my arm but it is useless. He grips my legs with his, an angry koala at my ankles.

In desperation, I prise him off, shut the door on him and call Leo's father on his mobile. He is at the cricket. With his parents and his new in-laws, who will all be most impressed that I need his help to discipline his son. Oh well.

'Leo is being physically abusive,' I tell him breathlessly. 'He punched me and now he won't do anything I tell him. I don't know what to do.'

'Well, send him to the laundry.'

'He won't go.'

'Make him.'

'I can't. I already tried.'

'You're bigger than him.'

'I know.'

Eventually, he offers to speak to Leo. I gratefully accept. As I said, I am desperate. I give Leo the phone and tell him who it is in ominous tones. He takes it reluctantly. I stand back and wait for a grim telling-off to begin.

I hear: 'So, mate. I hear you and your mother are having some problems. What's happening?'

Mark is chummy, inviting confidences. I listen to a few more lines of this before snatching back the phone.

'Be angry!' I say. 'You can't be *nice* to him. He *punched* me. Be *stern* with him.'

I pass back the phone and watch Leo listen to more of his dad's calm exhortations to please be good and *show your mother some respect*. To be fair, he listens. His eyes lose that possessed gleam, his body language softens, goes limp. I put away the green garbage bag—my concession to a truce. The rational part of my brain takes control again, my instincts and emotions receding. We have some stern words about respect and appropriate behaviour, language and attitude. I tell him to clean up his whole room, not just the recent mess.

I return to the study and sit at my computer. I smile inanely at Angus and Tom and ask them about their pictures, as if nothing has happened.

'Remember how you were going to give Leo's Bionicles to his friends if he was naughty?' asks Angus.

'Mmmm,' I mumble.

'Are you still going to do that?'

'That was before Christmas.'

'So, will you do it?'

'No.'

He returns to his drawing.

Leo comes to show me his clean room. He is meek and obedient. Peace reigns for a while. I make Leo grilled cheese on toast for lunch, with sliced apple on the side.

'Can we have that too?' asks Angus.

'You've got your sandwiches.'

Their faces fall. I return to the kitchen and cut more cheese and apple. The boys eat their identical lunches companionably, hunched over a *Superman* comic.

I'm reading a book on the couch and the boys are playing Pooland in the backyard when Tony calls from the relative safety of the shopping centre. I give him a brief run-down.

'Do you want me to talk to Leo?' he offers. I am reminded of how much I love him. I tell him I've got it covered. Tom appears at my side, grinning up at me.

'I'm Darth Maul!' he beams.

'Oh, Tom,' I say. 'No! You can't draw on your face with texta!'

I am about to hang up when Leo and Angus run past again, their bodies covered in texta swirls. They bolt into the bathroom, followed by Tom. Angus slams the door behind them, hard. The door is faulty and is never fully shut because it jams and can't be opened. Right now, it is jammed at a very strange angle.

'Oh *noooo*,' I wail down the phone. 'I *really* have to go now.'

I tell Tony to shop as long as he can. One of us might as well be sane tonight.

I peer through the crack between the bathroom door and the doorway. Leo and Angus's faces are worse than Tom's. They are all giggling madly.

'I'll open the window and we'll all climb out,' announces Leo.

'NO!'

It takes me roughly fifteen minutes to get the door open. It feels much longer. I catch the boys as they tumble out enthusiastically.

'I thought we were going to be stuck *forever*!' says Angus.

'I need to wash your faces.'

I do Angus and Tom first: a matter of priority. It takes a long time. The boys giggle as I come to Leo. He rolls up his sleeves.

'Look!'

'He did his willy too,' says Angus.

'And his bum,' adds Tom.

I inspect his handiwork and grimly deposit him in the shower, after squeezing a generous dollop of make-up remover onto a face-washer for him.

After the boys have been cleaned and scrubbed dry, I feel bad. They were being creative, after all. It was naughty to use texta, but what if I'd had face paint? I am inspired. I dig out a few old lipsticks from the depths of my bathroom drawers. I take them into the backyard and tell the boys they can use them to paint their faces, if they like.

'This is make-up,' I say. 'It's *meant* for faces.'

Ten minutes later, the boys visit me in the lounge room. Angus has covered his entire face in glitter-flecked orangey-bronze lipstick. He shimmers as he bounces excitedly before me.

'I look CHINESE!' he shouts.

I haven't seen any Chinese people with glittery bronze faces, but am too gobsmacked to respond. This time, it's my fault. He has also helped himself to my mascara, which he has used to paint his eyebrows.

I let them dance in front of my full-length bedroom mirror for as long as I can stand it. I take a group photo, then summon them to the bathroom for another round of scrubbing. They emerge with red-raw faces. I leave Angus until last. It takes a very, very long time. When I finish, his eyebrows are still tinged glowing orange, as is his hairline. I can't help laughing. He looks vaguely demonic.

'I'll have another go later,' I tell him.

He runs off, grateful for the end of his ordeal.

When Vanessa arrives to pick up the boys, she asks how they were. We stand on the back deck, watching them chase each other through the ankle-swallowing grass, waving plastic lightsabres.

'Oh, you know,' I reply. 'They were, um, interesting. There was a bit of fighting and Leo was pretty naughty at one point. But it was okay. They were fine.'

* * * *

Later that evening, after Tony has gone to bed, I sit on the couch alone, the television on and my mind whirring. The events of the day have mostly ebbed from my consciousness, but one scene keeps lobbing back to the forefront of my mind. Leo's temper tantrum echoes my childhood memories: the ferocity of his fury, the flood of his injustice—impervious to rules or consequence—is something I've seen before.

My youngest brother Nick, when he was Leo's age, would periodically erupt like this, usually in response to a ruling he viewed as unfair, or provocation from other kids, especially my brother Simon and me. As a toddler, he would scream and cry if Simon and I sang one of his favourite songs, especially the *Here's Humphrey* theme. ('That's *my* song,' he would wail to Mum. Of course, this made it extra fun to sing.) Nick's rages, once triggered, did not discriminate—they could be directed at us, Mum or Dad, or his school principal. He was often deeply apologetic afterwards, but couldn't seem to control his behaviour in the moment. Simon was once called to bring Nick in from the schoolyard after he trashed his primary school classroom then raced around the playground, climbing on equipment and ducking the teachers' attempts to catch him.

Leo has always reminded me of Nick. I wonder, with a sense of dread, if there are more tantrums like this in our future. My parents never really found a way to help Nick with his temper; he just grew out of it, eventually.

Then I comfort myself with my fondness for my brother, who is as kind-hearted as his tempers were explosive. He's like the nursery rhyme: *There was a little girl, who had a little curl, right in the middle of her forehead. When she was good, she was very very good—and when she was bad, she was horrid.* Nick's sense of injustice has also propelled him to do things like rip his mates apart for teasing an unknown girl in a pub, then make sure she's okay before going home in disgust. I comfort myself further with the thought that Nick has always adored our mum. If Leo is like him, maybe he'll always adore me?

Tony appears in the doorway, a glass of water in his hand. He blinks at me from the gloom of the hall.

'Why are you watching the cricket?' he says. 'You hate cricket.'

'Oh. I don't know. I was just thinking.'

He switches off the television, then stretches his hand towards me.

'Come to bed,' he says. 'You can think there.'

* * * *

29 December. My birthday. Leo wakes me by climbing into my bed with a home-made birthday card and a breakfast of an apple and Vegemite crackers on a plate. 'I'm not old enough to work the toaster by myself,' he explains. While I'm in the shower, Tony makes me pancakes from a packet mix he bought the night before. Leo collects fallen lemons from the backyard and we eat the pancakes with lemon and sugar, while poor Tony watches longingly over his rice porridge. I hide the uneaten Vegemite crackers in the top drawer of my bedside table, slip the apple into my bag and bring the empty plate into the kitchen.

'You ate it all!' says Leo. 'Was it good?'

'Definitely,' I say. 'Thanks so much, darling.'

Then I put the dogs on their leads and walk Leo across the park to Angus and Tom's house. It's Vanessa's turn now. I farewell Leo at the front gate, telling him to treat Vanessa with respect and *do exactly as she says.*

Tony tells me the day is mine, to do whatever I want with. We eat lunch at the Vegie Bar on Brunswick Street, he trails me around Fitzroy while I spend my birthday money on clothes, and then we finish the day at home, reading on the back deck.

At 6 pm, I return to Vanessa's house. She leads me into the kitchen where smoke is pouring from the griller. She makes me a latte as she scrapes blackened toast into the bin and puts two fresh slices of bread under the grill. As she froths the milk, she tells me about her day. Angus had a screaming tantrum when Leo wanted to play with his new toys. Tried to kick him out of his bedroom. Said he didn't want him to touch anything of his. Now, he is asleep in Vanessa's bed. They'd had an afternoon nap together while Leo and Tom watched a Batman DVD.

'It's been a tough day,' she sighs. 'They've been talking about sex again. They were teasing each other, saying they wanted to have sex with a girl at school. And they said something about boobs.'

I apologise, wishing the ground would swallow me up.

She places a hand on my arm and leans in close, her face just centimetres from mine. 'Why do you think Leo is so obsessed with sex?'

My mind whirrs. On Boxing Day, Angus was just as bad as Leo on the subject. I wonder whether to mention this.

'They were all talking about it a bit on Wednesday,' I venture.

'Mmmm. It starts, and then it just goes round in a circle, doesn't it?'

'I think it's about having just learned how babies are made and getting their heads around it.'

'I think it's his reading,' she continues, as if I hadn't spoken. 'Like that book he brought over.'

She gestures to Andy Griffiths's *The Bad Book*, which is lying, confiscated, on the counter. 'It is totally inappropriate and very rude. It's all about bums and things.'

I am momentarily floored. I didn't really think when I put that book in his bag, but it is suddenly obvious that I've made a bad decision.

'Miles brought home some Marvel comics the other day,' she continues. 'They were aimed at eight-year-olds, I think, but we couldn't believe it. There was some *very suggestive stuff* between Peter Parker and Mary Jane. Not explicit but, you know, *implied*. Leo must read that stuff. That must be where he's getting it.'

I reiterate that I think the 'subversive' reading material is *Where Did I Come From?* but once again, it's as if I haven't spoken.

Then she says, 'I think Leo's problem is his personality,' and it takes every ounce of self-control I have not to punch her. I call Leo, briskly, and track down his shoes. Vanessa makes small-talk as I tie his laces, but all I can hear is a furious buzzing in my head. I have had enough. Vanessa wishes me a happy birthday. At the front door, she hugs me and hands me a plate of home-made biscuits.

On the ride home, I lecture Leo about respect and lack of it and furiously interrogate him.

'Angus wouldn't let me play with any of his toys,' he complains. 'He was angry that I was in his room, so he said, "You want to sex with Cherie".'

'And what did you say?'

'I said *he* wanted to sex with her.'

I flick the switch on the talk about how, 'it's for adults' and, 'just because he said it, doesn't mean you should'. I tell him that Vanessa thinks he's a rude child now and that I'm not sure if he'll be welcome there again. I tell him that his behaviour is not a nice birthday present for me. On the back of my bike, he starts to cry.

Tony greets us at the door. I fill him in, confused. I don't know quite who I should be angry with and to what degree.

'That's fucked,' he says. 'What a bitch.' He takes Leo by the shoulders. 'Mate, no matter what Vanessa says, you're a great kid. We think you're great.' He hugs him.

'Your behaviour today was not great,' I add. 'But you are.'

I'm certain I haven't handled this situation well.

Fuck it. It's my birthday.

We all go out to dinner, to Leo's favourite local restaurant, where he orders lemon chicken, roti and rice, and pushes unsuccessfully for a blue heaven milkshake. I read to him from *The Bad Book* while we wait for our meals, holding him very close on my lap.

* * * *

We're not doing anything for New Year's Eve this year. I think I'm happy about it. The three of us eat our sausages and salad on the coffee table in the lounge room, in front of the television. Leo is in bed with a book at 8 pm, lights out at 8.30 pm. Tony and I watch a movie, then he goes to bed too, kissing me on the cheek to say goodnight.

'Happy new year,' he says, half joking.

'Aren't you going to give me a proper kiss?' I say, pouting up at him. He bends to brush my lips with his, then straightens to go.

'Why is it such a burden to kiss your wife?' I ask.

'It's just annoying when you ask for affection.'

'It's annoying to *have* to ask.'

'I'm just not very affectionate,' he says. 'You know that.' The twist of annoyance in his features softens into pity. 'You know I love you, though.'

'Yeah.'

He kisses me again—with conviction, if not passion, this time.

'Happy new year,' he repeats. 'Goodnight.'

It's 10.40 pm. I try not to resent him, knowing that he's been feeling particularly unwell lately. I miss passion, if not the uncertainty that always accompanied it. I do know he loves me, but sometimes I recall, with a mix of ache and alarm, the way he looked at me when we first met, as if he couldn't believe his luck. It makes me sad to realise he'll never look at me like that again, never love me like that again. It's over; the urgency of the past muted into weary duty-kisses.

I sit alone on the couch, trying to block out the pulsing doof-doof music from further down the street. I can hear it over the television, an alternative soundtrack to an old episode of *Family Ties*.

I make myself a bowl of ice-cream, my second tonight, and eat it on the back deck. There are whoops of drunken excitement from the other side of the house. The wheels of a skateboard grate on the unfinished bitumen of the street.

I don't think I've been this sober on New Year's Eve since I was a teenager, before I started drinking.

The shouts on the street become 'HAPPY NEW YEAR!' The air pops with gunpowder; the sky spews a glimpse of white sparks, tantalisingly close.

I leave my empty bowl on the bare boards of the deck and climb the railing to step up to the garage roof. It's a move I've perfected in order to rescue the footballs that Leo is always kicking up there. No matter how many times we've warned him to aim low, he can't help himself. I kick my thongs to the grass below. The corrugated iron is cool against my skin. Standing, I can see the fireworks over the rooftops, on the other side of the park. The house roof slopes above the flat of the garage. On the other side, people are still laughing and shouting. I stay above the garage until after the fireworks end. They don't last long.

Inside, I sit on the couch, listening to the sounds of the street. I sneak in to Leo's bedroom, edging through the half-open door, to kiss him goodnight. 'Happy New Year,' I whisper. Then I brush my teeth and go to bed. It takes a long time to fall asleep.

7. A WEEK OF GOODBYES

I step into the house to find the bedroom garlanded in laundry, the couch throw and cushions strewn across the lounge-room floor. I've just cycled up the hill from the train station, a hot wind whipping my ankle-length skirt above my knees. I'm limp and sweaty, exhausted from the juggle between steering my bike and controlling my wayward clothing. There's an hour for me to shower and change before people start arriving, and I feel like I've been rolling in hot chips.

There is a knock at the door. It's Tony's childhood best friend, Rob, a genial grin on his face and a sixpack dangling from one hand. I'd forgotten he was coming early. We're celebrating Tony's birthday and his trip to Mexico, all at once. He'll be in Mexico, alone, on the actual day of his birthday. He leaves in one week.

'Hello!' says Rob, as I fling open the door.

I force a smile. Tony follows him through the door, stooping to kiss me hello. I turn so it lands on my cheek.

It's not the first time this week that I've come home to a tsunami of mess. On Tuesday—my first day back at work—I got home to find my desk piled with even more debris than usual, expired food from the fridge heaped defiantly on the kitchen table and the bedroom floor carpeted in half my wardrobe. Leo's room was the worst: toyboxes on the bed; his comics buried beneath a heap of cushions and sleeping bags; and a litter of clothes, textas and crumpled drawings covering everything.

This is Tony's method of cleaning up, with the focus on getting all the stashed-away clutter into the centre of things where it can no longer be ignored. My method is the opposite—to scoop up bits of mess as I move around the house, putting it in drawers and cupboards, kicking it under couches and beds. He's going through a reverse version of nesting—tidying the house to prepare for the absence of one of its members, rather than the arrival of a new one.

I'd stayed up until late Tuesday night cleaning the rubbish from my desk and the clothes from my bedroom. But with Leo at his dad's this week, his room was less of a priority. The next night I was so exhausted that I didn't move from the couch except to go to bed. Thursday night we were out until early morning at a boozy farewell dinner with Tony's work friends.

Tonight, there's no escaping it: I have to fix Leo's room so the kids coming to the party can play in there. And so he can eventually go to bed.

Rob sits on the couch under the air-conditioner. He drinks his beer and pretends not to hear us shouting in the kitchen.

It's not unusual for Tony and me to fight before a party. We're as bad as each other when it comes to domestic order. But while I'm at one with my inner domestic slattern, he predictably morphs into a frenzied Martha Stewart just hours before people arrive. I grew up with the pointedly angry cleaning of my mother, whose only help with the housework came from whatever she could wrench out of her children. The cymbal clash of cutlery and clatter of plates would ring through the house while I sat trying to read in my bedroom, or watching television in the lounge. Tony's whirlwind cleaning inevitably triggers my nerves and we end up like this: wrestling in the hallway over a glass of water because I've idly picked up one of the new cocktail glasses bought specifically for mojitos and filled it from the tap. Tony insists he's saving those glasses for the party; I argue that *I'll drink out of any damn glass I want to*. Of course, it spills on the carpet.

When Linda arrives, with her partner and three boys, I am going through the mess in Leo's bedroom, armed with green garbage bags. I've set him up in the lounge room where he's playing Lego Star Wars on the PlayStation. I hear Tony greeting them at the front door, the boys joining Leo on the couch. I hurl the remaining toys and textas into toyboxes, which I push under the bed. The green garbage bags go in the cupboard.

Linda and John are at the kitchen table when I emerge. Tony is pouring the wine they've brought into glasses. He asks if I want a mojito. He's mixing them at a makeshift bar he's set up on the back deck, using the laminex table that we downgraded from kitchen use after his sister moved to London and bequeathed us a better one. The marbled top wobbles on its hinges, threatening to separate from the table legs. It is variously stained with coffee rings, paint and streaks of ink. I follow him out, supposedly to fetch my drink, but really to test the marital waters. He kisses me.

'No cheek this time?' he jokes, as I accept his kiss and return it.

I respond with a mock-pout. 'Do you love me now?'

'Always did.'

'Hey Jo,' says Linda as I return to the kitchen and take a seat beside her. 'The place is looking so incredibly *tidy*. You're not known for being neat.'

I dryly inform her that while usually I can laugh at myself along with everyone else, today is not the day for this particular joke.

Nikki arrives. Linda jumps up from the table; they look at each other and shriek. 'Get a room, girls,' says John as Nikki dips to hug me. Linda swipes at the back of his head. I wheel in wing-backed leather desk chairs from the study to accommodate Kabita and her husband Dane, then a painted blue stool from Leo's room for myself. Tony's friends pass through the kitchen and say hello on their way to the back deck, where they stay, dispersed on couches and chairs or standing on the back lawn under the darkening sky. A kind of Friend Apartheid develops.

We've always had very separate sets of friends. While I get along okay with most of his, none of them have become *my* friends, and vice-versa. Most of Tony's friends work in well-paid jobs—in government, business or finance. Their girlfriends and wives wear heels and talk about shopping or cooking; they somehow don't count me as one of them. My friends are all a bit quirky, one way or another. I met them through working for publishing companies, magazines or bookshops; we talk about books and politics and films and each other, and analyse it all, constantly.

If we ever split up, there would be no question about who would inherit what relationships.

Leo trails out to the back deck with Linda's youngest boy, Billy, three years his junior. They carry plastic cups of lemonade and handfuls of chips. Linda and I laugh about the surreptitious glances the boys shoot us, the way they carefully don't make eye contact as they pass through the kitchen. They think we don't know that they're breaking the rules, taking the food without asking. Actually, we don't care. It's a party.

As the sky deepens to black, the darkness punctuated by the fairy lights strung on the porch, Leo fetches a torch from the laundry. He and Billy bring a blanket from his room, squeezing nonchalantly past the grown-ups as they cross the deck to the lawn. Leo strings the blanket over the lower branches of the lemon tree to make a cubby and they sit there in the grass, playing Bionicles by torchlight.

Leo comes into the kitchen to ask me to open another bottle of lemonade. Dane, who is meeting him for the first time, makes the fatal mistake of asking questions about the Lego he carries in one hand; in return, he gets to hear all about the Bionicles universe. Leo talks on and on. I try to rescue Dane by changing the subject, but he ignores my efforts and asks another question about Bionicles.

'He's so confident with talking to adults,' he says, as Leo moves on to talk to Nikki. 'And so articulate!'

'Well, you did ask him about his favourite subject,' I say.

Kabita laughs knowingly; she has known Leo since he was two years old, though in the past couple of years since we both settled into long-haul relationships, we tend to meet up in the city for dinners or coffee rather than lounge at each other's houses like we used to.

'Sorry, he does go on about it.'

'He's passionate!' says Dane. 'I like that.'

Tony has made his own birthday cake for the occasion: a special concoction with no wheat, no eggs, no dairy, no sugar. No icing.

I carry it out to the deck and lead the singing. Tony holds Doug, his favourite dog, under one arm as he blows out the candles and cuts the cake.

I send Leo to bed after Linda and John leave. It's late, nearly 10.30 pm.

At 2 am, we call a cab to take our guests back to the inner north. After we wave them off at the door, we return to sit amid the party debris. On the back lawn, a blanket still hangs in the lemon tree.

* * * *

It's Tony's last day with Leo. The first in a series of 'last days'.

'What do you want to do?' he asks. 'We'll do anything you want, Leo.'

'Do you want to go to the beach?' I suggest.

'Yes!'

'Okay,' says Tony reluctantly. There is no air-conditioning in our car, a 1970 Holden Premier. We slide towels between our bums and the black leather seats. The heat still licks at my thighs. As we wait for the engine to tick over, we wind the windows down as far as they will go. A hot wind slaps at our faces and across my lips. I pick my hair out of my mouth and knot it into a bun.

Williamstown beach is crowded, but emptying fast. The sea, usually no more rippled than a curtain, is fierce with choppy waves. We shed our clothes and wade into the water beneath a shining grey sky. The water stings with cold, until our bodies adjust. The boys wrestle in the waves, Tony throwing Leo into the water and scooping him up again. Leo jumps on my back and ducks my head under. He laughs when I surface, spitting salt. The wind is now roaring in our ears. We shout above it to be heard.

'Let's go,' says Tony.

Our towels have blown down the beach; I run to rescue them. We walk against the wind back to the car, assailed by a fusillade of flying sand.

'Ow!' screams Leo. 'Help! Help! It hurts!'

'Wrap your towel closer,' I say. 'Put it over your head, like a hood or a cape.'

'I am!' he yells, pulling the towel from his waist up to his neck. 'It's stabbing me! The wind is like knives!'

He is exaggerating, of course, but he is also right. I guide my way by watching my feet, my head ducked against the tiny blows.

'*Hush*,' I say, sharper than I mean to. 'You're *okay*.'

He begins to cry.

Tony folds him under his arm.

At home, we take turns under the shower. No-one says that the trip to the beach was a terrible idea. I lie down on the couch and watch Leo and Tony play Lego Star Wars. When I wake up four hours later, they're still playing. They insist they had no idea it had been so long. After dinner, Tony assumes bedtime-reading duties. We all pretend this has no significance.

Tony goes to work for the last time. Leo will be gone when he gets home, off to the Gold Coast to stay with Mark's parents. Tony kneels on the lounge-room floor, where Leo is sprawled in his pyjamas making a comic book. He says a heartfelt goodbye. Leo nods. He adds feet to his superhero.

Tony stands and kisses me goodbye. Leo looks up. He follows Tony to the front door.

'Mum, we won't see Tony for a really long time, will we?' he says.

'No, we won't.'

He throws himself into Tony's arms. His head burrows into his chest. They stand like that for some time.

I watch from the hallway, crying.

Soon I will be leaving for Mexico too.

When Mark arrives, Leo holds fast to his bedposts and shakes his head. 'I want to stay,' he says. 'I haven't spent enough time here with Mum.'

Mark reminds him that he will be going to Sea World, Dreamworld and Movie World. He lets go of the bed.

* * * *

Farewell dinner with Margaret, Jordan and Edwina. Margaret has prepared a roast, as usual. Leo thinks she makes the best roast potatoes in the world. I try not to think of him as I pile them onto my plate. Jordan, seated to my left, is in a particularly chatty mood. I am not. Whenever he senses my attention waning, which is often, he comes up with something new, something like *Look in my mouth—see my food!*

'How are you feeling about leaving Leo?' asks Margaret conversationally. 'Are you nervous?'

I explode into great, heaving sobs. No one is more shocked than I am.

Margaret hastens to assure me that they'll be popping in on Leo while I'm gone, to see how he's going with Mark; that they'll make sure he's okay. I don't say that this doesn't help, kind though it is. I don't say that mothers shouldn't leave their children. That I am choosing my husband over my child, and I am ashamed. The conversation moves on to Tony's sister, who is living in London and miserable about it. It's Margaret's turn to cry, mine to join in the comforting.

By the time the fresh berries and cream are brought out for dessert, the funereal air has lifted, just a little.

Margaret takes us to the airport. At the departure gate, we both cling to Tony and cry. Especially me.

'I don't know why I'm doing this,' he says, as we sit hand-in-hand on a steel-mesh bench. Margaret is pretending to look at handbags on the fringe of a nearby shop. I tell him that he will have *a wonderful time* and it will be *an incredible experience*. That we'll see each other soon. We hug and cry. 'Now I'd better go,' he says. Another hug. 'Now I'd *really* better go.' Eventually, he does.

I slide my big black sunglasses from my head over my eyes. I know I look ridiculous, moving through the dim enclosed space of the international terminal. But I need some kind of shield between my ruined face and the world. Margaret sweeps me up in a hug and hurries me to the car in a swirl of chatter, suggesting coffee in Carlton on the way home.

In Borders on Lygon Street, I buy a DVD of *This Life*, a nineties television series about a sharehouse of lawyers in London. When I get home, I go to bed with a roll of Pringles and insert the first DVD.

I stay in bed all day, sleeping and eating and watching *This Life*. It is strange to think that Tony won't come home and pick up his dressing gown from the end of the bed or change the piles of CDs teetering next to the computer.

I get up to feed the dogs. I speak on the phone twice, once to Tony in Guadalajara, once to Leo at my mum's house in Adelaide where he has flown directly from the Gold Coast. He answers the phone with, 'IS THIS MY MUMMY?'

In Guadalajara, Tony is disoriented. He misses me, too. He says the city is nothing like he imagined. It's older, poorer, more run-down.

The road from the airport is lined with shells of abandoned cars. He is the only *gringo* on the streets near the inn where he is staying. At the Walmart he is calling from, they have all the familiar brands, with Spanish labels. He bought a packet of Doritos. He has been off the plane for half an hour.

'I don't know why I'm here,' he says.

I hang up feeling lucky to have two people who love and miss me.

The next day, I get up and go out for breakfast. I email Tony. I call Leo.

I don't return to bed, or my DVD, until it is dark.

8. CUTTING LOOSE

Margaret calls to invite me to dinner. She will pick me up and take me to their place in St Kilda, then drop me home, she says. I like the idea of a proper dinner, after the past few nights of baked beans or melted cheese on toast. And I like the idea of being somewhere I needn't pretend to be happy.

I sit on a stool in the kitchen and talk to Margaret while she chops asparagus for the salad. We exchange news from Tony. 'He'll be alright when he settles in,' she says. 'He's just got a bit of culture shock, I think.' Edwina pours me a wine, which I take into the dining room. I sit next to Jordan, who tells me stories about playing football with Edwina and the Lego fort he has built in his bedroom. I am reaching for my third serving of roast potatoes, hoping no-one notices, when I realise there is hardly a dent on Jordan's plate. I empty the last of the gravy boat onto my own.

'I'm sorry,' I say, in my best schoolteacher's tone. 'I can't hear you. I won't be able to hear you until you've had four more mouthfuls.'

He shovels in four hasty forkfuls of peas, then continues, open-mouthed.

Later, I ask him a question he is uninterested in.

'*Sorry*,' he says, putting his hands over his ears, as I had. 'I can't hear you.'

I have to laugh.

After dinner, I follow Jordan to his bedroom and read him two bedtime stories. At nearly five, he is just starting to love stories, though his concentration is waning by the end of the second one. I start skipping over words, condensing it as I read in an effort to turn the pages quicker. As I finish, Edwina comes in to give him his bedtime apple juice. Margaret takes me home, along the tramline and over the West Gate Bridge. As she hugs me goodbye in the driveway, in front of the dark windows of my house, she urges me to stay in touch.

I settle on the couch and call Dad's house in Adelaide to speak to Leo. He sounds a little perturbed to be called to the phone.

'What are you doing?' I ask.

'I'm watching a movie. *Fantastic Four*.'

'Oh. That sounds good. Is it good?'

'Yes.' Pause. 'I'm right in the middle of it, actually.'

'Oh. Would you like me to let you go, so you can get back to it?'

'Yes, please. Bye Mum.'

＊ ＊ ＊ ＊

It is my last day of work. At last. We go out for lunch to an Italian restaurant where I am presented with a card and present—a luscious hardcover book on the art and life of Diego Rivera.

'You'll visit his murals, I imagine?' says my boss. 'In Mexico City?'

I tell him we'll be staying in Guadalajara mostly, but will hopefully visit the capital, too.

It's the second time I've left a job with this man, whom I first worked with before I was pregnant with Leo. He was the publisher, I was the marketing manager (really a 'glorified publicist' as someone once said) of his list. Our meetings in his office had been dignified affairs. He would bring down his biscuit jar from a top shelf and solemnly offer it. His secretary would bring us plunger coffee and mugs, with a beaker of milk. We once took a business trip to Canberra, to visit the National Dictionary Centre. I was twenty-two years old and it was the first time I had been on a plane. When he found out, he swapped seats with me so I could sit by the window.

Over coffee, my boss tells us about his own youthful visit to Mexico City. He recounts walking from the airport to his hotel, intimidated by the crowds, the poverty—too intimidated to hail a cab or catch a bus. 'There I was,' he sighs, 'with my long hair and my suitcase full of books.' We all whoop with laughter, imagining his manicured sweep of hair, his pressed shirts and trousers, replaced by hair hanging down his back and rumpled jeans.

I end the day taking my successor through my files one last time, making a stab at editing a review, unpinning photos of Tony and Leo from the walls of my office. Wine swirls in my veins, in my head.

I walk to the train station one last time: terrifyingly free.

Adelaide. I stay in my mum's house, the home I lived in as a teenager: its five bedrooms, three living rooms and two studies now house my mother alone. Leo and I get the bottom floor to ourselves, with our own sprawling living room and a bedroom each. Mine has a single bed with a flowered bedspread and a wardrobe. Leo's has been decorated as a kind of shrine to him, though it sits empty for most of the year. There is a patterned quilt on the bed, an AFL poster on the wall, a box of Lego in a corner. A bookshelf stocked with our childhood leftovers: *My Naughty Little Sister*, Roald Dahl, Snoopy. We read, play Monopoly, trail my mother around the local shopping centre, catch the bus to the beach or the swimming pool.

Then we stay at Dad's house, in his unit. It was an investment unit before my parents split up a few years ago, now it's his. There are three bedrooms, a brick courtyard, two living areas. The few plants in the backyard are browning, shrivelling. He tells me, helplessly, that he doesn't know what to do with them. His two spare rooms are piled with gym equipment, computer manuals, tins of tennis balls stacked like blocks against the walls. I sleep on the futon couch in one living room; Leo sleeps on the fold-out couch in the other. Dad says the place is too small, that no woman would ever want to make a home there. I ask him what he would do with more space. He doesn't know.

My brother Simon lives literally around the corner from Dad's house. His backyard is as big as the house itself, a huge expanse of grass and fruit trees. An outdoor bungalow has a built-in bar, which he stocks generously with beer and vodka, Southern Comfort and Coke. The bricked front gate has a hole in it, where Simon drove his car through it on his way home from the pub one night. He has a new grey suede couch and armchairs, a flat-screen plasma television as wide as a window, a PlayStation. He works in mortgage finance at a bank, goes to work in a suit and tie every day.

Simon throws an Australia Day party at his house. There is backyard cricket and a barbecue. He invites both family and friends, which includes my high school best friend, Chelsea, whom I try to avoid, as well as his high school best friend, Toby—still his best friend. Chelsea is loud and brash and inevitably the centre of any conversation. She also dropped me, without explanation or warning, when we were in Year Eleven, after seven years of friendship. She would not answer my phone calls; when I went to her house, where she was allowed to write on her wall, there was a picture of a smiling deodorant can, labelled with my name, scrawled in texta. This still bothers me, though we became friends again six months later.

'Happy Australia Day,' Chelsea says to Leo, offering him a hat emblazoned with an Australian flag.

'Happy *Invasion* Day, you mean,' he says, frowning.

'What?'

'It's Invasion Day, the day when white people stole the country from the Aboriginal people. We shouldn't celebrate it, we should be ashamed.'

On a deckchair nearby, I am plaiting my sister's hair into twin braids. Chelsea is a curious combination of left-wing and self-identifying bogan; I wonder how she will react.

'Well, yes,' she says evenly. 'That's true, Leo. Very good. But it's also a day to celebrate being Australian, a day to have fun. I reckon you can do both, remember that *and* be proud to be Australian now.'

He peers quizzically back at her, but says nothing. He wears the hat.

'You can keep that,' she says. Calling across the verandah, she tells me, 'He's so smart, he is. Gorgeous. I want one like that.'

I can't do anything but smile and thank her.

My brother Nick mentors Leo through the backyard cricket game, calming him when he gets agitated at missing the ball or being struck out. I enjoy watching them together; it reminds me how similar they are. Later, Leo sits in the deckchair beside Nick, drinking lemonade while Nick drinks beer.

Simon's new girlfriend, Kate, sits under the verandah with Chelsea, sucking slowly on a Corona. She is quiet, contained, dressed simply in a black scoop-neck T-shirt and blue jeans, her feet bare and toenails polished. At first, I think she is aloof; I am inclined not to like her. But then she smiles at something I say, a throwaway comment about Simon, and I realise that she is shy—and possibly overwhelmed by this sprawl of family, of people who have been to school with each other, or lived next door to each other, since childhood.

Mum leaves in the late afternoon, along with Nana. Dad stays until after dark. Leo walks around the house bare-chested, eating from a packet of salt-and-vinegar chips as big as his torso. Crumbs stick to his skin. He hovers in the lounge room with the sons of Simon's friends. They break into shouts of collective joy when AC/DC appears on the plasma TV. It's late when I retrieve Leo's T-shirt from a corner and take him back to Dad's house, where I tuck a sleeping bag over him on the sofa bed, then change from my summer dress into jeans and long sleeves before returning to Simon's.

'You've done so well for yourself,' says Chelsea, as we sit together in the dark of the verandah. My outstretched legs rest on an esky.

I murmur modestly.

'Yeah, you're so smart at stuff I'm not so good at,' she continues. 'Like spelling and grammar. I wish I could hire you as my editorial assistant to proofread my PhD. You'd be really good at that.'

I think of my unfinished arts degrees: three of them.

'My dad buys *The Big Issue*, he reads your articles,' she says. 'He remembers you.'

'Really?' I'm genuinely flattered; I never think of anyone in Adelaide reading what I write.

'Yeah. Mum says she remembers you too; she remembers how you used to lie all the time.'

'What?' This is less flattering. I don't remember this at all.

'You know, to your parents.'

'Oh, *that*. You know they would never have let me do anything if I didn't.'

'True.'

'They wouldn't even have let me *be* at your place if they knew what we were doing.'

* * * *

Neither of us mentions that after my parents *did* find out what we got up to at Chelsea's house, after they read my teenage diary, after Chelsea had renewed our friendship as mysteriously as she had dropped me (following a six-month gap of me being invisible), they banned me from seeing her. They also made my best friend at the time choose between remaining friends with Chelsea or with me, under threat of telling *her* parents about what was in my diary if she didn't comply. She chose Chelsea, of course, rather than weekends under supervision at my house.

Chelsea had the kind of parents who said, *Better if you do it in the home* about alcohol and (I think) drugs. They might have said the same about boys too; I don't know. We talked about boys and crushes all the time; we wrote illustrated stories about them and found them in the phone book and prank-called them and walked accidentally-on-purpose past their houses. But we never actually had relationships with them. The boys we sat with at lunchtime and flirted with ineptly, as if for practice, were not the same boys we decided we were in love with. Neither of us had proper boyfriends until after we finished school.

The first time I drank alcohol was at a sleepover at Chelsea's, when I was thirteen. Someone passed around a minibar-sized bottle of Jack Daniels for us to share while we were watching *The Breakfast Club*. We only managed a couple of sips each before it was all gone, but we convinced ourselves we were drunk. We shrieked a lot, then we sang around the television, then we rang the boys in our class, one by one, and sang to them down the phone.

When my parents read my diary—okay, when Mum read my diary—I was sixteen and nearing the end of Year Twelve. She learned that I had recently singed my eyelashes lighting a joint in my bedroom cupboard; that Chelsea had offered to buy me a tab of acid as a present for an upcoming party, though I was apprehensive; that I had half-filled a pink drink bottle with Dad's cask wine from the fridge and brought it to school.

These were the things I suppose Chelsea could tell her parents about; the things I lied about to mine.

I lost all my friends, for a time, after the diary incident. It took me a while to make new ones. In the weeks in between, I studied obsessively for my Year Twelve exams and got into university, to my surprise, after a year spent writing letters and stories with my friends during classes and not handing in assignments. I walked for hours and did a hundred sit-ups every day, ate just bread rolls and yoghurt and apples, and lost twelve kilograms.

I filled the emptiness with careful planning and frantic activity.

Finally, Leo and I stay with my twin sisters, in the flat they share near the centre of town, in affluent St Peters. The streets are wide and leafy, hushed. There are sandstone houses, vast lawns. The Torrens River runs through the suburb, winding its way to the city. Leo sleeps in Sarah's double bed with her; I sleep on a mattress on the floor. Dad comes to visit and we play tennis in the park a few doors down from the flat. He teaches Leo how to wield a racket.

I have made plans to meet two blog friends for drinks on Rundle Street. Liz and Sarah think it hilarious that I am going to have a drink with people I have never met. I feel weird about it too, like I'm internet dating, but I don't tell them that while I've never met these people— Georgia and Clementine—I know them more intimately than I do many of my friends. I know that Clementine lost her mother to cancer, that she had an abortion, that she and her friends sometimes scale the fence of St Peter's College and swim in its pool. I know that Georgia writes with her cat pawing her keyboard and that when she walks on a beach, she remembers beachcombing with her dad who died when she was seventeen.

I walk through the back streets and across the Botanic Gardens to the pub where we have arranged to meet, iPod in my pocket, headphones on.

My natural tendency to be late means that I make a devoted effort to be on time these days. It usually means I arrive early—like tonight. I buy a gin and tonic, sit in a corner and wait. And then I realise that I have no idea what Clementine and Georgia look like. We hadn't thought to exchange photographs or descriptions. Or phone numbers. For the next forty minutes, I circle the pub, looking intensely at people, trying to gauge if they are waiting for someone, for me. More than once, I stare a little too long. The only way to fix this is to start asking people if they are Georgia or Clementine, but I can't do that. Instead, I walk slowly home, stopping for a solitary pizza along the way. As I pass St Peter's College, I think of Clementine, swimming.

Later, I check my emails and discover that Georgia and Clementine found one another. They had a great time, plan to stay in touch, and ended their night sharing a pizza at the same restaurant where I ate. We all agree to catch up another time. I am going home tomorrow, back to Melbourne.

* * * *

Leo says he's not looking forward to going back to school. But then, the day before he returns, he pulls out his new lettering set (a farewell gift from Tony) and asks if he can have an empty manila folder. He makes himself an intricately designed and illustrated 'school folder' with his name and grade in fancy print. Next, he stocks the folder with a map of the school and classrooms, and his class list, dug crumpled from the bottom of his schoolbag, untouched since last year.

'Are you looking forward to school now?' I tease.

'*No,*' he says.

After dinner, he tips the schoolbag upside down on his carpet and begins to pack. He includes a book about naughty schoolchildren, *4F for Freaks*, which he says he will ask his teacher to read to the class as an example of how *not* to behave. As I wash the pans and colander from tonight's spaghetti bolognaise, he parades a series of containers into the kitchen, arranging them on the table as suggested lunchboxes. They include a shoebox and a Lego container.

'So, you're really not looking forward to school?' I ask. 'You seem pretty excited.'

'Yes,' he admits. 'I am a bit.'

We select and pack his school lunch together. (Watermelon, a carrot, wholemeal crackers with cheese and two Arnott's Assorted Creams.) He solemnly packs it in a lunchbox I bought last week, along with the West Coast Eagles drink bottle Sarah gave him as a Christmas present.

I take his school clothes off the line and fold them.

He chooses *4F for Freaks* as his bedtime story. He instructs me to put it back in his schoolbag after I finish his nightly three chapters.

He literally wriggles with excitement as I leave the room and switch out the lights. Every time I pass his bedroom door, he is squirming on the bed, contorting his quilt into increasingly odd formations. I have to go in and shake it smooth again.

'Muuuuum.'

'What?'

'Is it really true that the quicker you go to sleep, the quicker you wake up?'

'Yes.'

* * * *

I wake to a small body against mine in the bed; he has burrowed under the covers to lie beside me.

'I'M GOING TO SCHOOL TODAY!' he trumpets.

As we're leaving the house, he ducks under my arm, darting back through the door. He returns with a dented Granny Smith apple. 'You know what you should give to your teacher ...'

I take this as a good omen for the year. As we set off down the road and across the park, I look at his head and suppress a sigh. During the holidays, he's decided it's cool to wear your hat backwards. In fact, he's told me he'll look like a 'nerd' if he wears it the right way round. I've tried, without luck, to convince him that the opposite is true. Now, he has tucked in the backflap of his school hat (meant to protect his neck from the sun) and turned it backwards so the visor shades his neck and his face is exposed.

'If a teacher tells you to turn that around, you must do it.'

'Yes, Mum.'

'Are you going to be a good boy for me this year?'

'Uh-huh. I have *no interest* in toilet humour.'

'You don't?'

'No. No interest at all. I mean, I think it's funny when, in *The Bad Book*, Terence takes off all his clothes. And when Horrid Henry shows his undies. But I would think to myself, "That is something I *should not* do".'

'Good.'

'What do you think the worst thing in *The Bad Book* is?' says Leo. 'I think it's when the little old lady swallows a poo, that'd be disgusting. Can you imagine how that would taste? And why would a little old lady swallow a poo? That'd be like your grandma doing it. My granny would never swallow a poo, but I guess it would be pretty funny if she did. If she thought she saw some chocolate sitting on the counter, like a little chocolate cake or something, and she was hungry, so she put in her mouth, but actually a cat came through the window and it pooed on the bench, and that's what it was. And then granny would be like— AAAAAAHHH! AHHHHHH! BLEEEURGH!'

'It sure sounds like you have no interest in toilet humour,' I say.

'EUUUUW! AHHHH!' continues Leo, as if I hadn't spoken. He puts his hands at his throat and sticks out his tongue, popping his eyes open wide. 'Then granny would have to run to the toilet to vomit, but she wouldn't make it, and she'd just vomit in the kitchen sink, and it would be all blocked up and disgusting. So she'd just keep vomiting, until it spilled on the floor. It would be the most disgusting thing ever—an old lady who swallowed a poo and then she didn't die, like in the story, she just vomited forever, that's even more disgusting, right? So I think Andy Griffiths shouldn't have made the old lady die, he should have made her …'

'Leo,' I interrupt. 'LEO!'

' … he should have made her vomit and then her cat eats the vomit,' he says, stubbornly finishing his sentence. 'And then it poos again.'

'Please don't tell that story at school today,' I say. 'At least, not around your teachers. They probably won't appreciate it.'

'Of course, Mum.' He gives me a look of grown-up disdain. 'I *know* that.'

'Anyway, Leo,' I say. 'You kind of didn't listen to me just then. It was a very funny story, but you were talking *at* me, not *to* me. Remember how we've talked about that?'

'Yep.'

'It's nice to give other people a chance to say things too, in between what you have to say.'

'Yes, Mum.'

We cross the creek and approach the start of the cul-de-sac that leads to the school. Leo squeezes me around the waist and beams up at me. 'I'm so happy!' he says.

Margaret drives me to the airport, with Leo. I am excited about leaving Australia for the first time; sick at the thought of leaving my son, who will stay with his dad during my weeks away. He sits quietly in the back seat on our journey down the Western Ring Road.

We snack at the Hudson's Coffee stand near the elevators and the payphones. Margaret and I have coffee in paper cups; Leo has an iced chocolate and a pink-iced doughnut. I manage a few sips. Leo eats and drinks steadily until his doughnut is gone and his drink reduced to cubes of milky ice.

At the entrance to the international terminal, there is a repeat of the scene of six weeks ago. Margaret hovers by the sunglasses stand while I hug Leo and cry. We stand under the departure board, with its orange neon grid of times, gate lounges and airline logos. Leo holds me tight, but he does not cry. His small face is solemn as the gates shut between us, his hand in Margaret's.

9. AWAY

The plane drops below the clouds. One minute I am staring impatiently at the flight screen, the next I glance at the window to see a ripple of bay and hills below, their colours muted by a screen of fog. It's as I had always pictured it, only without the sun and blue skies I associate with California, where I imagine oranges grow in winter and swimming pools are in use all year round.

As we roll across the tarmac, past the sign that says *San Francisco International Airport*, my eyes well with tears. I have entered the pages of a book, the other side of the screen. I am in America.

I decide I will save money and catch the train to the city centre, to find my way to the hotel from there. Considering I regularly get lost finding my way to an unfamiliar cafe or bar back in Melbourne, this is an interesting leap of faith.

Spat from the underground train station to a street pelted by rain, struggling under the weight of three bags, I stand blinking into the traffic, which runs in the wrong direction. A tall black man in a hooded rain jacket calls to me from the pavement. Like me, he is holding a tourist map. He is dry beneath his umbrella.

'Do you know where you're going?' he calls.

'What?'

'Do you know where you're going? Do you need a hand?'

I admit that I don't know, not exactly, and tell him the hotel I am heading to.

'How about I hail you a cab? It's not far for them to take you.'

I follow him to a street corner where he sticks out his arm and easily stops a cab.

'You wouldn't have any small change to spare, would you?' he asks as I thank him.

I scoop all the coins from my purse. 'I haven't worked out what these are yet, but you can have them,' I say.

'He shouldn't have asked you for money,' says the cab driver, shaking his head. He checks the address of my hotel and shakes his head again. 'That's a bad area,' he warns. 'Good hotel, bad area. There are some bad people there. Be careful.'

On our one-minute drive, the street front quickly segues from Bloomingdale's, Brooks Brothers and Westfield Shoppingtown to Payless Shoes, 7-Eleven and, opposite the hotel, a gaudily lit strip club, a drug store with boarded-up windows and a *For Lease* sign on the wall. The passers-by change from predominantly well-dressed and white, to predominantly black and obviously down on their luck. Clusters of young men gather on either side of the road, in front of the drug store and the cable-car line. None of this was featured on the hotel's website photos. Nor, I will soon discover, were the silhouetted naked ladies adorning the adult cinema outside my window.

I hand the driver a ten-dollar bill and let him work out the tip from the change. He doesn't take one.

I don't linger in my room; instead, armed with a map, a wad of US dollars and just one bag, I brave the walk across the street to the cable-car.

'So where are you from?' asks the woman who joins me at the stop. My head is uselessly ducked against the rain. 'Do you know where you're going?'

I am attempting to look confident and purposeful, but standing in the rain with no umbrella and a scared demeanour probably does not translate as such. I give in and confess my helplessness; she offers directions and comments on the rain, looking at me sympathetically from under her umbrella.

'Yeah, I thought it was never cold in California,' I say, aware as the words leave my mouth of how stupid I sound.

'Well, it's winter.'

'I know, I guess I thought it would still be warmer. And not so rainy.'

She makes a noise somewhere between a snort and a laugh. 'Oh, it's rainy alright!'

I stop to buy an umbrella at the tourist hub of Fisherman's Wharf, then wind my way through the sideshow alley of ice-cream and sweet stalls, and seafood restaurants advertising crab bisque, to look at the freezing ocean. It is my first up-close glimpse of the Golden Gate Bridge, its arch a lipstick scrawl against the steel sky and gossamer fog. Even as the rain soaks into the cuffs of my jeans and creeps up my calves, I feel my excitement return.

City Lights Bookstore is the legendary hangout of Jack Kerouac and Alan Ginsberg, owned by beat poet Lawrence Ferlinghetti. The shop runs a publishing company, too, and an events program. I've never been a big fan of the beats, apart from the requisite teenage flirtation with *On the Road*, but I like that this is a bookshop with a history. I stand in the doorway, admiring the dark polished-wood shelving, the handwritten and laminated staff recommendations, the web of interconnected rooms and stairs. I shake the water from my umbrella and wait for the staffer behind the counter to finish his phone call so I can deposit my bag and browse the shelves. For a moment, I feel at home.

I wake at 3 am to sirens outside my window and music blaring on the street. There is shouting, a scream. I get up. Someone is wielding an old-fashioned ghetto blaster on the pavement outside. Under the dim of the street lamps, I see that a cardboard city of sorts has sprung up along the cable-car line, people huddled under what look like fragments of boxes. I return to bed, deeply shocked.

I am in San Francisco for three days, before I travel to San Diego, where I will cross the border to Mexico. I walk and walk and walk. Then I write about what I have seen, in Starbucks in the CBD and taquerias in the Mission District: long rambling accounts that begin in my notebook, then translate to my blog. I don't eat enough; adrenaline has eroded my appetite. Besides, I am determined to save money for the weeks ahead.

Mum writes: *Glad to hear that you've arrived safely—but as a mother, a little concerned about your location … you sound as though you are being cautious though. Just ask yourself this as you go about your business—what would Mum be saying to me now? What advice would she give—wanted or not!!!! That you should keep safe. Nana says don't leave anything important in your room, carry it with you on your person.*

My sister Liz writes: *Take as many pics of the department stores and famous shopping strips as you can.*

The hour-long trip across the American border, from San Diego to San Ysidro then Tijuana, is long and fraught. My laptop crashes at 7 am when I turn it on to retrieve the details of my e-ticket. I use the computer in my San Diego hostel to email Tony. I try to call him on the payphone, but it's broken. He calls to assure me that all I need is my passport and the name of the airline.

I catch a cab to the trolley station where I ride to San Ysidro. As we move away from the city and towards the border, the housing gets shabbier and graffiti spreads like a virus along the fences by the tracks. Eventually, the fences start deteriorating: chips of wood peeling away, missing planks like broken teeth. The station signs become bilingual. We pass a temporary home—a one-man tent with a mattress inside and an American flag outside. This is just one cliché that my travels have proved true: Americans love their flag.

In San Ysidro, the trolley stops. There is a taqueria-style cafe, a worn tourist information office and a money-changer's. This is it. The end of the USA.

I expected the trolley to take me into Tijuana, but it doesn't. On foot, I cross a multistorey cement bridge lined with thick iron bars and guarded by uniformed policemen stationed at every bend. My bags cut into my shoulders; my back aches. I try not to look at the *WANTED* posters I pass. At the top of the bridge, I pause and look down at the highway below. Cars snake out in a queue with no end in sight, on their way into America. This, at least, is how I pictured it.

Twenty minutes later, I pass through revolving studded steel gates, two sets of them, and I am in Mexico at last. Tony and I are in the same country again.

'Welcome to Tijuana!' says the uniformed driver as I climb into the back seat of his cab. 'Where do you want to go?'

The streets fly past my window; I am too tired and bemused to properly take it in. A blur of Latino faces and bodies, pastel-painted houses, street vendors. At the traffic lights, a woman goes from car to car, brandishing pink candied hearts the size of dinner plates.

'*No gracias*,' the driver says politely as she pauses at our open window. It's Valentine's Day. In all the stress of getting here, I completely forgot.

At the airport, it turns out the driver doesn't take cards, only cash. I have none—no *pesos*, no dollars—and must run into the airport to use the ATM, then back to the carpark to pay him. Inside, there is a problem with my booking—it turns out my name, taken down over the phone, has been comically misspelled. There is a problem with my tourist visa, then my boarding pass, the last discovered just minutes before boarding—somehow, I forgot to collect it. I collapse into embarrassed tears and have to dig out my sunglasses to hide my face. Even after a kindly airport staffer tells me she has arranged for me to show my ID instead of a boarding pass, I can't stop crying. When I dare to look up, expecting disgust, instead I find sympathy in the faces around me—the woman with the toddler in Disneyland sneakers, the man in the cowboy hat. I sneeze and someone offers an accented *Bless you*. When it is time to line up, the woman with the toddler taps me on the shoulder and shows me where to go.

I am thirty-one years old and I seem to know nothing about how to get on in the world.

Tony's description of his arrival in Guadalajara to the sight of abandoned car shells and decrepit housing is still with me. But as I walk into the airport, I am reassured by gleaming modern buildings.

At the exit, a line of hopeful-looking people watches the sliding doors. Tony is among them, holding a long-stemmed red rose. He takes my sports bag and offers to take the others, though I assure him I'm fine. We hold each other tight as we walk to the carpark, shooting each other fleeting looks as if neither of us can believe we're together. He stops to kiss me along the way, more than once. We sit together on the back seat of the car. Tony clasps my hand in his and curls his other arm around me.

Our driver makes conversation from the front seat. He saw a documentary about Australia recently, he says. It was a tribute to a national hero of ours who had died, a great man. He thinks hard and eventually the name comes to him. Steve Irwin!

'It was a sad day for Australia, no?' he says. 'He was very, very famous. A national hero.'

'Yes, after he died,' says Tony.

We eat enchiladas and drink sangria at a restaurant near the city hotel room Tony has rented for the night. We are serenaded by wandering mariachis and bombarded by vendors with armfuls of roses for sale. Tony politely knocks back each of them in turn—*no necesito* (not necessary). I will quickly learn this phrase.

Back at the hotel, we stand on the balcony overlooking the narrow main street and the smog-streaked buildings on the other side of the traffic.

'So, this is Guadalajara,' I say. It is more modern, but less charming than I imagined, the few jewels of historical glamour—a domed church lit gold at night, a gallery with grand pillars and angels carved into its entrance—are set amid tired-looking shops stocked with cheap merchandise. It is, of course, a third-world country.

The hotel is one of the nicest in the city, Tony says. Our room has two double beds, with lime-green chenille bedspreads, and a bathroom with toilet paper in a bin next to the cistern. When I use the shower, water sprays the sink and the toilet, floods the tiles.

'I'm glad you're here,' Tony says, pulling me to him.

We come in from the balcony and shut the doors, alone together at last.

Our flat is in the relatively well-to-do suburb of Chapalita, a short walk from a strip of cafes and taquerias, a Starbucks (my one source of decent coffee) and an English-language bookshop. All the houses in this area are locked behind formidable gates; dogs guard the roofs of some of them—you see them pacing behind barbed-wire-topped fences as you pass. On the corner of our street is a crumbling abandoned mansion, shrouded in waist-high weeds and webbed with graffiti. Ivy climbs the walls and covers windows empty of glass.

Tony goes to university during the day; not all day and not every day. Occasionally he returns home because his professors have failed to show up. He says that teachers are highly respected here but poorly paid. As a result, it's accepted that sometimes they decide not to come to class, or show up late without comment. I sit in our shared courtyard under the jacaranda tree and read a sprawling 700-page history of Mexico beneath its bouquet of lavender branches. I spend hours with my laptop in the cafe down the road, earning my table and wireless connection by buying endless iced coffees or juices.

I am freer, more relaxed, than I have ever been in my life.

On weekends, we visit the markets in the city or in nearby villages. We eat and drink with abandon. We visit art galleries and museums. When I come back from the city, my throat aches and my sinuses are thick with the pollution. For hours, my nose runs black with mucus.

My relationship with Tony is freer, too. I have no responsibilities and he seems cavalier about his. He regularly skips his university classes: sometimes so we can travel, sometimes simply because he'd rather do something else, like go to the markets or visit one of the friends he's made here.

Most of the time, though, it's just us. It's just as cheap to eat out as it is to cook, so we eat every meal at the restaurants and taquerias at the end of our street. Tony largely disregards his diet; mysteriously, he is fine. He decides it must be because all his meals are freshly cooked, with no processed ingredients, and corn is more common than the forbidden wheat. We don't analyse it further.

We are drawn back to a time when life revolved around pleasure, when we both had jobs that ended when we left work. When we saw each other on the days I didn't have Leo—when everything was about us, about discovering each other and how we fit together. It's gratifying to discover that we still fit.

Kabita emails to tell me that my job at the bookshop newsletter is free; my replacement has resigned. I write immediately to ask for the job back.

The negotiations happen at the wireless cafe near our street. I consider a return to my old life while looking across the road at the piñata shop, its brightly coloured Supermen, princesses and soccer balls hanging in the window and over the footpath.

In the evening, I wander down the road to the internet cafe, with its lines of blocky beige PCs and the man taking your *pesos* from behind a desk in the corner. There is no deciding email from the bookshop, but there is another one from Kabita. *Stop worrying about the job*, she urges. *Enjoy your holiday. Stop checking your emails! You're not in Mexico for long. You'll be back in Melbourne forever.*

✳ ✳ ✳ ✳

I'm missing my boy. I talk to him on Skype, for the first time since I left him at Melbourne airport.

'I miss your house,' he says.

'*Really?*'

'Yeah, *don't tell Dad*, but the Lego is much better at your house.'

'Oh. That's nice. Okay, I won't.'

He is doing just fine without me. Mark reports that he is doing well in school—his teacher says that he has tested the boundaries a bit but there are no serious problems. This is an achievement. It's the first time since he entered institutionalised care (childcare, kindergarten, school) that a teacher or carer has begun the year with 'no serious problems'. He won a Best Listener award in assembly last week. My child, the dreamer, is not known for his listening skills.

He has formed a lunchtime football team, started music lessons and lost his first tooth, which he accidentally swallowed.

✳ ✳ ✳ ✳

I get an email from the bookshop, officially offering me my old job back, with the same salary and conditions as when I left nearly a year ago. I happily accept. I stop compulsively checking my email and choose a new book from the English-language bookshop.

* * * *

Tony and I are walking through a small plaza in Chapalita (an oversized traffic roundabout with trees and a fountain) when a small boy comes tottering towards us, arms outstretched. He is wailing: '*Ma-miiii, Ma-miiii.*' A woman with two small children is smiling over at us; I presume she is his mother, that he has walked the wrong way around the roundabout and has somehow got lost. I smile at the boy, who continues to come our way, still crying for his mother. I give him a little wave. The woman bends to scoop him up; she says something to me in Spanish. I wave at her, too.

As we cross the road, Tony tells me what she said.

'He thought you were his mother.'

'What? But his mother was there!'

'No, she was his carer, I think. She told you that he thought you were his mother. That's why he was following you.'

I burst into tears right in the middle of the road, surrounded by traffic, by shops and restaurants. Tony takes my arms and guides me to safety.

The idea that the little boy had thought that his mother was walking away from him while he stretched his arms to her and pleaded haunts me for the rest of the day. I think of my boy, on the other side of the world. If he calls for me, I won't hear him. I won't even know.

I am surprised, too. From what I'd seen of the children bagging groceries beside their mothers at supermarkets and sleeping in bassinets among clothes racks, I had the romantic view that in Mexico, children come to work with their parents. This, I'd thought, was a society where children are a welcome and inevitable part of life rather than lifestyle impediments.

Now, I realise that women on production lines, for instance (which employ mostly women) are unlikely to be allowed to bring their children to work. I don't think women bring children to law firms or newspaper offices or hospitals either.

The next day, around lunchtime, I notice a grandmother walking a toddler in a stroller, on the same street where the child had mistaken me for his mother.

* * * *

For our one-year wedding anniversary, we travel to the beachside town of Melaque, four hours away: over the mountains and past fields of agave (the main ingredient of tequila). We stay in a hotel with a path to the beach and eat dinner each night at a restaurant on the sand. Every morning, I swim in the pool outside our window, taking care to avoid the iguana that lives in the courtyard. For the first day, I can barely keep my balance due to an ear infection. In pain, I whine about everything, including the dusty streets, shabby hotel rooms and the beach towels festooned with sharks and the name of the town. ('Are there sharks out there?') Once recovered, I am enchanted by everything.

Tony, who usually declares himself not fond of water or beaches, has not brought bathers to Mexico. He swims in his cargo shorts, then buys board shorts from a souvenir shop. Each day, he spends a little more time in the water. In the pool, he teaches me proper swimming strokes and how to dive; I have never learned, while he was—as his mother has often told me—a swimming champion in his youth. 'Always boasting about me,' he sighs, when I remind him of her words.

By the time we leave, if I concentrate very hard, I can perform one reasonable dive among the painful belly flops.

Tony follows me across the border on my way home, to spend a week or so in New York, then California. New York seduces us both. I have always dreamed of going; Tony arrives ambivalent at best about America. As I rise from the subway to Midtown, I feel like Alice down the rabbit hole. Skyscrapers rise all around us, the street gratings breathe steam vapours, yellow cabs jam the road. Hotdog vendors and entrepreneurs are stationed on every street corner. The maximum temperature is three degrees Fahrenheit: I have never been so cold in my life. My jeans are damp on my legs, just from the moisture in the air.

I ice-skate in Central Park, eat cupcakes from the Magnolia Bakery; we walk across the Brooklyn Bridge. At a house where Truman Capote once lived, in Brooklyn, an old man sits on the stoop. Behind him on the steps lies an abandoned copy of Lonely Planet *Nueva York*. I am shy, but Tony photographs the spot, explaining to the puzzled man that this was Truman Capote's house. 'Who's that?' he asks. Park Slope, with its immaculate brownstones, is like the set of Sesame Street, but with independent bookshops and cafes strung with fairy lights. I expect to see Oscar the Grouch emerge from a trash can. We eat soul food in Harlem and visit Malcolm X's mosque.

In Greenwich Village, we meet a school friend of Tony's who lives here. He works in high finance. His one-bedroom apartment has a small kitchen with a stove and oven, and a tiny sitting room. Later, I learn that this is a mark of luxury. We go to a nearby comedy club where Richard shells peanuts onto the table as we drink and talk. He is dressed like Seinfeld in a T-shirt and blazer, jeans and sneakers. Tony longs to go to an NBA basketball game; I long to see Vanessa Redgrave in the play of Joan Didion's *The Year of Magical Thinking*. We do neither: both seem too expensive.

We double the length of our planned stay in New York at the last minute, leaving just a night together back in San Diego before we part ways again, each to return to different countries.

In ten years, we decide, we will come back and live in Brooklyn.

In San Diego, we enjoy simple pleasures. Back at the cheery hostel where I stayed before my entry to Mexico, we enjoy the luxury of a private room and double bed, after sleeping on bunk beds in shared dorms for the past ten days in New York. We eat fish tacos, browse the shops and walk the northern hemisphere's longest pier at Ocean Beach.

Then we catch the trolley to San Ysidro, where Tony will catch a Greyhound across the border to Tijuana airport. With an hour to kill in San Ysidro, our lunch choices are limited to McDonald's or Jack in the Box. We choose Jack in the Box because Tony is curious: it's the fast-food restaurant of choice in the movie *Boyz in the Hood*. Then we sit at the trolley stop, the only place with a bench and some privacy, looking at the hills of San Diego and the cement bridge ahead of us, holding each other and talking around the subject of our separation for as long as we can. I chase the Greyhound bus out of the terminal, waving, like something out of a bad Hollywood movie. Tony's face presses against the glass. We are both crying.

I catch the trolley back to San Diego for my last night in America, alone.

PART TWO

10. COMING HOME

When I emerge from Melbourne airport, a crowd is gathered at the exit barriers, waving excitedly, pushing for an early glimpse of the emerging travellers. Some wave hand-made signs with the words *WELCOME HOME*. As people take their last steps from the limbo of customs, they are swept up into hugs, greeted by squeals and kisses. There are carefully laconic greetings, slaps on backs, luggage taken from weary hands. I scour the crowd but find no familiar faces. Not yet.

I drag my luggage to a corner of the airport lounge: a Mexican soccer bag packed with presents and souvenirs, the grubby red sports bag with all my clothes and shoes and books from the past two months, my laptop backpack with my ugg boots crammed into it. I sit on the sports bag and wait. Half an hour passes, then an hour. The crowd has gone; I am alone. By the time I look up to see my mother, Mark and Leo at the sliding doors, an hour and twenty minutes have passed.

'He-llo!' says Mum, bending to hug me. 'Welcome home! How are you? How was your flight?'

'My *flight* was okay.'

'Oh boy, what a morning,' she says, oblivious to my mood. 'We rang the airport this morning and they said that your flight was delayed, so we came later, but then by the time we found out they'd made up the time, it wasn't delayed any more. But it was too late.'

'Hmmm,' I say, unwilling to relinquish my anger. I have already decided I don't want to be here.

Mark, trailing some metres behind her, catches up. Leo is at his side. Mark says a hearty hello and kisses my cheek. Leo looks at me, warily. I call his name, open my arms. He doesn't move.

'Why are you wearing that hat?' he eventually says, his voice small and uncertain.

I am wearing jeans, a hoodie and a straw cowboy hat I bought on our anniversary weekend at the beach. It cost the equivalent of five dollars. I have since worn it on the plane to Tijuana, the bus to San Diego and through a snowy Central Park in New York. I have worn it on the subway and through LAX airport, and now home.

'Oh,' I say, touching my head. 'Because I bought it in Mexico and I didn't want it to get ruined, so I had to wear it home. Do you like it?'

'You don't look like my mum,' he says, watching me through alien eyes. I take it off.

'Is that better?'

He nods.

'You want to give Mum a hug? I missed you so much!'

He steps hesitantly into my arms and I hug him hard, tears springing to my eyes. He hugs me back, but when I pull away he is only half-melted. He is still assessing me, unmoved by my tears.

'Look,' he says, showing me a magazine he holds at his side. Enthusiasm seeps back into his voice as he shares his treasure. 'I got the new *K-Zone*! It's so cool, look at this article here on the new Bionicles movie. *Return to Mata Nui*.'

He is frighteningly bigger, his face more mature, his clothes Mark's and not mine. But he is the same.

Mum climbs into the front seat beside Mark, who will drive us home before leaving Leo with me for the next month. Mum talks animatedly, telling me all about their trip this morning and the vagaries of their conversations with the airport staff. She tells me about the wedding that she was here to attend, along with my dad and my brother Simon, who are waiting for us at home. It was my cousin's wedding; I was invited too, but couldn't change my flights to get back in time unless I paid hundreds of dollars to do so. Selfishly, secretly, I was pleased to have the excuse. I love my cousin. But I lived thirty years without leaving Australia and may not leave it again for a very long time. I wanted those two extra days. Leo talks to me about the content of his *K-Zone*. The conversation often overlaps with Mum's, both of them addressing me at once, neither of them realising or caring that the other is, too. I am not really listening to either of them.

The car cuts through swathes of flat brown emptiness, punctuated by the occasional scrubby tree. A stencil design of a house hangs suspended in the air from a roadway bridge over bare fields. It's like the ghost of an absent city. Tiredness seeps into my veins. For the first time in my life, I feel just how far away I live from the rest of the world.

Then we are driving past factories, storage sheds, grim backyards glimpsed over fences. Sporting grounds perched on the edge of the highway. The West Gate Bridge, KFC, Coles. And then we are on the familiar roads that lead to home. Weatherboard houses, citrus trees, trampolines. We pass the fish and chip shop, the milkbar. We turn down a side street and stop in the driveway of my very own weatherboard palace, roses pushing through the white picket fence. There are houses everywhere, nothing but endless houses.

'You're home!' sings Mum. 'Does it feel good?'

'Yep,' I lie, squeezing Leo's small hand in mine in the back seat. 'It sure does.'

✳ ✳ ✳ ✳

The house seems older, dirtier, messier. I've always thought the seahorses galloping across the blue-tiled bathroom wall charming; now they seem sad. The broken dishwasher mocks me. The layers of papers and books and tiny Lego fragments seem endless and exhausting, the product of a slovenly mind.

The dogs, never exactly calm, seem possessed. They run barking around the house and yard, flinging themselves at my legs in a frenzy for days after my first appearance home. They gulp down every meal in a rush of competitive barks and flurries. Doug escapes approximately once a day, where his habit was more like once a week. Both dogs greet the diminutive Chinese woman from the unit on the corner as if she were their owner.

I learn that the dogs have spent much of their time over the past two months on the street; my neighbour, a dog-lover, has often rescued them and invited them in. She tells me, in her fragmented English, that our house-sitter—a friend of a friend—had rarely seemed to be home.

A note my parents had found on the computer desk had admitted as much, but claimed she regularly returned to feed the dogs. Nothing was said about having walked them.

The worst thing, though, is the mice that have made the cupboards and corners of the house their home. I sit in the study at night, ears cocked, and listen to mysterious scratching under the printer and in the waste-paper basket under my desk. I type cross-legged on my desk chair, my feet tucked under me. There is mouse poo amid the cereal boxes and cans in the cupboards. I have to throw out everything in packets or boxes, carrying them carefully to the bin to prevent their contents spilling from tiny ragged holes. I buy armfuls of sturdy plastic containers for cereal, flour, nuts, biscuits. And mouse traps.

I tell Leo that I am keen to move. He likes our house, he says. It's his home.

* * * *

After school one day, I invite Lucy and Conor over. The boys take a box of Lego onto the back deck while we sit at the kitchen table and watch them through the window. I offer to make Lucy a coffee. Tony bought me a coffee machine for Christmas so I could have my lattes at home, now that I'll no longer be having them on work breaks. I'm quite pleased with myself as I measure and brew the coffee and froth the milk, pouring it into glasses.

'Do you have sugar?' Lucy asks.

I open the cupboard door. As I reach for the sugar container, a mouse emerges from the dark, pausing between two tins of tomatoes. I scream and slam the door.

'Do you really want sugar?' I ask.

'No,' she says. 'Not really.'

I look out the window. Leo is building a Lego spaceship, brick by careful brick. Conor has abandoned his creation; he is kicking a ball through the grass.

Mark enlisted help in looking after Leo while I was away. Leo went to Conor's house once a week and to Angus's once a week, with three days a week in After School Care. I am both amazed and admiring of Mark's audacity: I would never have done such a thing. I try my best not to ask for help, to save it for if I really need it.

'I can't believe you had Leo once a week,' I say to Lucy. 'Thanks for that. Did he take Conor for you?'

'Oh, he couldn't,' she says. 'He was working. I have Thursdays off.'

'Well, thanks.'

'Oh, that's okay,' she says. 'As he said, he was a single dad for that time. I was happy to help.'

'Lucy,' I say, 'you're a single mum yourself. And he has a wife to help him. He's not exactly *single*.'

'Oh.' Her face transforms. 'You're right! I never thought of it that way.'

I offer to take Conor on Mondays to pay her back. She demurs but I insist, telling her that with my new part-time job, it's really not a problem. It would be a pleasure. This is true: I like Leo having friends over. It makes me feel good, knowing he has friends to play with.

I start work. It feels strange, entering the top floor of the bookshop again, reintroducing myself to all the staff. I go to my old in-tray, still marked with the name of the woman who replaced me, and start picking out books to assign for review, others to take home and read.

I'm nervous about seeing the bookshop owner again after having left and come crawling back like this, but he greets me with a hug and a flurry of new ideas, as if I'm just back from a short holiday. As if I never left.

On my first Wednesday back, I can't find Leo in the schoolyard. He's not outside his classroom. I find him a few classrooms over, with Angus. They are hunched over handfuls of AFL trading cards, giggling. Vanessa looks relieved to see me. Leo does not.

'But I play at Angus's house on Wednesdays!' he says.

'Not necessarily anymore,' I say, responding to Vanessa's closed expression. 'Come on, we're going home now.'

'Can Leo come and play?' Angus says. '*Pleeeease?*' Tom joins in. They clasp their hands under their chins and exaggeratedly flutter their eyelids.

Vanessa smiles with her mouth but not her eyes. Yesterday, she'd had a headache and I'd offered to take her boys.

'Oh, okay.'

'Yayyy!'

Together, the three of them race to the bike shed, leaving us alone.

I suggest we have the boys alternate weeks from now on—take turns having them. Or I could take them for several weeks in a row, to make up for when I was away. Mark had told me, laughingly, that Vanessa was often having a meltdown over the boys' behaviour when he arrived to pick up Leo. I can sense that she's not up to having him once a week.

'Yes!' she says, relieved. 'Let's do that.' Her starched demeanour loosens and she resumes her normal verbose style. 'You see, Tom was playing with Angus and Leo in the playground at the start of the year and I was worried and spoke to his teacher and she said that's fine, it's normal for preppies to hang out with older kids they know. Now Angus has been playing with Ryan in the playground instead, so that's good, but Tom is *still* playing with Leo. And he's been coming home saying rude words ever since he started school and he never did that before. So, yeah, it would be good to, uh, limit the amount of time they …'

At this point, it seems to dawn on her that I'm not suggesting the boys only play together every other week, but that they rotate houses. Perhaps she also realises that she is telling a boy's mother how relieved she is that her son is no longer so interested in playing with him.

'Yes, okay, let's do that,' she says, slowly. 'Swap houses every week. Okay.'

She sounds like she isn't quite sure how to get out of it. I'm sure this is just what happened when Mark asked if she'd take Leo once a week, because he was all alone.

I rush home across the park, keen to make a dent in the mountains of work I have to do. With Tony gone, I really *do* have Leo by myself, though his absence doesn't much alter the practical mechanics of our lives. I usually prepare our meals even when Tony's here; he kicks the football with Leo while I watch from the kitchen window. Now that I work from home again, I'll be taking Leo to and from school. But wrangling the dogs on my own is a chore. Tony's dog, Doug, has always been fractious, but now he has a hair-trigger temper; when I chase him down the street to bring him home, or try to beckon him from under the bed (where he's not allowed), he bares his teeth and growls. I've taken to poking under the bed with a broom.

I've just made coffee and sat down at my computer when the phone rings. I let it go to the answering machine, hovering to gauge whether I need to pick up. Whoever it is hangs up without leaving a message.

'Oh GOD,' huffs Vanessa as she arrives at her front gate to let me in. She grabs at Cujo who is hurling himself at the fence, lurching his great black head through the bars to gnash his teeth at me and my two dogs. I have been standing here for minutes already, shouting, 'Leo! I'm here!' accompanied by a chorus of barks: Cujo's deep sandpaper growl and the high-pitched yaps of Snuffy and Doug.

'I called you as soon as I got home,' she says, strongarming Cujo through the security screen and into the hallway. 'I wanted to say *I'm sorry, I can't do this*, and ask you to pick him up. But you obviously weren't home yet.'

'No. Sorry. What happened?'

'Well … it wasn't *really* his fault …'

It turns out that Angus had offered Leo his bike to ride home, then changed his mind, screamed all the way home, and told Leo he couldn't play with any of his toys once they got there. 'Angus is so *hysterical*,' she wails. 'He says such *nasty* things to me, to get a rise out of me. I don't know where he gets it from. Neither of *us* is like that.' I make sympathetic noises.

The boys arrive, Leo trailing his schoolbag. Tom scales the gate, giggling as it swings open. Angus and Leo exit; Tom wriggles down to the footpath.

'I think,' says Vanessa, 'that we should not have Leo over anymore, until further notice. You know, to punish Angus.' She puts a hand on my arm.

I step back. 'Okay.' And I stalk off down the front path, collecting Leo at the end of the driveway, the dogs straining at their leashes. The two brothers follow us on their scooters.

'Leo was *naughty*,' calls Tom, panting with the effort of talking and keeping up with us at the same time.

'Tom,' I snap, without slowing, 'every time I see you, you tell me Leo was bad. He never tells me anything bad about you. Maybe he will if you don't cut it out.'

'He took my brother's *bike*,' he says.

I swing on him. 'Well, I heard that your brother was naughty. That he gave Leo the bike and then threw a tantrum about it.'

I quicken my pace so that Leo has to jog beside me. 'You won't be playing there anymore,' I say. Leo's face crumples. 'It's not you,' I add. 'I'm sorry.'

I visit Leo's teacher, Kaye, to see how he is going, and to volunteer for classroom reading. She has yellow hair and rectangular glasses; a hardness squats in her eyes, contradicting her bright tone and the smile she wears like a borrowed outfit.

She shows me Leo's writing book, leafing through to point out an especially interesting creative piece. *On the weekend I got some new Lego! But it is not the same as Mum's Exo-force or Bionicles.* A voice brusquely addresses him, telling him to *Calm down just one more week.* Leo again: *Sorry I can't!!!!!!* Then someone, presumably his stepmother, huffs, *All this fuss about Leo's Mum coming home!*

I am hollowed out by the intensity of it, by what I recognise as canny ventriloquism. 'Wow,' I say. 'That's really something.'

'He has a good command of voice,' she says. 'It's really great writing.'

I had assumed she was showing me because she was concerned about the impact my absence has had on him. But she speaks blithely on.

'I thought you'd like to see how well he's doing.'

'He seemed fine when I spoke to him from Mexico,' I can't help saying. 'He didn't seem bothered.'

'I think he really missed you,' she says. 'He's happy you're back.'

We arrange that I'll come in every Friday after assembly to help listen to kids read.

She walks me to the classroom door as we talk and leans against the doorway, edging me out to the hall.

I set up a new food shelf on a bookshelf in the kitchen. I take out all the cookbooks and move them to a pile in the hallway, replacing them with containers of flour and sugar, tins of tomatoes, marshmallows and biscuits. I don't open the cupboards anymore, except to occasionally throw poison in them.

* * * *

On Anderson Street, I eat a soggy pie and salad, and mope at the bill. I resent spending fifteen dollars on lunch, remembering my ten-dollar meals in New York, five-dollar feasts in Mexico. In our local cafe in Guadalajara, Tony and I would keep ordering food until we were full. Tacos, empanadas, enchiladas. It was so cheap, the bill didn't matter. I look out the window at the same old shops and imagine seeing them forever.

I accept a freelance job writing a history of a soon-to-be-defunct government agency and plan to use the money to go overseas again. Maybe I'll take Leo with me. I tell him about the pyramids in Mexico and the Legoland in San Diego. He wants to go to San Diego.

The floor of the study is carpeted in an interlocking domino snake of papers and annual reports. I sit up at night to pick out relevant titbits for the corporate history. During the day, I work for the bookshop and am Leo's mother. At night, I do my second job and talk to Tony on Skype. A microphone is plugged in to the computer; I sit and talk into it when he calls, like I am a guest on a talk show.

There is a certain luxury about being able to—on a whim—have toast for dinner, about dominating the television (or even better, having the blessed silence of *no* television), about reading in bed as late as I want. But I miss having someone to talk to about my day, or to sit with in the evening. I miss being with someone who cares about Leo as much as I do, who is on my team, who has become my family. That's the difference between now, living the life of a single mother, and before, when I was one. That's why Tony's absence is an itch, even an ache, but doesn't keep me awake at night, or mutate into the kind of anxiety that makes me want to scratch my way out of my own skin. I know he is there at the other end of our emails and Skype calls; that he is coming back. I may sometimes *feel* alone, but I know that I'm not.

* * * *

Tony alerts me to an email Leo has sent him, about his AFL Dream Team account:

> *As you know it is very hard for me to work out my dream teams'*
> *passwords because I have two.*
> *JUST TELL ME WHO THE PLAYERS ARE!*

I am amazed. He used the plural apostrophe correctly! It's a Sunday, which means I'm cooking a roast dinner—as has become my habit. I call Mum for company while I peel and chop the vegetables; this has also become a habit. I read Leo's email to her.

'That's wonderful!' she says, when I note the apostrophe. 'Some of my Year 12 students can't do that.'

'That wasn't my point,' says Tony, when we talk on Skype later in the night. 'I thought it was very rude.'

'Oh,' I say, mentally re-reading the email. 'Of course. Yeah.'

'I didn't notice the apostrophe,' he says, sounding more than a little exasperated.

Tony writes a long reply to Leo: it is a brilliantly pitched mini-essay on manners, effort and how to appropriately handle frustration at not getting things right, or needing help—all within the framework of a fable about Chris Judd's (fictional) less successful brother. (Who was too proud to learn better ways to do things or ask for help, and therefore never made it into the AFL, unlike Chris Judd, who did the opposite and thrived.)

> *The rewarding thing about finding things that you can't do or work out is learning how to do them. Because once you've learnt how to do them it's an extra thing you can do. Sometimes it's challenging, but you feel really good once you have learnt how to do it. Remember when you hated to kick the footy because you didn't know how? Well, maybe you don't remember, but you used to hate it and never wanted to go outside and kick it. Now look at you, you love it, you can't stop kicking it, it's all about footy for you. And it feels really good when you do a good kick, doesn't it?*

Leo's eyes grow wide as we read the email together; I read aloud while he skims the screen.

'Wow,' he says when we finish. 'If I keep going the way I am, I'll end up like Chris Judd's brother, won't I?'

I post Tony's email on my blog, in full. I am showered with comments about what a wonderful (and wise) stepfather he is, how lucky I am. Georgia writes to say how impressed she is by my seven-year-old's ability to use an apostrophe properly.

* * * *

Lucy finishes work early on Thursdays. We develop a sometimes-habit of leaving the schoolyard together, Leo and I going to her townhouse across the park. The boys raid the freezer for ice-cream which they scoop into bowls and heap with Milo. Or they take packets of chips and handfuls of biscuits from the cupboard. Lucy and I sit on stools at the breakfast bar with mugs of hot drink or glasses of red wine.

I don't drink wine much anymore; I certainly never drink it on a weeknight, in my lounge room. It makes me sleepy and dissolves my brain so that I can't focus on putting words on the page, or organising them into good sentences, paragraphs and pages. And there's never a day I'm not working. It fills the gaps after Leo goes to bed and when he's at school; sometimes it competes for my attention while he's watching television or asking me to take photographs of his Lego creations. But sitting at Lucy's counter, my feet hooked under the rungs of a stool, watching our boys build Lego on the carpet side-by-side, I relax and accept the wine, to be companionable. To be a normal schoolyard mum, whatever that is.

Often, Conor will tire of the Lego and wander off to play his piano keyboard in a corner, or come to rest his head on Lucy's shoulder as we talk. Leo will stay where he is, concentrating on the Lego city expanding across the living room.

'It's great that Leo loves the Lego so much,' says Lucy. 'Conor barely touches it when we're here alone. It's good to see someone get some use out of it.'

I wish Leo weren't so stubborn; that he would follow Conor and play something else. That he would be a better guest. The same thing happens at our house every Wednesday. Then, I wish Leo would be a better *host*. Neither Leo nor Conor seems capable of doing something they don't want to, to make the other person happy. Sometimes this causes fights (*Can you ask Leo to stop reading books?*) but more often they are content to be at opposite ends of the house, one of them outside on the swing-set, the other in the bedroom drawing.

'They play *together* more often than they used to,' says Lucy. 'They interact more.'

'Yeah,' I say, dipping a cracker into a tub of hummus. 'I guess so.'

* * * *

I try seeing Melbourne as a tourist would. I have a new habit of visiting the nearby beach suburb of Williamstown on the weekends. On impulse, Leo and I ride the ferry from Nelson Pier, boarding next to the navy ship that doubles as a museum—going through Port Phillip Bay, down the Yarra and into the city. As we sail slowly down the river, the sky darkens. Leo gets bored when he can no longer squint at his comics through the dimming light.

'Look at the water and the lights,' I tell him. 'Isn't it beautiful?'

He is still bored.

I take photographs of the West Gate Bridge as we pass under it, a twinkling tiara against the black sky and mirroring water. It is no Golden Gate Bridge, but in the dark it is still enchanting. I tell myself a tourist would be impressed.

At home, I upload my photographs to the computer and make the West Gate my screen saver. It replaces my previous photo of the Golden Gate, its bright arms curving over the bleak sea.

'Why do you like bridges so much?' asks Leo when he sees it.

We are in the lounge room watching television when a mouse runs across the polished floorboards from the direction of the kitchen, tracing a diagonal path past the couch and behind the stereo cabinet. We both scream and jump onto the couch, where we stay standing until we are sure the mouse won't re-emerge.

'Mum,' says Leo at breakfast the next morning, 'I think we should move house.'

'Me too,' I say. 'Why?'

'I don't like mice.'

11. LOOKING A GIFTHORSE IN THE MOUTH

Walking home from school, Leo tells me about his terrible day. There were bullies. A kid hit him. Another punched him. Someone else poked him. I hear this sort of thing often, on and off. I know it's not all black and white. I know that Leo can be an antagonist, that I am hearing one particular side of the story.

'That's terrible,' I say mildly.

'Yeah,' he continues, dragging his backpack on the footpath. 'Then I spent half an hour hiding behind the garbage bins, crying.'

'Pardon?'

'A teacher found me. She took me to the principal.'

He was crying, he says, because he realised he doesn't have any friends and nobody likes him. We have a big talk, and I carefully listen, making sure I neither tell him he's imagining things, nor confirm his fears by giving them too much credence.

'What about Conor?' I say. 'What about Angus? Or Seth?'

'They play football,' says Leo. 'I don't want to play football.'

'Why not? I thought you had your own team.' He's been telling me stories about his informal football team, the Melbourne Dinosaurs, since I came back from Mexico; he says they win every lunchtime, by hundreds of goals. I've asked Conor and Seth about it—they don't know anything about being called the Dinosaurs and they tell me they don't often win, but they *have* confirmed they play football with Leo at lunch.

'Some kids took my ball last week,' says Leo. 'They said Conor and Angus could join their game, but not me. They said I was boring and stupid. I don't want to play footy at school anymore.'

I promise to go up there the next day and talk to the principal. I tell him he's a great kid and repeat some nice things that Lucy said about him over coffee last week—how kind he is, how mature for his age, how much Conor likes him. I hug him; he lets me. I suggest that he try playing football at lunch again. He shrugs; I don't push it.

He plays football on Saturday mornings, when we cycle to Yarraville Oval for Auskick. During the drills, where it's all routine and no competition, he is happy, if more engaged with play-fighting Conor or Angus than with developing his skills. But the official games often devolve into tears: he throws himself to the grass when he doesn't get the ball, or mooches around the field, frowning at the running, shouting pack rather than joining in. He's new to playing sport; the few times we've tried to enrol him in the past, he's been disengaged at best. But I've enforced Auskick this year. It's an opportunity for him to socialise outside school and learn skills like teamwork. It's torture, though—for Leo and me. I see the coaches' frustration, hear the whispers of other parents—*What's wrong with that kid?* It is mortifying. But how else will he learn to share, to work with others, to cope with losing or doing badly? He's already behind on these things. Maybe other kids learn with friends or siblings in their backyards, before they venture out to the public arena of the local sports oval and the critical gaze of their neighbours.

We go to Margaret and Edwina's house for dinner. While the grown-ups talk about Tony and how he's going in Mexico, Leo and Jordan pull faces at each other and whisper rude words until we release them to play Lego in Jordan's room. They come back for dessert, bowls of ice-cream topped with frosty blackberries, freshly chopped strawberries. Leo eats carefully around the fruit. He listens to the adults' talk of Tony.

'Do you miss him?' asks Margaret, catching his eye. He nods.

'I miss him too!' says Jordan.

'We all miss him,' Margaret agrees.

Soon after, Leo returns from Jordan's room with a miniature guitar which he announces he would like to play for us all. He has written a song, he says. We move to line up along the couches while he turns a chair from the dining table to face us. Solemnly, earnestly, his eyes firmly on his guitar strings, he plucks them randomly and sings about how we all miss Tony. *Come home, come home soon,* he sings. Margaret and I wipe away tears. When he finally puts down the guitar and looks up at us, she draws him into her arms.

'That was beautiful, Leo,' she says.

Mark picks us up. It is his night to have Leo; he drives me to a taxi stand, a little bit further down the road towards my place. Leo and I sit together in the back seat. He begs to come to my house, saying he has had a terrible day and it would make it *just that bit better* if he could come home with me. We tell him I'll see him tomorrow. When Mark's car stops at the taxi stand, Leo's whimpering lurches into real sobbing. He clings to me. I unclamp his arms from my waist and get out of the car to talk to Mark.

'He's really upset,' I whisper. 'Please let me take him.'

'I'm his father and I need to deal with this too.'

In the back seat, Leo's head is buried in his own lap.

'Please. I can't tell him he's not welcome with me when he's this upset.' I burst into tears.

Mark looks at us—me standing in the street, crying in the dark, his son now howling on the back seat—and shakes his head. 'Fine.' He gets back into his car and drives home.

Half an hour later, Leo lies still in his bed as I stroke his hair and kiss him goodnight. Usually, he wriggles and talks in an attempt to keep my attention as long as possible. Tonight, he is so content for me to leave him to sleep that I perversely turn back to sit beside him again.

'Mum,' he murmurs eventually, turning onto his back to face me. 'Today I realised that I was weak.'

'Why?'

'Because I couldn't defeat the bullies, no matter how hard I tried.'

'What did you do?'

'Nothing.'

'Well then …' I scramble in my mental odds-and-ends basket, hoping to come up with some homespun wisdom that will suit the occasion. 'That means you're strong, actually. They're the weak ones, because they needed to make you feel bad in order to make themselves feel tough. Cowards do that. By doing nothing, you showed that you're not like that.'

It's hard to know what to do, how to fix this. It's not that he doesn't have friends, as I pointed out to him. It's more that those friendships don't always seem to fit. It doesn't help that he only wants to play with his friends in the schoolyard if they're playing what he wants to play. But I also know that sometimes he tries to play with other kids and they tell him to *get lost*. I know that friends of his won't play with him because their other friends *said so*. I remember these things from my own schoolyard days. It breaks my heart.

The next day, I break down in the deputy principal's office, telling her what has happened. *He is really unhappy*, I say. She is sympathetic, but reminds me that Leo has a temper, that he can aggravate some of the 'bullying' he gets.

'Does he really know what bullying is?' Eliza says. 'I don't think he does. Often, that's not actually the issue.'

I tell her I've heard through another parent—Vanessa, in fact—that there is a school counsellor who can consult with parents or kids on behavioural or social issues. I ask if I can make an appointment with this counsellor. She agrees, and makes a time for me.

That afternoon, Leo says he told a kid who was teasing him that he was weak, that he was being mean to make himself feel tough. He tells me this, almost cheerfully, while heaping teaspoons of Milo into a glass of milk. I am pleased and surprised; it's hard to know what will sink in, what will give comfort.

In the absence of Tony, in the waiting period before I meet with the school counsellor, I pour out my anxieties about Leo on my blog. *I want him to learn to compromise, but not to change who he is*, I write. *I like his wavelength. Where do I find other kids who are on it?*

Now that I work from home, visiting the office approximately once a month, this online community I've tapped into has become more than a fun distraction. I talk to the other freelance writers about juggling jobs and appropriately faking enthusiasm for topics like interior design. And, increasingly, I talk to the other mums about balancing kids and careers, about trying to bring up children in line with our own philosophies, about the mistakes and small wins along the way.

Bright or eccentric kids with slightly underdeveloped social skills have it tough in school (just ask me how I know …) writes one freelancer. *Gee, being a mum is hard*, sympathises a mum of two, who assures me that not wanting to change him is a big step in the right direction.

Another commenter suggests: *I don't want to be presumptuous or alarmist about a child I've never met, but several of the behaviours you're describing sound like signs of very high-functioning Asperger Syndrome or another Autistic Spectrum Disorder.*

Others write to me privately to say that it's absurd to suggest such a thing based on my blog. I'm not offended; the idea of Asperger's has occurred to me, very vaguely, once or twice before. And the commenter means well. But I'm sure he's overreaching, guessing at a trendy diagnosis just as I did a couple of years ago after listening to a radio program on the subject. I asked an aunt, who works with autistic kids, what she thought; I told her about how excited he gets by the things he's passionate about, his resistance to joining in group activities at childcare and kindergarten, his detachment from other children. 'I doubt it,' she said. 'He's nothing like the kids I work with. But check it out if you're really concerned.'

I wasn't.

* * * *

'I think the teacher has found out my secret,' Leo announces over dinner. 'She announced it to the whole class.'

'What's your secret?'

'That I play alone in the playground because I have no friends.'

'Oh, darling. What did she say?'

'She said, "If Leo comes up to you in the playground and wants to play with you, let him. Say, Hi Leo, of course. Make him welcome."' He frowns into his bowl of noodles. 'It was so *humiliating*.'

I don't know what to say.

'It was a pretty stupid thing for her to do,' I admit. 'I'm sure she was trying to help, but that does sound humiliating.'

We have extra-big bowls of chocolate ice-cream for dessert. I chop up some squares of chocolate, leaving dark smears on the breadboard, and sprinkle them on top. Leo gets coloured sprinkles, too. We sit on the couch and watch *The Simpsons*, bowls on our laps. It's an episode we've both seen at least twice, but it doesn't matter at all.

I run into another mother, a friend of Lucy's, in the schoolyard. Leo and her son Jack were briefly friends in Prep. Then Jack became part of the 'in crowd' and Leo, well, didn't. Jack is good at everything— sport, lessons, making friends. He is tall for his age and handsome, with brown curls and a sprinkling of pinprick freckles across his nose. He is smoothly polite to adults, though with his peers he is capable of a top dog's mean streak.

'How's Leo going?' she asks.

'Oh, okay,' I say. But I seem to be incapable of lying that things are fine when they're not. I go on to tell her that he's having trouble with friends, that he feels alone, that it's heartbreaking. She looks pained, almost guilty.

'He's a great kid,' she says. 'He's lovely. Maybe, you know, he's just so smart that he's not on the same wavelength as the other kids. They just don't get him.'

'Maybe,' I say. I've been wondering the same thing.

'He really *is* so smart, you know,' she says. 'I remember listening to him read when Jack was in his class and I was amazed.'

I smile and try to look modest, though I'm burning with pride.

'How's Jack?' I remember to ask.

The schoolyard is empty when I arrive to see the counsellor. The kids are in their lessons, so the yard is eerily quiet, the hallways hushed. I walk past Leo's classroom and glance through the window, hoping to get a feel for how he's going today. The kids are bent over their desks, working; Leo is too. He doesn't stand out in any way. I am vaguely comforted.

The counsellor's office is off an alcove near a back stairway. It feels appropriately discreet, though it's actually a temporary measure while the school offices are renovated.

Jennifer is friendly; she listens carefully to my concerns. She seems to take them more seriously than the assistant principal did. I tell her that Leo plays alone, that he was found crying behind the bins because he was lonely, that I think he's being bullied. I tell her about the theory that the other kids don't get him because he's so smart. She hands a box of tissues across the desk, but I don't cry. Then she asks me a series of questions about his reading level and how he does in his school reports.

'Hmmm,' she says. 'I think it sounds like Leo might be gifted. Have you thought of that?'

'Well, yes,' I admit. 'His Prep teacher thought he was gifted and wanted him to do tests, but the school said he was too young, that what he needed to focus on was fitting in.'

'I'd like to get him tested,' says Jennifer. 'I'll talk to Eliza and sort it out.'

She tells me that if he *is* gifted, we can apply to accelerated learning programs in selected schools that offer them.

'Like University High?' I ask.

She confirms that yes, that's exactly the kind of thing she's talking about. She says there are also special camps and holiday programs for gifted kids, giving them the opportunity to connect with others on their wavelength.

I walk home elated. *Gifted.*

12. NEIGHBOURS

Mark is late. I sit on the couch, watching the street through the window, thinking *any minute now*. There seems to be no point in doing anything—I've already packed our bags to go out when Leo arrives. But *any minute now* stretches for ten minutes. Fifteen. I call Mark on his mobile; he tells me breathlessly that he is *on his way*.

I am ready to be angry, but he doesn't take much longer than the promised minute. He really had been on his way, sort of.

'Sorry we're late,' he says, pre-empting me. 'You'll never guess where we've been!'

He was driving down the main shopping strip nearby when he saw an ex-girlfriend standing in the front yard of his old house. It was the place where he'd lived for four years, between leaving the house we'd shared when Leo was born and moving to the house he bought with Rachel not long ago.

'Friends of Karen's are living there now,' he says. 'They're moving out, actually. Having a garage sale before the move.'

Leo had loved that house. He'd had a friend next door, a small boy just a year younger than him. Every time we walk past—which we do often on our way to the neighbourhood cafes and supermarkets—he comments that it doesn't look as well looked after as it did when his dad lived there. 'It looks messy,' he'll say, disapprovingly. I'll agree, but it doesn't. Its native front garden is planted with wild grasses and spreading trees, carpeted with bark chips; it requires no maintenance at all.

'Anyway, I'm sorry,' Mark says. He offers us a lift to the train station.

In the car, an idea hatches.

'So, they're moving out?'

'Yep.'

'Do you know if there's anyone to replace them yet?'

Mark doesn't think so. He still has the landlord's phone number; he urges me to call him.

'It's a great house,' he says. 'Good luck.'

I once house-sat there, for a month. Mark was overseas and I was living in a two-bedroom flat with no backyard. Leo would play in the carpark, or on the stretch of cracked concrete outside our lounge-room window—the communal driveway. I'd have to accompany him, to watch for cars and to pick the concrete clean of glass splinters and cigarette butts. For some reason, broken glass was always seeded in the cracks of the concrete and amid the expanse of gravel that stood in for lawn at the front of the apartment block. The cigarette butts made sense, but I didn't understand why, no matter how long I'd spend sifting through the gravel, the glass would be back within days, as mysterious and persistent as weeds.

The carpark was good for rollerskating or riding bikes. It was perfect for games of skating-soccer (I'd wear rollerskates and Leo would be in his sneakers). Or we'd race each other from one side to the other— me on skates, he on his scooter—slamming ourselves into the decaying wooden fence to stop. But as Leo got older, I longed for him to have a patch of outdoor space to call his own.

House-sitting Mark's house was a trial run for moving to the inner-west. Rents were much cheaper than in North Fitzroy, where I lived. And I wanted to put some space between me and Tony, who had broken up with me (again) and lived a short walk from my flat. After a month living at Mark's, near the train station and shops, a short walk from Cruikshank Park where Leo and I could ride bikes and explore the creek, I decided that I could trade living near my friends (and Tony) for a backyard (and space from Tony).

I moved to a tiny triangular suburb next to Mark's, reclaimed by real estate agents and named after the nearby train station. It was the first house that was every truly mine, with no housemates: a whole house, with two bedrooms, two living areas, a paved backyard and a strip of lawn at the back. There was an outside toilet and a tiny clapboard kitchen. And opposite a shed the size of a cupboard, there was a wooden cubby house raised on stilts, with stairs leading up to it and large open windows. It sheltered under an enormous tree. When Leo, who was sceptical about moving, wandered into the backyard from the kitchen, he was won over. 'A TREE HOUSE!' he screamed. 'Mum, we have to have this house!'

We lived there alone for a while, paying just ten dollars a week more in rent than I had for my flat. Then Tony and I reunited for the last time and he moved in. A week later, he went to the Lost Dog Home and came home with Doug, 'his' dog.

We had been dating, on and off, since Leo was two. We met at work; we got together at the Christmas party. The first time I went back to Tony's flat, above a fire station in West Melbourne, he had an exercise ball in the corner of his bedroom and a poster of a girl in a bikini above his bed. A poster of Michael Jordan hung near his cupboard. He was twenty-three years old. He moved back in with his mother soon after we started going out, after a fight with his flatmate.

Tony and I didn't really think about our relationship at first. We just got drunk together (and then went home together) a lot, for several weeks. It seemed impossible that we'd ever have a serious relationship. He was still in the grip of a kind of adolescence while I had a two-year-old child. He loved sport and I hated it; he told me on our second date that he was not interested in politics at all, while I had just joined the ALP and was studying politics and media part-time. But we'd both had complex childhoods, we both loved books, and somehow we just got along.

And while Tony almost didn't call me after our first drunken encounter, because I had a child, he quickly loved Leo, and vice-versa.

'I used to be really worried about how to act like a stepfather,' I once heard him tell a friend during a dinner party. 'And then I figured out—I don't need to be a father figure. He *has* a father. I can just be his friend.'

They watched cartoons together and played PlayStation and wrestled. We went swimming and to the zoo. Tony got down on the floor and helped build Lego cities, reconnecting with his own childhood.

For a long time, he wasn't sure if he wanted this relationship to be *it* for him; he hadn't travelled, he hadn't finished uni, he hadn't really had any long-term relationships before. And he wasn't sure he could live with my moods forever; my downs frightened him in their intensity. He loved me, but I was needy and insecure. He worried my malaise could be contagious.

The last time we were officially 'off' (for nearly six months), Tony stayed in touch with Leo. He wrote him letters and postcards, he visited, he even had him over to his flat for sleepovers.

I went out with someone else, briefly. A poet I met when he was selling his book on consignment to my bookshop. He was 'on a break' from his marriage and sharing custody of his two kids; he was still dating his wife. He was the kind of person you go out with when you are seriously messed up. So was I.

He came over for dinner. He stood at the doorway as I said goodnight to Leo, gave a friendly wave.

'I want Tony,' said Leo, looking at him with angry eyes.

Tony came over for dinner the next week; I was helping him prepare for a job interview. He helped me tuck Leo in. I withdrew to the doorway to let him say goodnight on his own. Leo held his hand tight.

'Will you be here in the morning?' Leo asked.

'I don't think so, mate.'

'I don't want you to go.'

'Neither do I,' said Tony. Tears spilled down his face. In the doorway, I was crying too. Tony had to unclasp Leo's fingers to free his hand. He promised he'd be back to visit him again soon.

When Tony and I got back together a month or so later, we both knew that it was for good, though it was another two years before we would marry. When we told Leo that Tony was moving in with us, he shouted with happiness. And so my first independent house became our first house as a stitched-together family. Until, predictably, we were evicted so that the landlords could renovate and move their daughter in to it. The first thing they did was cut down the jasmine that had threaded beguilingly through the iron lacework over the verandah. And we moved to our current house, ignoring the poor public transport and the distance to the shops, because I was enchanted by the creek and the park.

* * * *

I call the landlord, David, from a payphone next to the train station. He's not there; I leave a message.

I met David once, when I was house-sitting for Mark. I thought I heard noises in the roof at night and used the emergency phone number left on the fridge to call him. Trying to sound sensible and sane, I explained that I'd heard noises in the roof and was *simply ringing to find out* if there was some way that an intruder could have got into it. Or maybe, I allowed, I was imagining things. David said that it was likely a possum, and that the only trapdoor into the roof was on the inside of the house, in the hallway. *Oh okay*, I said. *Thanks, I'm sure it's fine then.* But he insisted on coming over and checking it out himself, to put my mind at ease. He was younger than I'd expected: about Mark's age, with a beard and a bulky knitted jumper. He brought his own ladder, with which he climbed into the roof cavity. Of course, it was nothing. But he didn't seem annoyed at having driven over in the rain and the dark at 10 pm. Instead, he cheerfully wished me a good stay.

Our current landlord is often shadowed by his father, who bought him the house. He is prone to turning up unannounced, ostensibly to do maintenance we haven't asked for. Once, we arrived home to find saplings we'd planted scattered on our back lawn like trash, trailing newly naked roots. Our landlord's father had let himself in while we were out. He doesn't like trees.

'Would you like to live in Dad's old house?' I ask Leo.

'YES!' he shouts, jumping up and down with excitement. 'I can play with Steven again!'

I tell him nothing is certain, that I still have to talk to the landlord.

'Oh, he's really nice,' Leo assures me. 'I'm sure he'll say yes.'

I have to talk to Tony, too. I'm not sure how he'll feel about living in my ex's old house.

I'm surprised to find that David remembers me, if vaguely. He especially remembers Leo.

The rent has gone up a little, but it's still good. The only thing to have changed about the house is that it's repainted: the once salmon-coloured cornices around the doorways are now the same neutral cream as the walls. David was planning to advertise the house next week, but guesses he could save the money and hassle and simply let me have it. He'll talk to his wife and let me know.

I tell him I'll talk to my husband.

* * * *

My head is full of the possibilities of this house. We walk past it every time we go to the shops or the train station. Every time, I think *nearly there* as we pass. I imagine being able to stroll a few houses down the road to go out for lunch, or to collect a take-away coffee. To decide on a whim to go to the beach, or the city. And the chance for Leo to reconnect with the boy next door. At this moment, when his friendships are so precarious, his confidence so dented, this is the most alluring opportunity of all. A friend his age living next door is something no other house can offer.

Tony is predictably wary about living in Mark's old house, but lured by the cheap rent and proximity to shops and train. He is quick to say we should do it, though he's worried about me having to move house alone.

'Are you sure?' he says. 'I'm so sorry.'

* * * *

David says his wife wants to meet us before they decide if we can have the house. Just to be certain.

I clean for their arrival, mopping the polished wood floors and scrubbing the bathroom. Clutter is swept under beds and crammed into cupboards. The papers scattered around the study are stacked together and shut away in drawers. Half-drunk cups of coffee are collected from around the house—beside my bed, on the kitchen table, on my desk—and washed.

Leo is in his pyjamas when they arrive; red flannel patterned with racing cars. It's a little past his bedtime, but I have kept him up to meet them. David's wife, Fiona, is charmed by his solemn greeting and outstretched hand. I have told him he must be very polite.

'Hello, I remember you,' smiles David, bending to shake Leo's hand.

The couple sit together on our red velour couch. They ask some general questions about what I do and why we're leaving the house we're in.

'Do you remember me?' David asks.

Leo squints. 'Yes,' he says unconvincingly. It's as if he's trying to match his memories with the man in his lounge room.

'You've grown so much!' says David. 'You were two years old when I met you. You used to play with the boy next door, what was his name?'

'Steven!' says Leo, brightening.

'Yes, we're really hoping he could play with him again,' I say. 'If we get the house, I mean. It would be so good for him to have a friend next door.'

I leave the room to put Leo to bed. When I return, David tells me they've decided we can have the house. I thank them profusely.

'You can do anything you like with the garden,' he says. 'Consider it yours. There's just one thing I ask.'

'Sure,' I say, 'what is it?'

'The native trees and bushes in the backyard, I'm quite attached to them,' he says. 'I put them in myself. So please leave them as they are.'

'Of course,' I say. 'I think we can do that.'

We move in two weeks.

Leo screams when I tell him the good news. He shrieks at the top of his lungs, then throws himself to the floor.

'We've got to tell Steven!' he says. 'We have to tell Steven I'm coming back!'

I hope Steven remembers Leo as fondly as Leo remembers him. Steven came over to play one afternoon about a year ago. His mother, whom I'd only met in passing on the footpath of Mark's house, rang to ask if Leo might like to have a play-date some time. I invited Steven over that weekend. The boys were happy to see each other but played awkwardly, an imperfect fit after a year apart. Once, I looked out the kitchen window to see them on Leo's swing-set, one on the two-person metal swing, the other on the simple platform swing. They were just swinging, not talking. Other times, I looked out to see Leo talking at length, Steven politely attending. Still, they wandered around the house together all afternoon and Steven had seemed pleasantly engaged when we drove him home. They hadn't contacted us again.

We walk in to Yarraville the next day, to go to Leo's favourite bakery for coffee and cake. At least, that's what I say. Really, it's an excuse to walk past our new house.

'Can I tell Steven now?' Leo asks as we pass his house. 'Please? He'll be so excited.'

My excuses about it being rude to knock on someone's door without warning are easily dismissed, and I nervously agree. I hate taking the initiative with strangers.

We unlatch the wooden gate and make our way through the roses planted on either side of the garden path. Flowerboxes line the windowsill. A bronze plate hung by the door says *Nirvana*.

'Why do they have "Nirvana" on their door?' asks Leo, whose guitar teacher is fond of 'Smells Like Teen Spirit'.

'It's not the band,' I say. 'It means peace. Or something.'

Doris, Steven's mother, opens the door to us in open-mouthed surprise.

'Hello,' she says. 'Leo, haven't you grown?'

'I'm coming back!' he shouts, ignoring her niceties. 'Is Steven here? I have to tell him I'm going to be next door again!' He pauses a beat. 'Does he like Yu-Gi-Oh? I love Yu-Gi-Oh!'

'Hi,' I say, as Doris stares uncomprehendingly. 'I hope you don't mind us knocking on the door out of the blue like this.'

'No,' she says, a little uncertainly. 'Of course not.'

'We came to introduce ourselves, as it were. We're moving next door, into David's house.'

'What?' she says. 'Pardon? Really?'

'Yes.'

'Wow,' she says. 'Sorry, that's great news. Steven will be over the moon to have Leo next door again.'

'Wonderful!' I am relieved at her enthusiasm.

'That's so strange though, isn't it?' she laughs. 'He's lived there with his dad, and now he's living there with his mum?'

I agree that it is very strange.

Steven is at the barber's, having his hair cut, Doris explains. His dad takes him once a fortnight. We can find him there, if we really want to.

'Yes!' says Leo. 'Let's go! Come on!'

We pass the newsagent on the way and stop to buy Leo a packet of Yu-Gi-Oh cards. He rips open the foil packet on the footpath, as usual, and is elated to find a rare card. It must be his lucky day, he tells me. At the barber's, Steven's dad is seated in the chair before the mirror, a white smock pinned at the back of his neck. Steven is seated on a plastic chair against the wall behind him.

Leo flings open the door and catapults in ahead of me before I can urge him to be calm.

'Steven!' he shouts. 'Steven, it's ME!'

'Leo?' says Steven. 'Hi, Leo.'

His dad, Roger, jolts in his chair. I wave meekly at him as I follow Leo through the door.

'Oh, hello,' he says mildly, adjusting his glasses. 'Walking by, were you? How are you?'

Leo is shouting frantically, waving his card at Steven. 'I got an Elemental Hero Necroshade Yu-Gi-Oh!' he says. 'Look. It's really rare. Do you like Yu-Gi-Oh? Do you collect the cards?'

'Actually, Doris told us you'd be here,' I say. 'Sorry to barge in, but Leo really wanted to talk to Steven.'

'Oh. Okay.'

'He wanted to tell him,' I say, watching Leo and Steven hunch over the card, 'that we're moving next door to you, into the house where he lived with his dad.'

Roger graciously says that this is wonderful news as the barber continues to snip at his hair, politely oblivious.

'Oh YES!' says Leo. 'I'm moving next door to you!'

'No WAY!' shouts Steven. 'Awesome! Wow!'

I let the boys shout together for a moment, then say my goodbyes and pull Leo away, leaving Roger to finish his haircut in peace.

He says he looks forward to being neighbours.

13. HELL IS CHILDREN'S BIRTHDAY PARTIES

Saturday. We are on our way to the bookshop to meet Leo's idol: king of the kids, Andy Griffiths. Leo is a big fan, thanks to Andy's wicked sense of humour … and his wholehearted embrace of bums and toilet gags. Leo reads Andy's *Just* series—*Just Kidding, Just Annoying, Just Stupid*—so often that the books look as if they've been buried under a few acres of landfill. (Not an entirely inaccurate picture of his room.) He reads them on the train, in bed and on the toilet. More often than I'd like, an hour before bedtime, I'll open the door to the bathroom and there he is, sitting on the loo, pants around his ankles, frowning intently at a *Just* book with the look of a boy who has been in there for a very long time.

We're sitting on the train, books on our laps, talking about what to get Angus for his birthday. After weeks of no contact from Vanessa, Leo brought home an invitation to Angus's birthday party. Apparently birthdays are exceptions, when Leo is allowed to be friends with Angus. The party is tomorrow; Leo is excited, I am nervous.

'Maybe we should get him a book?' I suggest.

'Yes!' says Leo firmly. 'Do you know that they don't have *any books*? Really, Mum. Their bookshelves are full of toys. Toys! Angus is *not* that into reading. All he reads are comics. We *must* get him a book and get him into reading.'

I am amused and tickled and pleased for so many reasons. As a bookworm, it's nice to be reminded that Leo loves books by his own volition, not as a result of me pushing them on him. As a profound disliker of Vanessa, I am amused by his observation. As his book-loving mother, I am tickled by his passion for reading. And as a lazy woman embarking on a lazy Saturday, I am pleased that we can kill two birds with one bookshop.

'But we can't get an Andy Griffiths,' says Leo. 'Vanessa hates Andy Griffiths. She says he is inappropriate.'

'Ah, yes,' I say. 'Though we could get him *The Cat on the Mat is Flat*. That's not rude. It's just silly.'

'We'll get him *Maxx Rumble*. Angus is into footy, so he might be into that. And it's illustrated by Terry Denton. Will he be there? He might sign it.'

'Oh. I think he is.'

'Good, that's settled. Do you know they don't even get bedtime stories?' says Leo, full of seven-year-old scorn. 'They just get bedtime *toys*.'

'I'm sure that's not true. I'm sure they have books. Maybe they're somewhere else, not in their rooms.'

'They don't! I've *seen* their house.'

I'm not so sure. Vanessa is a crazy bitch, but I know she reads.

The children's buyer is an old friend as well as a colleague. We worked together with Emily and Tony in another bookshop, many years ago; we were all members of its original staff. Kathy and I stocked the shelves of the children's section together before the shop opened. She brought in Natural Confectionary Company lolly snakes for us to eat while we worked.

Leo looks at the table of Terry and Andy books and asks her where the *Maxx Rumble* books are.

'You're so clever!' she tells him. 'I forgot about them.'

Leo fetches them from the shelf, feeling very important, and hands them over, keeping one book for himself. He takes a place near the signing table and sits between a couple of older boys; they look to be around eleven or twelve. One of the boys clutches a stack of *Just* books.

'Oh, I have them,' says Leo.

'I love the *Just* books,' says the boy. 'I have the whole series.'

'Not *Just Shocking*,' says Leo. 'That's not out yet.' I don't know how he knows that. I work for a bookshop and I don't know it.

'I *know*,' breathes the boy. 'I have the whole series except that one. I *have* to get it as soon as it comes out. If I don't get the whole *Just* series, if I don't get *Just Shocking*, I will *die*. My life *will not* be worth *living*.' This boy is talking exactly like Leo.

Leo looks at him in solemn admiration. 'Me too,' he says.

The three boys begin an animated discussion about the bumosaurs in the new book and the characters in the *Just* series. I leave them to it and buy the new book and the *Maxx Rumble* at the counter.

When I get back, Andy and Terry have arrived. Leo shows all the signs of growing up to become one of those really annoying people at writers' festivals. The ones who just want to demonstrate how clever they are. The ones who make a statement instead of asking a question.

'I was wondering, the other day I made a new comic about Bum Man. And his power is earthquake farts.'

'And your question?' says Terry.

'Well, Andy, I wondered if you would write a story about him in *Just Shocking*?'

When the kids are asked to demonstrate farts, his is the grossest. He suggests that Terry add poo to his butcher's paper drawing of a bumosaur.

When it's Leo's turn to have his book signed, Andy greets him by name, without even having to consult the Post-it note stuck to the title page of his book. Next, Leo moves on to Terry with his *Maxx Rumble* book.

'Hi Leo.'

'Terry, my friend's mum is *not impressed* with Andy.'

Terry laughs. A lot. 'Why is that?'

'She thinks his books are *inappropriate*.'

Terry laughs some more. 'Tell Andy. Hey. Andy!' He plucks at his sleeve. 'Andy! Leo here has something to tell you.'

Leo repeats his statement. Andy splutters with laughter.

'I think *she's* inappropriate!' He gathers himself. 'No, really, she's absolutely right. My books *are* inappropriate.'

Leo goes home happy. So do I.

I tell him many times NOT to tell Vanessa what Andy Griffiths said about her. I tell him as we leave the bookshop, as we board the tram for home, as we walk in the front door and when he goes to bed.

I can tell he is dying to do it.

Sunday morning, as we cross the park, Leo recalls the incident in loving detail, relishing the words on his tongue. I remind him not to tell Vanessa. I do it again as we approach the front gate.

'Yes, Mum.'

I remind him that there always seems to be trouble here and that he must behave.

'Yes, Mum.'

Another parent is lingering at the gate, watching Cujo throw himself at the bars in a frenzy. We make small-talk while we wait for Vanessa to come and rescue us. She wrestles the dog inside the house and out the back door, returning to unlock the gate and let us in.

'Hi!'

'Hi,' says Leo. 'I went to see Andy Griffiths yesterday!'

Vanessa looks at me and rolls her eyes, then turns to Leo and makes a disgusted face, looking back to me as if for support. It's as if he told her he went to Sexpo yesterday.

'Oh *did* you?' she says wryly. 'And was he *rude*?'

Leo runs past her down the hallway, thrusting his present at Angus who greets him with a delighted shriek. Crisis averted. For now.

At 3 pm, Cujo is nowhere to be seen so I am able to ring the doorbell instead of shouting from the footpath. Vanessa sweeps me down the hallway, past the table of iced cakes and chocolate crackles, to where a huddle of small boys in football jumpers is watching television. But no Leo. The boys swing to look at me.

'Leo said a bad word,' says Angus.

'Right.'

I give Vanessa a questioning look.

'I think he might be upstairs. In Angus's room?'

I nod crisply and climb the stairs. The door is locked. I knock. No answer. I call his name. Vanessa is close behind me. She pokes a wire into the lock and gives it a deft twist. It seems she's done this before. Leo is glowering behind the door, arms crossed.

'I have had *the worst day* in my entire life.'

'What's wrong, Leo?' asks Vanessa, bending so her eyes are level with his and putting a comforting hand on his arm. 'Don't exaggerate, now.'

'I don't want to talk about it.'

'We'll talk on the way home,' I decide, grabbing his hand and leading him downstairs. He grunts out a goodbye to Angus, under duress.

Angus waves cheerily as Vanessa gives Leo his lolly bag and follows us down the hallway and to the gate, waving us down the footpath.

They had a fight over footy cards. Angus said his were lame. He said they weren't. They bickered.

'And you said a rude word?'

'No.'

'What did you say?'

'I said Angus was an idiot.'

'And that was the rude word?'

'Yeah.'

'Did you get sent to time-out?'

'Yeah.'

'Vanessa shut you up in Angus's room?'

'Yeah.'

'What did she say to you?'

'She told me never to use that word again.'

Vanessa runs across the schoolyard to catch up with us, greeting us with white-hot charm. She launches into a monologue about a headache and her annoying mother and reading George Monbiot. I focus all my conscious attention on not being rude. Which translates into curt nods and lots of 'yes' and 'really?'.

'Have you recovered from yesterday, Leo?' she asks.

'Yes.'

As we near the end of the cul-de-sac, she turns her attention to our dogs. Doug lurches at her, barking. Leo looks her in the eye. 'He doesn't like you,' he says.

14. THE 'A' WORD

It's the day of Leo's test, the one that will prove what we've always known: that he is gifted. I try not to think about it, but it seeps into my consciousness as I sip coffee at my desk, clean thick fingers of dust off the study bookshelves, then stack the books into cardboard boxes. I line up the hardbacks and wide B-format paperbacks, putting aside the smaller Penguin Classics and A-format paperbacks to pack in their own boxes, or to plug the gaps between the piles of books. Then I use spiky newspaper balls to plug the gaps again, so that when the box is lifted, the books don't move. It's soothing, once you get into the rhythm of it. Pleasing, to see the perfect symmetry of the finished boxes. The stacks of books are then stacked again, in wavering cardboard towers that line the hallway and grow from the corner of the study in Tetris-like piles.

I break for lunch, walking through the park to the shops, stopping along the way to silently admire the new house. I let myself in the front gate and sit on the wooden slats of the verandah. My chin rests on my tracksuited knees as I watch passers-by through a veil of trees. The house is empty, awaiting our arrival. I like the view from here.

Lunch is in my favourite cafe, less than five minutes' walk from the new house. *I'll come here every day soon.* It serves falafel wraps, chicken pies, comfort food. A painted orange flower unfurls across one wall; a coloured-glass chandelier hangs over the counter, resplendently kitsch in its sculpted shards of red and yellow, blue and green. Leonard Cohen sings mournfully overhead as I browse the newspaper and eat my pie.

* * * *

The answering machine blinks hello as I open the front door. *The test!* It is 3.10 pm. I drop my grocery bags in the hallway and press play.

It is, as I suspected, the counsellor. There are twenty minutes until school pick-up; plenty of time to call back and get the good news.

'We'll need to make an appointment to discuss the results,' she says cautiously. 'It'll be a month from now. There are school holidays between now and then.'

'Okay. But do you have any idea what the results are?'

'Ye-e-ees, we do.'

'And?'

'He's very strong in some areas, like language. He has an excellent memory, which explains why his reading is so advanced. He's learned through memory, not comprehension. And there are some … significant areas where he's quite behind, where he has social problems. Social comprehension.'

'Oh yes. I knew that, I guess. But he's not gifted?'

'No.'

'So, he won't get into University High?'

'No. He won't.'

I am horrified to find tears in my throat, threatening to overwhelm my voice. At first, it's disappointment that we won't, after all, get into the private school of public schools, which had seemed a certainty—at least, to me. But in the next second, something clicks in my head. Something that seems wrong. It makes sense, but it doesn't.

'He's not … *autistic* or anything, is he?'

'Um … well, yes, I do think he's on the autistic spectrum. I think he has Asperger's Syndrome.'

And my world collapses in on itself, changes forever, just like that.

Seconds pass.

'Why did you ask that?' she says.

'I don't know.'

'I'm sorry, I didn't mean to tell you like this, over the phone … but when you *asked* … well, you must have wondered.'

'No. Not really, no. I mean, it had gone through my mind a long time ago, but I dismissed it.'

'We'll talk about it properly in a month,' she says reassuringly, as if that closes the matter.

And then she is gone.

I hang up the phone and pick it up again, to ring Mum at work. I need to speak to someone, to share this news before I drown in it. I am crying before she even answers.

Her voice rings with the sing-song *he-llo* that means she's happy to hear from me, idly curious to know what I want. I can barely speak through my panic; she can barely understand me, but draws me out, millimetre by millimetre, with her cool logic.

Drawing on her professional knowledge from years of teaching kids of all kinds, she tells me what Asperger's is in the practical tone she'd use if she were giving me a tip on extracting a splinter or getting a temperature down. She does not collapse. She does not take it as a disaster. She tells me it's not at all certain, that I need a professional with expertise in the field to confirm it.

'Who is this woman?' she scoffs, faintly mocking. 'What does she know? Is she even a qualified psychologist?'

Mum says it's completely unprofessional to tell someone on the phone like that. *Disgraceful.*

'It was my fault. I asked the question. She wasn't going to tell me anything before next month's meeting, but I asked if he was autistic. I don't know why.'

'Still.'

Mum tells me that in the staff room with her is a teacher who specialises in *these things*, things like Asperger's. Their disability coordinator. She asks me to hold, just for a second. She tells me that this teacher has some really good handouts that she can photocopy and send me. And that … she pauses … she is listening … the teacher says *that you need at least two qualified professionals to make a real diagnosis.*

'Don't panic,' she says. 'You don't know anything yet, not really.'

And then I have to go, to pick up Leo.

* * * *

Somehow, I swim through the crowded courtyard, navigating the schools of shouting children and smooth grown-up faces. I manage to avoid eye contact until I reach Leo's classroom, about five minutes late. He is standing outside with his new mate, Ryan, and Ryan's mother, a crop-haired hippie type in jeans and a polo neck. I bend to envelop Leo in a hug that he wriggles expertly out of.

'Mum, can Leo come to our place?' asks Ryan. Leo looks at Ryan and then at his mother, his eyes pleading with them.

'I don't see why not. If that's okay with you?'

'Sure, fine.' Ryan's mother scrawls her phone number and address on a scrap of paper. I flee homeward, to pull myself together like a proper grown-up.

Back in my dining room/study, surrounded by books and papers, I plunge into the world of the screen, grasping for information. One website has a checklist of 'typical' features of an Asperger's child. *A fascination with a topic that is unusual in intensity or focus. Difficulty with the communication and control of emotions. An unusual profile of learning abilities.* It sounds like a description of Leo. Despite the fact that they seem to bolster the diagnosis, the on-screen facts calm me down, lure me afloat. They are less judgmental, less grimly damning, than the school counsellor seemed today. Not that she said much, of course, but her tone was heavy with meaning. *There are some problems … social comprehension. We think he has Asperger's Syndrome.* I linger on the websites that balance the advantages and disadvantages in matter-of-fact, upbeat prose, rather than the ones that talk about 'disorder' and people who 'suffer from' Asperger's Syndrome. Not all of the advantages fit. *Asperger's children are very honest and rarely lie.* Others do. *Distinctive sense of humour.* And the root of Leo's problem, the issue that led us to the school counsellor—and to the words *Asperger's Syndrome*—in the first place, is there on all the checklists, on the good sites and the bad. *Difficulty making friends and often teased by other children. Impaired ability to identify social cues and conventions.*

While I desperately surf the web, the computer trills. Tony is ringing from Mexico, on Skype, as he does most afternoons. I spill my new knowledge into the machine.

'What do they mean, Leo has some kind of syndrome?' he says. 'There's nothing wrong with Leo, he just needs to learn how to compromise more. And it sounds like some of these kids are being little shits.'

Between the talking and the crying, I lose track of time. It's too late to walk—I find myself dialling a cab to pick up Leo. I grab a warm jacket for him on the way out.

In the cab, I am frenetic, distracted. My directions are, to put it frankly, crap. We need to circle back the way we came at least once to turn onto the right street.

Ryan's mother greets me cheerfully at the front door and leads me through to the kitchen where she is chopping vegetables for dinner by the stove. I hear muffled thundering and shouting overhead.

'Was he good?'

'Oh … they were *very* good. Very good. Do you want some wine?'

'Yes, please.' It's just what I need, I think, unspeakably relieved that there has been no trouble. Ryan's little sister appears at my knee as I sit at the kitchen table and watch her mother dice celery. The girl is slight, with fine hair and a blunt, fringed bob. She wears a skivvy and cords and plays football. She brings me paintings to admire, like a cat with offerings of mouse, dropping them on my lap and trotting off for more as I exclaim over them. Her father sits at the other side of the table, reading *The Age* at a leisurely pace, popping his head up with the occasional comment. It is down-to-earth and familiar and comfortable, and I relax a little too much.

Apropos of nothing, I exhale into my wineglass and tell Ryan's parents about my afternoon. I have been cracked wide open, and haven't yet had the chance to begin closing in on myself again. The words pour out with my first tentative sips of wine.

I tell them about the message on the answering machine from the school counsellor, how I rang back right away so I could hear the results from the test that was going to tell us if he is gifted. The way I guessed at autism from her comments. *There are some significant areas where he's quite behind … like social comprehension.* Not really believing it, just saying it. And how it turned out to be true. *On the autistic spectrum.*

I am distantly aware that I hardly know these people and that it is vaguely indecent to be burdening them with something so private and consequential, let alone with my raw emotions. But I can't help myself.

They are kind. They ask me questions. They are appalled at the way I was so casually told; horrified that I have to wait a month to hear more before these strings of words are matched with concrete explanations. This is their son's school.

'I always thought he had a kind of accelerated only-child syndrome,' I sigh. 'Because we don't really know people with kids, and he's the only child in two households, with lots of adult attention. So I thought it must be to do with that.' I am thinking about his ease with adults, compared to his difficulty navigating the codes of friendship with his peers. About my failure to cultivate friendships with other mothers, making it harder for him to practise those codes of friendship.

'You thought it was your fault, then?' ventures Ryan's dad, his curiosity palpable as he leans over his forgotten paper.

'Yes. I did.'

'And you thought it was because you split up with his father?'

'Yes.' I surprise myself. 'I think I did.'

'And it's not that?'

'No.'

I tell them about the phone call with Mum.

Ryan's dad leans across the table, still interested. 'What did Leo's dad say?' he asks. 'Have you told him yet?'

I'd rung Mark after Mum hung up—the next step in my telephone daisy chain. He was as shocked as I was, but calm. He, like Mum, talked me back into the world with logic and plans for action.

'He wants to talk to the school tomorrow,' I say now. 'He wants more information.'

Leo is reluctantly dragged out of Ryan's bedroom where he has been putting together all Ryan's Bionicles.

'Ryan said I could keep this one!' he announces.

'No, you can't,' I scold.

'It's fine,' says Ryan's mum, a little too kindly. 'He got them all as presents and he's never known how to put them together anyway. He's never played with them.'

I realise that I've left Leo's jacket in the back of the cab. It's cold outside, the damp cold that comes at the end of a winter evening and a rainy day. I'm zipped snugly into my quilted parka. Despite my embarrassed protests that I plan to give this to Leo, Ryan's mother lends us her son's duffle coat for the walk. Ryan's father offers to drive us home; they both try to insist on it. I wave them away gratefully. I need to be alone.

The wind whips my hair and slaps our cheeks as we push through the darkness. We skirt the traffic on truck-heavy Somerville Road and turn into leafy Severn Street, trudging deserted footpaths beneath the streetlights, passing lit windows behind picket fences. It is a long walk home: nearly half an hour. Leo is excited by his new toy. He talks all the way home in a rambling, unbroken monologue about the Bionicles universe. *Toa Jaller is friends with Toa Kongu, but I reckon that actually Kongu wants to trick Jaller so he can take the Mask of Life first. He doesn't really want to save Mata Nui …* I'm in the habit of interrupting him after a while and instructing him to change the topic, just to develop the art of conversation. Tonight, I let the wave of it roll over me, too numb and exhausted to intervene. And of course, tonight, the real meaning of the Bionicles monologue is painfully clear. *Asperger's children do not comprehend the give-and-take nature of social interactions.*

We disappear into the unlit reaches of the park. The darkness swallows us whole as we approach the bridge that will take us to our street, home, dinner, bed. And I wonder, for the first time since this afternoon's phone call: *how could I not have known?*

* * * *

After Leo has gone to bed, I write a blog post titled 'Bad Day', a few sentences long.

> *I found out that my son has Asperger's today. Not that the school psychologist is available to share any of the details until a month from now. That's what happens when you don't pay for services.*

Over the next few days, I will be flooded with understanding, with offers to talk any time, with the story of one blog friend whose brother has Asperger's, too.

Though I won't have the energy to engage, not for some weeks anyway, I am mutely grateful that the opportunities are there.

15. LOOKING FOR ANSWERS

After I drop Leo at his classroom, along with Ryan's duffle coat, I head for the principal's office. I have work to do at home, but I sit in the school office lobby anyway, waiting. There is no point in going home. There is nothing else I can think about.

I am desperate to get hold of the elusive report; the one that explains how and why Leo apparently has Asperger's Syndrome. Without it, I can't accept it. I won't. I need details. What are the specific shortcomings that led the school counsellor to think it's Asperger's? And what exactly does this mean? Does she really mean that he *has* Asperger's, or that he has *characteristics*? Did I exaggerate what the counsellor said on the phone? Who would tell someone something like this *on the phone*, then disappear for a month? I must have it wrong.

Finally, after half an hour or so, the deputy principal arrives. She ushers me in, looking slightly harangued. She sits behind her desk and waves me towards a chair, her smile tight as I sit down.

'So, what's up?'

'Have you spoken to Jennifer?'

'Yes.' Her smile escalates to high-beam intensity, all light and no warmth. 'Yes, she told me.'

'Have you seen the report?'

She has, yes, but can't tell me anything about it. 'I'd really better leave it to Jennifer to talk to you about it.'

Does she know that Jennifer can't see us for another month? Yes. She seems unsurprised by this turn of events. She is calm, breezy, upbeat; her surface unruffled. She explains what Asperger's is, in basic terms, and tells me it's a very good thing we've found this out now.

'We have a fair bit of experience with this,' she assures me. 'There are other Asperger's kids at the school. In fact, there's another kid in his class who has it.'

I guess who it is. I'm wrong. She doesn't enlighten me. I'm relieved, really. It's confidential information; at least I hope it is.

She tells me they have some 'great' information sheets. She fumbles through the newly unpacked shelves of her office and unearths a sheet on autism from a cardboard box. I can take it home, she says. I hope my face is not reflecting how I feel as I look at it. Even my few hours on the web have taught me that autism and Asperger's, while on the same 'spectrum', are not the same thing. Luckily, I know that autism is the more severe of the two. I don't know if this list of points on 'How Your Child is Thinking' is entirely relevant.

'I'll find the other stuff when we unpack,' she promises. 'But this is a really good introduction, here. A lot of parents find it useful.'

'Okay. I've actually found some very good stuff on the internet.'

'*Good.*'

'Actually, when I found out, I rang my mum, who's a teacher, and she was in the staffroom with a teacher who specialises in kids with special needs. She's sending me some information. But thanks.'

'Oh.' She blinks at me as if a cartoon light bulb has flashed above her head. 'Are you up*set* about this?'

I am stunned. How could she not have immediately realised this? How could I not be upset?

'Yes. Well, I was yesterday. I think I'm okay now.' This is not remotely true, but I feel the need to prove that I am sane and rational. 'It was a real shock, to be told on the phone like that.'

She makes sympathetic noises, reminds me that this diagnosis is a good thing, that it will enable me to help Leo, and gently manoeuvres me out of the office and into the empty lobby. I stand alone under the fluorescent lighting before heading for home, autism handout in hand, none the wiser and still desperate to know more.

* * * *

At home, I head straight for my desk and dive back into the internet. I find an Asperger's test from *Wired* magazine. It won't give me anything definitive, but in the absence of the concrete information I crave, I'll try any likely substitute. I do the test, pretending I'm Leo as I consider the answers. *I frequently get so strongly absorbed in one thing that I lose sight of other things.* Strongly agree. *I find social situations easy.* Strongly disagree. *When I talk, it isn't always easy for others to get a word in edgewise.* Strongly agree. He 'scores' as Asperger's.

Asperger's runs in families. Fifty per cent of people with Asperger's have someone in the family with the same diagnosis.

I do the test as Mark. He scores on the borderline. In my imagination, he is classified as Asperger's by just one point. It is him.

I do the test as myself. There are some strands of questioning that put me in the Asperger's camp. *New situations make me anxious.* Definitely agree. *I prefer to do things the same way over and over again.* Definitely agree. I'm nowhere near the Asperger's score, though. Loving fiction and hating numbers has something to do with it, I think. (*I find making up stories easy.* Definitely agree. *I am fascinated by numbers.* Definitely disagree.) It's funny, I've always said that Leo may look like his dad's family (he does, without the nose) but he's very much a Case personality. Now that I discover his personality is shaped by something that carries a label, my first thought is that he must get it from his dad. I realise this smacks of hypocrisy. Or something. Later, I will learn that Asperger's often presents differently in males and females. For instance, while my answers in favour of fiction and imaginative play earn me high scores on the 'not Asperger's' side in this test, many girls and women with Asperger's are interested in exactly these things. So is Leo.

Work is forgotten for the day. The stacks of government reports on the polished boards of the study lie ignored in favour of Google and the search term *Asperger's*. I need to know what this means. I need to figure out if it fits. Any other thoughts are crowded out. There is only room for this.

* * * *

Dad writes to me:

> *After the shock of hearing this possibility, I think that it might*
> *provide a few valuable leads to parenting strategies and might*
> *make you feel less responsible for some of his eccentricities, which*
> *are not too hard to adapt to anyway. Perhaps more importantly,*
> *Asperger's might help others to realise that those eccentricities are*
> *not wilful rudeness directed at them. I'm thinking of a particular*
> *mother you wrote about …*

Mum calls. She tells me she has booked a flight and she's coming back this weekend to help me move. This, after having spent last weekend driving around Melbourne to find boxes, then helping me pack them.

'I can't let you do it by yourself,' she says. 'This is so shitty already. You find out Leo has Asperger's—*might* have Asperger's—and you move house two days later.'

I know I should tell her not to worry about it, that I'll be fine, but I can't do it. I'm not sure that I will be fine.

'Thank you, Mum. Thank you so much.'

I tell Mum that I've been thinking about an incident from last weekend. It was deep into the evening—say, 9.30 pm—and Mum and I were washing down newly emptied bookshelves in the hallway. Leo padded out in bare feet and flannelette pyjamas, his head peering from behind a tower of stacked boxes by his doorway.

'I'm scared.'

'It's okay, we're here. Go back to sleep.'

'I'm scared of the straight lines.'

We shepherded him back to bed together, and tucked the quilt over him. Dinosaurs roamed beneath his chin. We each landed kisses on his cheek, indulgent where our normal instinct would be almost military at this time of night. ('Get back to bed!') Once we were back in the hallway, his small voice rang out from the darkness.

'I'm still scared!'

'Go back to sleep.'

'It might be the boxes,' Mum ventured. 'They form straight lines.' We relented and went back in, to turn on the bedside lamp *just this once*.

'What an autistic-sounding thing to say,' I reflect now, expecting Mum to tell me not to be silly. It's not so much anything I've read about autism as the images I can't quite banish, despite knowing they're nothing like Leo: Dustin Hoffman in *Rainman* or the kid in Mark Haddon's *The Curious Incident of the Dog in the Night-Time*. Robotic geniuses with odd but specific fixtations, like counting licence plates or refusing to fly any airline but Qantas. Or not liking straight lines.

'Yeah,' Mum concurs. 'It is, a bit. But I'm sure it's nothing. We're probably analysing everything too much.'

'Probably.'

* * * *

The internet backs up Mum's advice that I need to confirm the diagnosis by making an appointment with a professional who specialises in the field. Technically, we then need another expert to confirm it.

The school counsellor is not an expert, or even a psychologist. And she's not available for a month. Mark takes on the task of tracking down an expert and making the appointment while I become as much of an expert as Google can make me. I find Tony Attwood, a British-born Queenslander, who I've been told is the world authority. I like the soothing manner of his website, the calm assertiveness: 'From my clinical experience I consider that children with Asperger's Syndrome have a different, not defective, way of thinking.'

I collect a list of successful famous people with Asperger's: Albert Einstein, Mark Twain, Bill Gates, Mozart, Woody Allen. Of course, it's all (mostly posthumous) conjecture, but it's another small lifeline, proof that people with Asperger's can live a successful life.

* * * *

Mark speaks to Eliza himself. He tells her that we're making an appointment with a specialist and that we'll fill her in on how it goes. She is indignant. She tells him that if we insist on doing our own thing, the school won't be able to work with us. Mark says something uncharacteristically sharp, to the effect that they will *just have to*. She backs down.

While I've reacted to Leo's diagnosis the only way I know how—with a tidal wave of emotion—Mark has been practical, logical, even cool about it. He deals with the facts, with the tasks to be done, and seems somehow able to withhold any judgement or emotion, until he knows just what we're dealing with. Of course, this could all be a front. Maybe he cries in a corner of his lounge room when he hangs up the phone, unseen and unheard by me. Maybe he feels he should be the sensible one, to balance my focused hysteria. Maybe he feels superior, because he can control himself and I can't. Part of me admires his control, envies it. I feel it would be useful. But I can only be myself. We don't talk about any of this—we talk about what we can do, we pool information, and we let off steam by bitching about the school.

The house is a cardboard maze. The wall of boxes winds its way down the hallway and rises in towers along the edges of newly naked rooms. I have managed to tear myself away from the internet to channel my nervous energy into packing. The movers have already been booked for Friday, when I'll move into the new house by myself. Mum arrives on Saturday morning.

Moving is a good way to temporarily divert my thoughts. My laptop is packed into its bag, blocking me from the internet. I'm focused on stacking boxes and clearing paths for moving the furniture. It's not the first time I've moved house alone, but it still feels strange—and somehow lonelier—to be doing it as a married woman.

The movers are impressed by my organisation and with the fact that I pitch in to help load and unload the truck. I don't tell them I'm doing it to save time, and therefore money. It takes four trips and as many hours to move all the boxes and furniture. On the final trip, the movers let the dogs ride with us in the front of the truck, to save me from having to go back to collect them on foot. I hold Doug firmly on my lap during the short ride, so he won't bite them—which he's been attempting to do since they pulled in to our driveway. The movers also reassemble my bed and take care to place the furniture exactly where I need it.

By the time they leave, the sky is dimming. Taking advantage of my new location, I walk down the road to pick up Cambodian for dinner. When I get home twenty minutes later, I discover that I've locked myself out. The house proves impossible to break into. Luckily, Emily has recently moved to the neighbourhood; she lives around the corner, so I sheepishly interrupt her dinner preparations to find and call a local locksmith, before walking home through the dark to wait for him. I eat my cold vermicelli and chicken meatballs with my fingers on the front porch, listening to the dogs bark in the backyard.

Saturday morning, there is a knock at the door. It is Lucy, offering to help me unpack. I make the appropriate noises about being fine on my own before relenting and gratefully accepting. It's nice to have company as I slice open boxes and unfurl the contents, slowly populating shelves and drawers with evidence that I live here. Lucy takes the kitchen while I unpack my books. When Mum arrives, I've filled half a bookshelf; Lucy has organised the cutlery drawer and is in the process of stacking plates below the counter.

'You've taken the kitchen?' says Mum. 'Good plan. I'd never try to organise her books! She's got her own systems for them—she's so finicky.'

Lucy laughs and agrees.

'Have you got them in alphabetical order?' asks Mum. 'Can you believe she alphabetises them?'

'No I don't,' I say. 'Not anymore. I'm just taking them out of boxes and putting them on shelves.'

'So, there's no system at all?'

'Well, the fiction goes on this side of the room, the classics are in the hall and the non-fiction goes over here. That's all.'

Mum agrees that this is really quite laidback of me, while Lucy giggles conspiratorially. I leave to collect take-away coffees and when I return with a cardboard tray and a bag of muffins, they are arranging framed photographs and ornaments atop my shelves and cabinets. Tony's carved Japanese figurines, inherited from his sister, are all in a row, facing one another as if in conversation.

'Look!' says Mum, pleased with herself. 'Doesn't this look nice?'

'Sure,' I say. 'Though he'll probably want to move them his own way when he gets home.'

'Of course,' says Mum. 'But I think he'll be pleased with this arrangement.'

Sunday is the day we go back to the old house to clear the last of the rubbish and clean. A hired skip takes up most of the driveway. We pack Mum's car with piles of things to keep—handbags and backpacks, hangers, plants, papers. I am seized by a desire to get rid of everything; I just want this to be over so I can get back to my life. Whatever that is right now. Mum holds up a Crumpler satchel of Tony's, her eyebrows posing a question mark.

'Bin it,' I say.

'Are you sure?'

'Yeah, he never uses it anymore.'

Earlier in the week, I'd arranged for Goodwill to take away some old furniture, including two tall, stained-wood cabinets inherited from Tony's dad. Tony had told me to get rid of 'anything you want', but when I said I was getting rid of the cabinets, he was furious. They're family heirlooms, he said. (They're ugly, I said, but this was not a valid argument. His dad had designed them and had them made especially to fit the stereo that Tony had also inherited. And besides, he didn't think they were ugly.) Luckily, I was able to retrieve the cabinets before it was too late.

Margaret comes over to help. She takes Tony's Crumpler bag for safekeeping, as well as the plastic climbing frame and slide that Leo has grown out of, for Jordan. She helps shuttle carloads of belongings to the new house, which she agrees is better than the old one.

Mum, Margaret and I go out to lunch down the road.

'Leo is a very special boy,' Margaret says over her pasta. 'I don't know about this Asperger's thing, but I don't think he needs a label put on him. I don't see how that's useful.' She tells us a story about a time when well-meaning teachers had tried to put a label on one of her children and she'd resisted. 'He's just a great kid,' she says, about Leo. 'And we all love him.'

'That's right,' says Mum. Later, she adds that she thinks a label could be useful if it would help other people understand Leo.

All weekend, with Lucy and Mum and Margaret, I have the same conversation, over and over: Does Leo have Asperger's Syndrome? What are the signs that he does, or doesn't? What does it mean? And does it matter?

Leo comes to the house for the first time on Sunday afternoon, shortly before his Nana leaves to drive back to Adelaide. He greets her with the 'wiggly hug' they've invented for each other—a kind of vibrating bear hug. As always, she is delighted. 'He hasn't grown out of the wiggly hug yet!'

'Never!' he says. And then he asks to go next door and see Steven.

'Hello,' says Roger, opening the door wide. 'Steven's been asking and asking when he can come and see you. I'll get him.'

Sure enough, Steven rushes down the hallway behind him and grips Leo by the shoulders. They squeal each other's names and disappear, shouting, into Steven's bedroom. I promise to collect him in an hour or so; Roger says he'll just bring him home when it's time for dinner.

I wave Mum off from the footpath as she drives away, then turn inside. The sky is darkening, just a little. It's time to look through my cupboards and see what I've got that I can turn into a meal. As I begin to chop onions, I hear the thud of a ball against the other side of the fence.

16. STARFISH

On Friday mornings, when listening to kids read in Leo's classroom, I get a feel for how he's doing in class. Not his reading level (I've never had any concerns about that), but how he's behaving, how he's fitting in. With this new information, the new question of Asperger's Syndrome, this seems more important than ever.

Leo gets to go first. He sits very close to me, his back straight and eyes solemn with pride. He leans into me, the sleeve of his jumper warm against my arm. Two girls in the class, Mikhela and Bhanu, regularly joust for position as second reader. Leo looks on with pleasure, as if to say, *they're fighting over my mum!* The girls slip as much conversation as they can into the reading: pausing between pages or three-line paragraphs to admire my long fingernails or squint at my hair. ('It's too short,' Bhanu told me after a haircut. 'You need to grow it back.') They tell me what they do on weekends and what music they listen to. I enjoy Mikhela's shy smile and Bhanu's serene cheekiness. There is a third girl who likes to have me listen to her read. Her name is Jenny. She has wispy red hair and a sprinkling of freckles on her nose. I want to like her more than I do. She's a nice girl, but it's a struggle to get her to read at all. She only wants to talk, about her tree house and her little brother and her dog.

As the children disappear into the schoolyard for recess, I get to snatch a few words with the teacher: a quick progress report on how Leo is going. It's the main perk of being a classroom helper. This week, Kaye beckons me over to look at a book she's read to the class: *All Cats Have Asperger's*. It has a cutesy photograph of a cat on each page, with one-liners like, 'Sometimes I feel like I belong on another planet'.

'Guess what?' she says, excited. 'After I read it to the class, Leo came up and told me he feels like that.'

'He did?'

'Yes. He said, "That's me".'

'Wow.'

'A couple of other kids did the same thing too.'

'*Really?*'

'Yes. Conor and Ryan.' His two best friends.

'How interesting,' I say.

'Yes,' she smiles. 'I know.'

Leo asks me if he can take his skateboard down the road to the skate ramp. I say yes. I grew up watching my brothers and friends skateboard on the ramp at the end of my street; there's something nostalgic about watching Leo do the same thing. The one time I tried skateboarding, I sat on the board and went down the ramp on my bum, playing it safe. The board flew out from under me, flipping me into the air and over on my side. My skirt flew up, giving the boys I was trying to impress a mortifying glimpse of my underwear. My next-door neighbour who was there with me hooted in delight. 'Oh my god! Did you see her knickers?' she shouted, just in case anyone had somehow missed it.

Simon and his best friend Toby used to line up the bins on our street and jump over them on their skateboards or rollerblades, having competitions to see who could jump the most bins. They borrowed our parents' camera and took photos of each other mid-jump.

I sit on a bench at the top of the skateboard ramp, under the naked tree threaded with dangling sneakers. Leo sits on the board and lets go, whizzing down the ramp and up the other side. I clap my hands and hoot with relief.

'I knew you could do it!' I say. I like that he's brave, braver than I ever was. He does it a couple more times sitting down, then wriggles onto his stomach. Tense with trepidation, I watch him push off with his hands. He shoots down the slope and up again; whole and perfect, utterly unharmed. On the way back home, he struts a little.

We rug up in waterproof parkas and catch the train to Williamstown for ice-cream. We go to the playground near the primary school first, the one with the tunnels and high slides. I devise a monkey-bar course for Leo to run and time him as he completes it, counting down the seconds. It goes: cross the monkey bars, do a backflip on the horizontal bars, run to the second set of monkey bars, another backflip—and back. He challenges me to do it, too. I'm good at backflips, but drop to the ground after two monkey bars. 'Just ten minutes,' calls a parent as her two small children burst onto the equipment, breaking our solitude. 'It's too cold today.'

We do another obstacle course (this time, the slide circuit) at the other playground, the one opposite the harbour where the boats are moored. Then we reward ourselves with ice-cream at the parlour that boasts fifty flavours. We always get the same ones: mint choc-chip for me, bubblegum for Leo. We eat with our parkas zipped to our chins and hoods on, standing under the eaves of the shop and watching rain fall on the footpath beyond our feet.

Ice-creams finished, rain faded into drizzle, we trail the skirts of the sea, walking around the tennis courts and past the boat sheds, along the path by the water. Leo spots an empty plastic water bottle under the fence at the sailing club; he declares it perfect for collecting mussels or shells. I wriggle onto my stomach and reach my arm under the wire, just managing to grasp it. We cheer and jump up and down on the spot.

We don't see any mussels, but starfish are visible on the rocks at the bottom of the seabed, along the fringes of the rock-wall we are stalking.

'Do you want a starfish?' I ask Leo. 'Do you want me to catch one?'

'Yes!' he says.

I take off my sneakers, socks and parka, followed by my hoodie; then I roll up my jeans and my sleeves as far as they'll go. Knees and elbows bared, I wade into the sea, stepping carefully on the rocks. The shock of the cold seawater makes me shriek; Leo echoes me.

'Mum!'

'I'm okay,' I say. 'I'm just cold.'

'Oh.'

I reach for the starfish, straining my arm as far as it will go, but I can't grasp it and give up. Barefoot, I leave my discarded shoes and clothes by the water's edge and keep moving, urging Leo to follow. Soon, we find another starfish, this one tantalisingly close—surely within arm's reach. I am more confident, less careful; maybe this is why my foot slips on a rock and I fall with a scream, landing on my bum in the water, submerged to the waist. Leo screams, too, just as I start to laugh. When I catch my breath, I reassure him I'm fine and climb out of the water to prove it. Water streams from my sodden jeans, puddling on the footpath.

'Oh, it's my fault!' wails Leo. 'I'm so sorry Mum!'

'No it's not, why is it your fault? I'm the one who climbed into the water.'

'But I told you I wanted a starfish.'

'It was my decision to go get it,' I say. 'Really, I'm the grown-up. It's my responsibility.'

I decide to climb back in and retrieve the starfish; I'm wet anyway. It's easy this time, now that I'm not worried about keeping myself dry. But of course, it doesn't fit in our water bottle, not even close. I put it down on the footpath and we watch the tiny tentacles on its underside quiver.

'Cool,' breathes Leo.

When I pick it up, it leaves a damp, star-shaped outline on the cement.

'Let's get a container for it to live in,' I say. 'We'll go to the supermarket.'

My jeans soak into my socks, which squelch in my sneakers with every step up the road. In the shopping complex, I keep my eyes fixed straight ahead, as if I don't know what a ridiculous sight I make in my dripping jeans, as if I don't notice the wet trail I am leaving down the aisles. I ask Leo to hold my purse as I retrieve the money to pay for the clear plastic lunchbox I've found. I'm holding the starfish in my other hand, its tentacles wriggling against my fingers. On the footpath, we put the starfish in the lunchbox and Leo fills it with seawater from his plastic bottle. It seems to settle in the water.

'Wow,' says Leo. 'It's my pet. I'm bringing it to show my class.'

By now, I can feel my legs going numb, prickling with the last sensations of feeling. We go to the surf shop. I send Leo in to explain that his mum is very wet and ask if she can come in anyway because she needs new pants. I stand in the doorway, craning my neck to watch. He rests his container of seawater, the starfish floating inside, on the counter. The salesgirl seems baffled. She comes to the door and asks me how wet I am.

'I just mopped the floor,' she explains.

'Well, I fell in the sea.'

'Oh.' There is a silence.

'It's okay,' I say. 'I'll go, I understand. I just wanted to buy some dry pants.'

'No, no, come in.'

I browse the rack of tracksuit pants and select an armful of pairs to try on. The girl turns her attention to the starfish. She tells Leo that she did a school assignment on them. She tells him the scientific name for starfish, and that they are actually called 'star of the sea' these days, because they're not fish. She rustles beneath the counter and comes up with some scissors, which she punches into the container for us: breathing holes.

'Did your mum get that for you?' she asks Leo. 'Is that why she fell in the sea, because she was getting that for you? Is it your fault?'

She is teasing, but I turn from my rack of 75-per-cent-off jeans to see his stricken face.

'It's not his fault at all,' I say. 'I'm the grown-up. I should have known better. Right, Leo?'

His face returns to normal. I turn back to the jeans.

'You're very lucky to have a mum who takes you to the beach, huh?' I hear her say.

'Oh yes,' he says. 'She takes me *all the time*.'

I buy a pair of tracksuit pants that are slightly too long in the leg, and transfer my wet jeans to a plastic bag. On the way home, we stop to buy hot chips. The girls at the counter admire Leo's starfish.

At home, I shut all the doors to the living area and turn the heater on, full blast. I make roast dinner, with a slab of beef, slivers of carrot and as many potatoes as I can fit in the baking dish. Leo puts his starfish on the front verandah and sits at the dining-room table to write songs.

I write an email to Tony, who is now in London, visiting his sister on his way home from Mexico. It is his last stop; for the past three weeks he has been travelling with Carlo, visiting remote beaches and

Mayan ruins. I have resented this post-university leg of the trip since he announced it at the end of last year. He's a married man: why is he spending our money on fun, just for him? Why is he not coming home, to see his family, at the end of his six months?

But by now, I have shed my resentment—or at least I think I have. He has written to me almost every day, and has called often. He has apologised, again and again, for leaving us for so long. *I was selfish*, he's said. *You're not selfish*, I reply. *Just enjoy yourself, now you're there.* As I say it, I believe it.

Tony writes back to say we shouldn't be taking starfish out of the sea.

Mark and I finally meet with the counsellor, Jennifer. Eliza is there, too. I'm surprised when they usher us in to the empty staff room for our meeting.

They explain the results of the test Jennifer administered—and why they've both concluded Leo has Asperger's Syndrome. They point to a graph, with the above-average marks in memory and reading skills, the below-average marks in social comprehension. Such a set of strengths and weaknesses, coupled with the difficulties Leo has been having in the schoolyard, they say, points to an autistic spectrum disorder.

Jennifer asks Mark and I to complete a checklist called a Pragmatics Profile, which we answer together, sitting at the communal table with the graphs spread out in front of us. Newspapers and magazines sit further down the table.

A teacher wanders in to make coffee. She sits at an opposite corner of the table while the kettle boils. I want to stop talking, to push her out of the room and shut the door. It seems such a very private thing we're doing, judging whether our son might have a developmental disorder that will affect his whole life. It seems to me that we should be able to do it in privacy. But no-one else pays any attention to the teacher, or to the next one, who settles in a corner with a fragment of newspaper.

We talk through skills like:

makes/responds to greetings from others
observes turn-taking rules in the classroom or in social interactions
agrees and disagrees using appropriate language
responds to teasing, anger, failure, disappointment appropriately
knows how someone is feeling based on nonverbal cues

We rate them always, often, sometimes or never. Leo mostly rates 'sometimes', with a few 'often' and a few 'never'. There is no 'always'. His overall score is below the average for his age level.

Jennifer explains things like Leo's absence of empathy (being able to understand what others are feeling and respond appropriately), his lack of role-playing or modelling skills, his lack of imagination.

'But he has empathy!' I argue. 'He often knows how I'm feeling and responds. He comforts me all the time when I'm unhappy. He hates to feel that he's hurt others.'

'He's the most imaginative kid I know! He's always making up games and stories!'

They don't convince me. The Leo they describe both is and isn't the boy I know. And I can tell I'm not convincing them either.

There are some observations that strike a chilling nerve. The lack of eye contact (which I'd never thought remarkable), the fact that he still doesn't start or finish conversations appropriately, but introduces them mid-thought. ('Do you like Yu-Gi-Oh, Steven?') None of these things had seemed significant before, but now I realise they just might be.

Maybe he is a little bit Asperger's, I decide. He might have elements of Asperger's.

I have bought a copy of Tony Attwood's bible, *The Complete Guide to Asperger's Syndrome*, by now; I read it at night before I go to bed, or browse it between television ads on the couch.

It's not just Leo I sort of recognise within its pages.

17. BACK TO THE FUTURE

It's the night before Tony comes home. Leo and I stay with his brother, Jamie. We will all travel together to the airport, early in the morning, to pick up Tony. Jamie and his partner live in a narrow two-storey terrace, on a leafy inner-city street. Leo and I share a double bed at the top of the house; moonlight leaks in through the bare window. Neither of us can sleep, and after a while I give up trying to keep Leo quiet, or willing myself to shut down. We are both electric with anticipation. Our talk circles around what it will be like to see Tony again, what we will tell him, whether he will like the new house.

'He'll never go away like that again, will he?' says Leo. 'He's back for good?'

'Of course.'

'How do you know?'

'Because he said so.'

'Okay.'

This is true.

'Tell me a story,' says Leo. 'Please.'

So I do, about his favourite semi-imaginary character, a naughty little girl named Brenda. She's based on a classmate who chopped off one of my plaits when I was in primary school. The story involves Brenda publishing naughty stories at school, getting into trouble, being discovered by Andy Griffiths, then becoming a superstar; the story within the story has the punchline: 'And then she sawed the cat in half'.

'I think this is the best story you've ever made,' says Leo. 'Except for one thing. Brenda wins! You have to fix that. In Andy Griffiths stories, the naughty kid always learns their lesson.'

We sink into sleep as the sky begins to lighten; an hour later, Jamie knocks on the door.

Tony hugs us all, hard, as if snatching a rare chance. He holds me for a long time. He looks exactly the same, except for a beard that wasn't there before. His eyes are tired; a wariness lurks in them that I recognise from my own arrival home. He sits in the back seat of the car, between me and Leo, refusing Jamie's offer to let him ride in the front. He holds our hands, and is quiet while we take turns talking to him. Leo offers to tell him the story of Brenda and the cat, then plunges into it without waiting for an answer. Tony looks out the window as Leo talks, but though he doesn't seem to listen, he frowns at the punchline, 'And then she sawed the cat in half'.

'That's horrible,' he says, over Leo's and my laughter.

'I know,' I say. 'I made it up in the middle of the night. We couldn't sleep; we just couldn't wait to see you.'

Tony squeezes my hand, kisses the top of Leo's head.

Tony's favourite dog, Doug, snaps at him as he comes through the door, barking and biting at his pants legs. Snuffy barks with happiness, leaping at his legs and licking his hands and face when Tony bends to pat her. Tony stretches his arms out to Doug, crooning to him, but the dog runs to me—me, who can't stand him!—and cowers at my feet.

'He doesn't remember me,' Tony says sadly.

'He will.'

'You won't leave again?' says Leo.

'No way,' says Tony.

'You're not allowed to,' Leo adds. 'Mum said so.'

Tony is disoriented. He looks around the house with a grim expression—at the bookshelves half-stocked, the piles of boxes stacked behind the couch.

'What do you think of the new house?' I say proudly.

'It's okay.'

'I haven't quite finished unpacking. I've been really busy the past couple of weeks. You don't mind, do you?'

'No, of course not,' he says slowly, in a voice that implies he minds quite a bit.

'You can help me unpack them. I saved some for you, so you wouldn't feel left out.'

He looks at the Japanese figurines on top of the bookshelves in the dining room. They are still arranged as if in conversation with each other.

'What's that?' he says.

'Oh, Mum did it. She thought it was funny. You can move them if you like.'

'Hmmm.' He turns the row of figurines so they're all facing in the same direction, towards the centre of the room.

Tony unpacks gifts for everyone: a Mexican soccer shirt and a poncho for Leo, plus an acoustic guitar with a colourful painted design. Jewellery for me: earrings and seeded pearls, an embroidered peasant top and matching skirt. He unpacks colourful striped rugs and blankets, carved onyx Aztec figurines, purple embroidered placemats.

'I'm sorry I wasn't here to support you,' Tony says later, after Leo has gone to bed. 'That you've had to cope with this Asperger's thing on your own.'

'That's okay,' I say. 'You didn't know that would happen while you were gone. How could you?'

I am okay with it—just. But I feel like he owes me something. I'm not sure what. Recognition?

The next day, I plunge back in to work: it's deadline day for my newsletter and I have to go in to the bookshop to put through corrections and get the file ready for the designer to take over. Life returns to normal. Tony offers to pick up Leo from school and take care of him while I'm gone. He kisses me goodbye at the door.

I get home as soon as I can—early evening. I open the front door to see the formerly tidy house—*my* house—in disarray: the hallway jammed with furniture, living area strewn with bookshelves at right angles, couches in reversed positions, boxes and papers and books in piles around the room.

'Hi,' says Tony mildly, an edge to his smile. Leo stands beside him, also smiling.

I start to yell.

Basically, I ask what the hell he is doing, why he has taken apart all the hard work I've done in arranging the house—work I did with no help from him—without asking me. He tells me he was hoping it would be a surprise, that he wasn't expecting me home so early and that he'd thought he'd be closer to finishing when I did walk through the door.

That he'd arrived home shocked at how little work I'd done in unpacking and organising the house; he didn't expect to get home and find boxes everywhere. He didn't like the way the house was set up; he doesn't feel like it's his home. I tell him it's not my fault he wasn't here when I moved, that it was his choice to go to Mexico, and then his choice to extend his trip with backpacking with Carlo, and a stay in London with his sister. That I've been working hard and dealing with a lot on my own while he's been gone, and how dare he judge me for not doing more.

And then I leave.

I don't know how we're going to learn to live together again. Maybe I've got used to living alone. Maybe I'm not as okay with his long absence as I thought I was.

I call Mum from a payphone at the train station, feeding it with coins as long as I can.

Tony apologises when I come back, half an hour later. He says he thinks he does feel weird about it being my ex's house, after all. It's too late for that, I say. He agrees; he's sure he'll get used to it. We agree to rearrange the house together, later.

'I'm sorry,' says Leo, when I find him in his bedroom. 'I shouldn't have let Tony mess the house up.'

'Don't be silly,' I say. 'That's not your job. Everything's fine now, anyway.'

And it is, mostly.

The next day, Tony gives me another piece of the puzzle. He'd been furious when he realised his sister's fridge was missing, the one we'd been storing for her since she moved to London with her husband four years ago.

'What am I going to tell her when she wants it back?' he says.

'I'm sick of storing your sister's stuff. We don't have the room and it's a pain every time we move house.' I'd never been consulted about storing the fridge; it was simply delivered to my back verandah one day, just weeks after Tony moved in with Leo and me.

'Well, you should have told me. It was better than our fridge; we could have at least swapped it. Or I could have moved it to my dad's garage.'

I've also thrown out a television cabinet Tony wanted. There's a jacket he can't find anywhere; I'm sure I didn't get rid of it, at least *pretty* sure.

Tony opens box after box of papers he empties straight into the recycling bin.

'Why did you keep all these papers,' he sighs, 'but throw out important things, like my sister's fridge? And my dad's cabinets, if I hadn't rescued them?'

'I didn't know what was important,' I argue.

'Couldn't you have thought about it? Surely it would be obvious if you did?'

It does seem obvious when he says it. But the things I'd be most devastated to lose would be my boxes of papers: old letters, photographs, university essays, scraps of stories. To me, keeping all the bits of paper, just in case they were important, seemed like the obvious thing to do.

* * * *

There is a framed wedding photo in the hall: me and Tony, his parents, my parents, Leo. Tony hangs it in the study, over my desk.

'Look!' he says, expecting me to be pleased.

'I don't want a picture of my family in here, where I work,' I say, taking the picture down immediately. 'I don't want to think about my family when I sit at my desk.'

'Why not?'

'Because this is where I *work*.'

During my average working day, I rotate loads of crockery in and out of the dishwasher or hang clothes on the line. I walk Leo to and from school; I respond to questions about homework and listen to anecdotes about Lego. I pay bills and take phone calls from Tony, about anything from what we'll have for dinner to who he ran into on the street. This is what I have chosen; it's the way I like it. But I draw the line at hanging my family's faces over my desk.

Steven is at our house every weekend, or Leo is next door at his house. Sometimes he comes over after school, too. They call over the fence to each other; sometimes they climb onto it—Leo standing behind the native bushes, Steven trampling his mother's rose garden—so they can look at each other while they talk.

I make the back shed into a clubhouse, with blankets covering the old velour couch that Tony doesn't want in the house; the dark wood cabinet I loathe is banished there too, now stocked with books and comics. There is an old school desk in a corner, with pencils and textas and paper. Leo makes a sign for the door: NO GIRLS ALLOWED. They add to it: LEO AND STEVEN ONLY. Soon after, Jordan's name is added to the door, then Conor's.

Sitting in my study, I can hear them digging for treasure in the dirt outside my window, or kicking a football in the backyard—either ours or Steven's. They prefer our yard; Steven's mum is protective of her roses. The native bush that covers the fence between our yard and Steven's is growing a hole at its centre, as small branches bend and break with the constant pummelling of the football. I'm torn between protecting the bush—and our lease—and not wanting to ban playing ball in the yard. In the end, I wilfully ignore the decimation of the bush.

'Hi!' chirps the voice on the other end of the phone. 'It's Vanessa!'

'Oh.' My stomach drops. Somehow, I know this isn't about reinstating play-dates or inviting Leo over for cheese on toast.

'Well,' she says, her voice dropping from perky to tragic in one beat, 'I've had the *worst* day!'

'Oh no.'

'It's been a bad time, really. I'm sorry to call you like this. The dog has been eating all the plants in the garden and the electrician, I called him and then he called me back and then I missed him and he didn't leave a message and … oh. Anyway, I've reached him now and he's coming.'

'Uh … good.'

'And the *boys*! Angus just kept on and on at me while I was trying to talk to the electrician on the phone. He wouldn't *stop*. It was *awful*.'

'Oh dear.' I am mystified, and growing increasingly alarmed at the actual reason for the call.

'And it's so *cold*, isn't it? Are you cold?'

'Um, yes, it has been a terrible day.'

'It's just been *like* that. Terrible. And the reason for my call, that's terrible too.'

She tells me that Tom is very upset: Leo has snatched all his football Tazos. He took them from his hand, ran off and wouldn't give them back. This is not good. In playground currency, Tazos are gold. All Vanessa's worst fantasies about him are coming true: Leo is behaving like a thug, a thoroughly bad influence. Which is why she's on the phone.

'Shall I give you a list of the Tazos Tom is missing?' she says. 'I'll tell you what they are. Ready?'

'Leo isn't here right now. He's with his dad. But okay, tell me what they are and I'll bring them to school tomorrow.'

And so she tells me, consulting with her boys as she goes.

'So, which team do you go for again?' she asks me, mid-list.

'I don't have a team.'

'Oh. Okay.'

'So, what exactly happened? What did Leo do?'

'He snatched the Tazos and ran away with them. Hold on, I'll get Tom. He can tell you.'

A small voice comes on the line, somewhat nervously. 'Hello?'

'Hello, Tom. So, what happened?'

'Um.' He pauses. 'Um … do you know, I *actually* can't remember if Leo took them from me or if we had a deal, for him to borrow them and then give them back.'

'WHAT?'

He repeats himself.

Vanessa comes back on the line. 'Oh,' she says. 'Did you hear that?'

'I did.'

'Maybe Leo will have a … a better memory of what happened.'

'I'm sure he will. Okay, I'd better go.'

'No, no! How are you anyway? Is your heater about to *overload* with the cold?'

I want to kill her and her stupid, lying, dobbing children.

I tell Rachel, who answers the phone at Mark's house, that I've had a complaint from a mother, who says Leo has stolen some Tazos. It seems he's actually borrowed them, but I need to read him a list and make sure he brings them to school.

'Sure,' she says. 'Was it Vanessa?'

'Yes,' I say, surprised. 'How did you know? Have you had trouble with her?'

'No. But I know you have.'

'Oh.'

'She is really odd though, isn't she?' says Rachel.

It's Leo's birthday. Again, I'm up until midnight making cupcakes for the class. I've unwittingly started a tradition.

This year, the theme for his party will be *rock* so I ice the cakes with words like *rock* and *AC/DC*. The words are limited to those short enough to fit on a cupcake, so Led Zeppelin becomes *Led Zep*. Mum stays on the phone with me throughout the hour it takes to mix and bake the cakes, offering advice on matters from how to get the cakes extra fluffy (lots of stirring with a wooden spoon—it hurts) to what to do about them not being *at all ready* at the designated fifteen-minute mark. ('Don't whine. Just put them back in the oven.') When I finally hang up, my neck is cramped.

Tony thinks they look a little pale and undercooked; he wonders why I used two patty pans on each one.

'You've never baked a cake in your life!' I scoff. 'Mum told me to do it, and she knows what she's doing.'

Leo is delighted.

'Mum, they look *lovely*,' he tells me the next morning. 'Even better than last year!'

I write him a letter to take to his teacher, explaining that I'll be picking him up early today because we have an appointment.

'*Don't* tell her what the appointment is,' I say. 'Don't tell anyone.'

'Why?'

'Well, I think what we're doing is totally fine, but it's not worth drawing attention to it. And the kids in your class might get jealous.'

'That's true,' he says. 'They *totally* would.'

When I enter the classroom to pick him up, he stands importantly from his chair. Whispers erupt around him. *Where are you going?* He looks at me, then back at the kids on his table. Reluctantly, he says, 'To an appointment.'

Bhanu grabs my sleeve. 'Hi Jo,' she says. 'Where is Leo going? Why does he have an appointment on his birthday?'

'We're going to see *The Simpsons Movie*!' he bursts out. 'Sorry Mum.'

'Don't tell anyone, Bhanu,' I whisper.

'Why not?'

'Just because. It's fun to have secrets, isn't it?'

'I guess.'

We walk home, where we drop off the cupcake container and Leo's schoolbag. Then we run down the road to catch the bus, so we can make the 3 pm session at the local shopping centre. It's Mark's turn to have Leo for dinner tonight; I am squeezing in this special occasion by stealth. Because it is his birthday, Leo gets a choc-top and popcorn *and* Coke. The cinema is barely populated. We spread out in the dark, with a clear view ahead, unobstructed by fellow viewers.

We sit on the back seat of the bus on the way home and pick from the popcorn bucket. Leo takes a fan of football cards from his pocket and begins to read aloud—chains of player statistics. A man sitting in front of us turns around, his face bright with interest. He wears a navy-and-white-striped beanie pulled down to his eyebrows; grey hair puffs from beneath it.

'Like your footy, do you?' he says. 'Good lad!'

'Absolutely,' says Leo. 'Actually, my team is the Eagles. We beat Carlton last week, by 82 points. We beat you last time we played you, too. By 17 points.'

'Don't knock Carlton!' says the man.

They settle into a fierce but friendly exchange of opinions and statistics, reaching back over years of football history and delving into the details of particular players' performances. I am used to this, to men—usually older men—making friends with Leo on public transport after hearing him spout statistics.

'You look after this one,' says the man, as he stands and presses the button for his stop. 'He's smart. Real smart.'

I smile and assure him I will.

18. DIAGNOSIS

It's taken almost four months for us to get to this stage: an official diagnosis of Asperger's Syndrome (or not) by a specialist.

Mark has done the work of finding the professional: a clinical psychologist who specialises in autism spectrum disorders. Her clinic is in a little weatherboard house opposite a pub. She's been referred by the Children's Hospital as one of the best in the field.

There are three parts to the diagnosis. First, the psychologist talks to Mark and me about Leo while he sits in the waiting room with Dad, who is sleeping on our couch for the week. Then, Leo talks to the psychologist alone. We've told him—deliberately nonchalant—that we're here for some standard tests; we don't elaborate and he doesn't ask any questions. He is diverted by the novelty of a day off school. Lastly, Dad takes Leo home while Mark and I hear the diagnosis.

The psychologist shares an office with an ear, nose and throat doctor. The waiting room is full of his patients, an assembly of winter coughs and crumpled tissues. There are a few toys and a chalkboard in a corner, glossy magazines on the windowsill.

We talk brightly—over-brightly—while we wait, talking around the subject for Leo's benefit.

The psychologist, Naomi, seems youngish for an expert. She wears thick rectangular-framed glasses and a long tapered cardigan. She is both warm and brisk, her manner reflecting the fact that her time is costing us a great deal of money.

She asks a series of questions about Leo. Why is he here? What are our concerns? What was he like as a baby? When did he start to talk? Did he go to childcare at all? From what age? What was he like playing with other children?

We fill in the gaps as best we can. Sometimes Mark makes observations I've never noticed. Is he impervious to pain? *No*, I say. *Yes*, says Mark. *He's very stoic. He often doesn't realise he's hurt himself until I comment on it.* I've always thought he's just being well behaved. *At other times he's very sensitive to pain*, I say. *Once he notices he's hurt, he makes a huge fuss.* Both these things are true. Naomi notes it all down. I can't quite imagine the picture we're making for her.

Does he have any sensory issues? *He doesn't like scratchy clothes*, I say. *He won't wear knitted jumpers, for instance. He doesn't like how they feel on his skin.* But this seems pretty normal to me. Most kids don't like scratchy clothes. *He doesn't like having his hair washed*, says Mark. *He doesn't like the feel of the water on his scalp.* I am sceptical. I've never noticed such a thing. *He doesn't seem to feel the cold*, I venture. *I'm always having to tell him to wear jumpers or jackets, or put warm pants on. He's always arriving underdressed at my house. Mark tells me Leo says he's not cold, even if it's freezing outside.* Mark laughs and says I'm obsessed with Leo being cold. I laugh too. Because he's English and went to boarding school in Scotland, Mark doesn't feel the cold, I say. He doesn't realise what's appropriate for Leo. Naomi writes it all on her notepad. I wonder if she's writing that Leo's parents fight about stupid things like whether or not he wears enough layers.

Is Leo responsive to our feelings? Does he notice if we're happy or sad or tired or cranky? *No*, says Mark. *Yes*, I say. I notice him respond to my moods all the time. If I'm unhappy, he's either unhappy too, or he's especially solicitous, trying to pull me out of it. It's no coincidence—I sense his moods shift in parallel rhythms to mine. *He's very responsive*, I say.

Does he have any obsessive interests? Well, yes. Football. Yu-Gi-Oh. Lego. Yes, he likes to talk about these interests at length. Yes, he has always had special interests. Some past ones? Thomas the Tank Engine, Care Bears.

Does he have any special preferences when it comes to clothing? He used to insist on wearing a skivvy every day underneath his school shirt or T-shirt. But then again, I used to buy armloads of cheap red skivvies and let him draw on them with permanent texta. So he had

Spiderman skivvies, spy skivvies, a collection of Fire X skivvies. (Fire X was a superhero he invented. I cut flames out of red fabric and hand-sewed them onto the leg of a pair of pants for him. They were his official Fire X pants. He was pretty fond of them, too.)

Did he get agitated if he couldn't wear his skivvies? Um, yes. I tell the story of how Leo once ran away from school because I'd punished him that morning by banning him from wearing a skivvy. He was found in the park by himself, trying to cross the creek, by another mother from the same primary school. She asked him what he was doing and he said he was going home to get a skivvy. I'd watched him walk into the school grounds. He'd waited until I disappeared before following me.

Naomi hoots with laughter. 'That's pretty determined,' she says. 'It's a great story.'

I decide I quite like her.

The deputy principal had not been amused at the time. Then again, neither was I.

And then it is Leo's turn to talk to Naomi while we sit in the waiting room with Dad.

He comes out of the room in a great mood; he's been regaling her with football statistics.

'He's very bright, isn't he?' she says as we duck in to collect him.

Dad takes Leo home on the tram.

Mark and I walk down the road to a cafe where we get take-away coffees and Mark buys some kind of gourmet sandwich. I can't eat pre-made sandwiches (they go soggy, and I don't like butter on them) so I buy a muffin for lunch.

We talk about what we think the outcome will be as we hurry back to hear the verdict.

I don't think he'll be Asperger's; he'll just have traits. Or he'll be just the tiniest bit Asperger's. Mark thinks he will be Asperger's, but he agrees it will be a close shave.

'I think my dad's Asperger's,' I say. Mark agrees.

'That could be the answer,' he says.

Dad has always been different; an individual. I'd never thought about why until I was introduced to the concept of Asperger's, to the idea that it might be in my family. I've always thought he just *is* how he is.

Dad spent half my childhood in his bedroom, reading; in his study, inventing computer code; or on a tennis court. He doesn't like small-talk; he'd often walk away from Mum (who *loves* small talk) when she was mid-conversation. Sometimes she would follow him, still talking—he would ignore her. (And she would ignore the fact that he *was* ignoring her.) His views are strongly held: brought up Catholic, he is so anti-church that he once sat outside in a parked car while we all attended his niece's christening. He never does anything at all because it's conventional; only if it makes sense to him. I have always admired this about him.

Naomi tells us that, in her opinion, Leo definitely has Asperger's Syndrome. It's a classic case, she says. Straight down the middle. No doubt.

I am shocked.

'But what about his empathy? He has empathy. I told you he reacts to my unspoken moods.'

'He's very tuned in to you,' Naomi says. 'That can happen with Asperger's boys, in particular, and their mothers. It's a close bond. But he doesn't seem to sense people's moods in general.'

(Soon, the 'no empathy' element of an Asperger's diagnosis will be largely discredited. Evidence will suggest that people with Asperger's Syndrome actually have extreme empathy—more than most people— it's just that the triggers for it are different.)

'What about his creativity? He plays imaginatively all the time. And he writes stories.' Naomi points out that his creative play is usually within the framework of a particular storytelling universe—like Bionicles or Yu-Gi-Oh.

'It's not always,' I say. 'He makes things up from scratch. He conjures stories out of the air.' She asks for an example. I tell her he used to have imaginary friends. I tell her that when he was younger, we'd catch the tram home together from work and childcare and he'd say things like, *Look Mum, there's a fairy, and he's picking that man's nose.* 'That's imaginative!'

'Who would start those games?' she asks.

'Pardon?'

'Who would start those games? Who first came up with the idea of an imaginary friend? Was it you or him?'

'I don't know.'

'Did you imagine seeing things?'

'Of course.'

'Do you think you might have pointed out, say, the fairies on the tram, first?'

'I might have.'

'It's called scaffolding,' she says. 'You modelled imaginative play for him. He was joining in.'

'Oh,' I say.

Naomi has an answer to all my questions, all the niggling doubts that made me seriously doubt the school counsellor's diagnosis. For every significant deviation from the classic Asperger's Syndrome framework, Naomi has an explanation for how it's not really a deviation at all.

Something clicks in my head.

For the first time, I believe this is real.

* * * *

Naomi thinks Leo will adapt well. He wants to fit in and he's bright. People with Asperger's can learn social skills, she says. It's just that they need to learn them intellectually rather than instinctively. They need to work at it. Intelligence helps.

She tells us that school will be hard for him. Making and keeping friends will be hard. Fitting in to the classroom environment and in the playground will be hard—in the playground, there are no rules or structure.

He has no learning problems, but these may arise in future, especially as homework becomes more of an issue.

We'll need to work closely with the school, including regular meetings once a term to assess his progress.

He'll continue to need our help with developing and managing friendships, probably for many years to come.

It feels a bit like a life sentence.

* * * *

We've been advised to tell Leo about the diagnosis. There's a book we can order, from a specialist Asperger's publisher in the UK. It's called *Can I Tell You About Asperger's Syndrome?*

But we tell him as soon as we get home. Mark drives me. We sit Leo on the couch, in the lounge room that used to be Mark's and is now mine, and we tell him.

'It's just the way your mind works, it's the just the kind of personality you have. There's nothing wrong with it.'

'Some things are harder for you—knowing how to behave in groups, organising yourself—but other things are easier. You're so interested in the things you really love, that you're really good at— and so much of your brain is concentrating on that—that there's not much room left for the little things in life, like remembering where you put your shoes.'

I tell him about the famous people with Asperger's Syndrome, the ones whose existence comforted me. Mozart, Bill Gates, Einstein.

'Albert Einstein had Asperger's Syndrome and he was the smartest man who ever lived.'

He is a little impressed about Einstein.

But mostly, he doesn't say much. He just nods and shrugs and goes conspicuously quiet.

I feel sick. Did we do the right thing? Should we have waited and ordered the book? Would he be fine about this if I was fine? Was there another, better, way of telling him? One that would make it seem like a gift, not a curse?

Naomi had showed us the book in her office. It suggests you tell your child, 'Congratulations! You have Asperger's Syndrome.' This seems stupid to me, blindly optimistic. I wasn't going to say it. Mark did though; he opened with it, his voice wilfully bright.

He seems, as always, calm—relieved we can move on to the next step, to practical solutions. I think he accepted the truth of it long ago. Is it easier to accept difference that comes with a label when you don't think it stems from you, from your genes?

I don't think it's a disaster, but I don't think it's a cause for celebration either.

Or maybe I do think it's a disaster. I don't know.

* * * *

I ring Mum and tell her after Leo has gone to bed. I cry down the phone.

Tony cooks dinner: a stirfry with chicken and snowpeas and bok choy. We eat it in front of the television, balancing our bowls on our knees, watching an episode of *The Simpsons* we've all seen before. We don't talk, not about anything except for the food in our bowls and the events on the screen.

'It doesn't have to mean anything,' says Tony, when we are alone. 'He's still the same Leo. I don't think we should make too big a deal of it. Especially not with him.' I agree: he's making sense. But I can't help thinking it does mean something, that it is a big deal.

Dad goes down the road to get a kebab from the fish and chip shop; he doesn't eat stirfry. He's not sure about his kebab either. He's not convinced they've managed to make it the way he likes it, with the right ratios of garlic and tomato sauce, beef and shredded lettuce. I don't say anything when he quietly slips it, half-eaten, into the kitchen bin.

The next day, Leo gets into a fight in the schoolyard over a football. He swears at a kid, in a way he hasn't since first term. When I pick him up from school, his art teacher tells me that he had a fit of perfectionism over a painting. He made a stroke he didn't like, then scribbled over the page, painting it black. He demanded she not hang it on the wall with the paintings by the rest of the class.

'It feels weird, being Asperger's,' he tells me while I'm cooking dinner and he's reading a book at the dining table. 'It just feels wrong.'

'Does it help to talk about it?'

'No. It makes me feel worse.'

'Does it help that other people in the family have it?' I've told him that my dad and my brother do. I'm almost certain this is true.

'No.'

'Does it help that other kids at your school have it?'

'A little.'

'Does it help that another kid in your class—we don't know who—has it?'

'Yes.'

We take turns trying to guess who it might be.

✳ ✳ ✳ ✳

Dad joins me as a classroom helper. We sit side-by-side on miniature plastic chairs, each of us paired with a child to read to us. Dad was an English teacher for most of his working life; his specialty was working with kids who had learning challenges, though he's been working in IT for several years now.

Dad starts with Leo; I start with Bhanu. She asks me why I don't wear nailpolish.

'Your nails are so long,' she says, stroking the curve of my middle fingernail. 'Why do you grow them so long if you're not going to wear nailpolish?'

'I don't grow them on purpose; I'm just too lazy to cut them.'

'Hmmmm.' She frowns at me. 'You'd look good with blue nailpolish, I reckon. Or maybe silver.'

'I'll think about it,' I say.

Next to me, I hear Jenny telling Dad about her dog, and what he did last night. He looks at least as impatient with her reluctance to read her book as I usually am.

When we leave the classroom, Leo looks content.

Dad and I cycle home across the park; he's borrowing Tony's bike while he's here.

'I can't believe this,' he says, returning to his theme of the past few days. Dad has been reading Tony Attwood's *Complete Guide to Asperger's Syndrome* and he thinks he has Asperger's Syndrome, too. I agree with him. So does Tony, my mum, my brothers and sisters, and Mark. 'This has changed the way I look at my whole life!'

'It must be pretty weird,' I say.

'But I can't be, really,' he says. 'I didn't learn to read like Leo did. I had trouble learning to read. My sister had to teach me, or I probably still wouldn't be able to.'

'Like I said, Dad, it can go either way. You can either pick up language really well, from memory, or it can come late, can be hard to decode. There's more than one way of being Asperger's.'

'Maybe,' he concedes.

'But I love sport!' he says, after a pause. 'I play tennis every day, I ride, I run. It's very important to me to be fit. People with Asperger's don't have an aptitude for sport.'

'True. But Dad, you work really hard at being good at what you do. Like you say, you play tennis every day. You're obsessed with tennis! It's your special interest.'

'Mmmm,' he says.

'And Leo loves sport.'

'You're right. He does. Yes, I think I *am* Asperger's.'

He changes his mind again before we reach my front gate.

I wish he would make up his mind. Or shut up. It is exhausting to be doing this now when all my energy is focused on dealing with Leo's diagnosis. I don't want to be responsible for his, too.

And I suspect he knows that the diagnosis fits. He just doesn't want to believe it. His rejection of Asperger's—when I no longer have that luxury for Leo—feels like a rejection of what Leo is. It feels like a tacit admission that being Asperger's is being defective.

Inside, he sits on the couch with Tony Attwood, turning the pages and marvelling aloud. I give up engaging; instead, I try to block him out.

Later that afternoon, I'm both relieved and sorry to see him go.

19. BULLSHIT

I can't think straight or write properly. Which is a bit of a problem, considering I write for a living. I can't answer the telephone properly either, not without letting it go to the answering machine first and checking who's there. It's a blend of self-obsession and Leo-obsession. Do I have it? (I see my own thinking in his.) Is he okay? How does he feel? How is he doing at school? How are his friendships going? How much will we need to do for him in terms of special needs—the social stories, the social skills sessions with a speech pathologist, possible 'extras' at the school? How much will it help and how much will it add to the problem of making him feel different?

I walk through school in a fog. I don't feel ready or especially able to engage with the other parents, even the ones I know. I don't want to talk about it, but I don't want to talk about anything else, either. Then I see them avoiding me and I feel angry. Or maybe I imagine it.

Somehow, in the absence of a tangible target, a person or an institution I can blame for what has happened, I transfer my cocktail of emotion to the nearest substitute.

Three am. I lie awake thinking about what I could do to Vanessa, the woman who has separated my lonely, socially handicapped boy from one of the few friends he had at school. Spit on her. Slap her face. Throw water at her. Shout at her, really yell at her. Simply say, if she ever speaks to me again, *Please don't ever speak to me again*, even if it is in front of a group of parents.

I fantasise about getting out of bed, dressing, walking through the night to her house, passing through the unlit pitch-black of Cruikshank Park and stopping to throw black paint all over her perfect front lawn and white picket fence. Paint BITCH on the footpath in big black letters. Sneak back home and get into bed. Tony will be my alibi. I'll have to be careful not to spill any paint on my clothes. That would be evidence.

Of course, I don't actually have any black paint.

I imagine ringing up the local paper and booking an ad. The ad would have a photograph of Vanessa and underneath, the sentence: 'Vanessa is a bitch'. That would be it. Everyone would see it. She would be humiliated.

My sleep, once it descends, is streaked with paint, swims with newsprint. I don't remember losing consciousness, but I wake up in the morning so I must have.

The next day, the next afternoon, I grudgingly accompany Tony on a walk with the dogs. 'It will do you good,' he says. 'Exercise is good for you.' As we cross the train line and pass the cafes, I think about running into her. I look hard at the faces of the people lingering by the fish and chip shop, carrying plastic bags or dragging shopping carts from the supermarket.

The Yarraville Gardens are quite ugly. Palm trees and straggly eucalypts. A playground. A couple of mottled statues. Nothing like the leafy serenity of North Fitzroy's Edinburgh Gardens or the picturesque duck pond of the St Kilda Botanic Gardens. In the west, you get a yellowing patch of lawn framed by main roads choked with trucks and the heavy machinery and sun-bleached containers of the river port as backdrop.

Even here, in the dog park, I look out for her, though I know she won't be here, have never known her to come here. Cruikshank Park is nearer her house. If she wants to walk her dog, she'll do it there. Still.

Tony walks the dogs around and around the oval, where they are permitted unleashed. Most of the dog owners stand clumped at the edges while the dogs run circles around them, sniffing and tackling each other excitedly. I do one circuit of the oval, stopping to get a plastic bag to pick up Doug's shit, then sit on a bench overlooking the grass and the dogs and the trucks and the containers. My lungs feel tight with invisible exhaust fumes. I'm not sure if the feeling is real or imagined.

Leo comes out of his classroom frowning.

'Tom punched me in the head five times today,' he says. 'And now I have a headache. He tried to kick me here, too.' He points to his stomach.

My own stomach clenches in response. 'What happened?' I ask, trying to sound calm.

They were playing football. The ball went over a fence, from the oval to the playground. Tom collected it and Leo offered to kick it back for him, saying, 'I can kick further than you.' Then Tom attacked him with multiple punches to the head and an attempted kick.

'Did you tell a teacher?'

'Yes.'

'What did she say?'

'It was the yard-duty teacher. She did nothing.'

Leo starts to cry.

'That's IT!' I shout. I know that I'm not just angry because a kid beat up my son. I know this is complicated, highly nuanced fury. It mixes all the week's tension, all my added worry for Leo, all my hatred for this family who never seem to stop making our lives harder.

* * * *

Tom's teacher is Louise. She's the Prep teacher who thought Leo was 'very special' and wanted him to be tested for being gifted. If we had done it, we would have saved two years of misunderstanding and heartache.

Louise will help us, I think.

'Don't worry Leo,' I say. 'I'll sort this out.'

On our way to Louise's classroom, we pass Tom and Vanessa. I am far too angry to take up the matter directly with Vanessa; I am afraid of what I might say to her.

Louise looks up in surprise as we knock on her door, but invites us in and listens as I explain what's happened.

'Who was the yard-duty teacher?' she asks Leo.

'I don't know her name.' Leo wrinkles his brow. 'She looks like a teenager though. She's very short.'

'Oh, I know who it is,' says Louise. 'I'll talk to her. I'll tell you what: I'll set up a meeting between you and Tom tomorrow. Here, I'll write it on the board.'

Leo visibly relaxes as we watch her uncap a texta and write his name and Tom's on the whiteboard.

And that's when Tom and Vanessa enter the room. They sit on a chair behind Louise, Vanessa pulling Tom onto her lap.

'Um, here they are!' I say.

'Oh!' says Louise. 'Speak of the devil!'

'What's going on?' asks Vanessa.

Louise explains.

'Oh,' says Vanessa. 'Well, we're here because Tom didn't get his pancake today and he had no lunch.'

'I'm sure he did,' says Louise.

'No, I didnnnnnnn't.' Tom dissolves into noisy tears. Snot runs into his mouth. 'I didn't get a pancaaaaaakkkke.'

'We'll talk about this tomorrow, okay?' says Louise, turning to me.

I'm a bit pissed off that not getting a pancake takes precedence over punching someone in the head.

I go to Leo's classroom.

'Did you know about what happened in the playground today, with Leo and Tom?' I ask Kaye.

'Yes,' she says. 'But Ryan says it didn't happen.'

'I am SORRY,' I say, surprised by my vehemence. 'But I don't believe a word that Tom Green says. He's a little liar …' And I go on to detail various instances of Tom lying to get Leo into trouble, while the teacher looks increasingly dubious.

'Well,' she says when I finish at last, 'it was Ryan who said it didn't happen. He was there.'

I kneel to zip Leo's jacket, not looking at her.

'Well, okay,' I say. 'Anyway, Louise has it in hand. We'll just keep talking to her. It's fine.'

And I sweep out of the classroom, dragging Leo by the hand.

As we collect our bikes and pedal through the school gates, I assure Leo that I will make them take him seriously.

'Tom is a passive-aggressive little shit!' I splurt.

'Mum!'

'Sorry. I didn't say that, okay?'

'Okay.'

At the bottom of the street we pause, side by side, our feet planted on the bitumen as we wait to cross the road. Leo's face crumples a little.

'Do you know what the worst thing is?' he whispers. He dissolves into fresh tears, this time erupting from deep within his gut. 'When I was on the ground, in pain, they said I was faking. And then ... then ... Conor was trying to comfort me, and they ... they pulled him off me. They didn't want me to feel better.' He is almost incoherent with grief.

I pop my bike stand and climb off to hug him close. A sea of kids in school uniform parts to flow around us, then they continue on their way home. I fumble in his schoolbag for a tissue; I hold one to his nose and instruct him to blow. I am so sad for him that I want to cry, too.

'I'm sure they didn't mean that.'

We get back on our bikes; we keep going. He streaks ahead. I can't help but repeat, loudly enough to be heard by the mothers with prams but not loud enough for him to hear: *passive-aggressive little shit.*

At home, Leo goes straight to bed. I make him a hot Milo and bring it to him. It cools on his bedside table, untouched, as he burrows into sleep. When he wakes, his forehead and cheeks flame with fever.

He stays home sick the next day, Friday. We pack him off to his school sleepover that night anyway, with a bottle of Panadol we give to the teachers in charge.

'Am I doing the right thing?' I ask Tony.

'Definitely,' he says.

I don't want to take him away from social situations right now.

I fall asleep on the couch, the television running, soon after dropping him off. Tony wakes me up when the film is over and escorts me to bed. We wake at 8 am the next morning, the time we are meant to collect Leo from the sleepover.

We arrive late, to find him sitting in a corner of the library, deep in a book he's pulled from the shelf.

'Hi!' he says, unfazed. He tells us he had a great time.

Later in the day, Tony, Leo and I are crossing the road to the bakery when we pass Vanessa and her husband, coming the other way. Our eyes glancingly meet, before they quickly look away. It's a relief that they do it first.

Monday morning, I leave Leo in the schoolyard and go to speak to Louise. Her classroom door is locked; she's not there. I go to Leo's classroom. Kaye is sitting at her desk, bent over a fan of papers. I tell her I want to make sure the meeting between Leo and Tom will still happen.

'But Leo was away on Friday,' she says.

'Yes, he was sick. That's why I want to make sure they talk about it today.'

We glare at each other.

'It didn't happen the way you think it did,' she says.

'Well …' My chest trembles with the effort to keep the anger in my throat from rising. 'That may be true, but my son was still punched in the head and I want something done about it.'

'There was blame on both sides.'

'Yes. He made a smart comment and he was punched. That's still not appropriate. I want it resolved.'

'I don't think that was it. Look, you can trust me with this. *I'm very fair.*'

'*Look,* I know Leo can exaggerate. But I also know he's telling the truth now. He was very, very upset on Thursday. And he was punched in the head and you weren't even going to tell me about it. He came home with a splitting headache.'

'I'm very fair,' she repeats.

We flounce off in opposite directions.

All I want is for the school to set up the promised meeting between the two boys so they can resolve things—and so that Leo knows he has been heard.

If he did something wrong, they're free to punish him for it. But there is no way in hell that I'm going to let them decide that the Asperger's boy exaggerates, that he's oversensitive, that his story doesn't need to be heard. They are not going to use this diagnosis as a convenient way to dismiss him.

* * * *

After school, I send Leo and Conor to the oval to kick a football while I talk to Kaye. She doesn't look pleased to see me.

'I've spoken to the boys involved,' she says. 'Leo snatched the football from the other boy and kicked it.'

'He shouldn't have done that. But Tom still shouldn't have hit him.'

'He hit him *with a flat hand*,' she says, in a withering tone. She demonstrates, holding up an open palm. 'Like this.'

'So? He still shouldn't have hit him.'

'Well, maybe Leo shouldn't have *bullied* him.'

I don't think a boy snatching a football from his friend is bullying. I've seen it happen a million times. I've seen Leo snatch from his friends; I've seen them snatch from him.

'You still don't hit someone,' I say.

'He's a *Prep*!' the teacher sneers.

'So? I don't care. I don't want anyone hitting my son, whether they're a Prep or not.'

She puts a hand on her hip and rolls her eyes.

'I should have been told about this,' I continue. 'I spoke to my mother on the phone this morning. She's a teacher. She says schools are meant to have *policies* about these things, especially when kids are hit in the head. She says it's compulsory to tell the parents.'

Kaye is momentarily stuck for words.

'Leo and Ryan were interrupting my class talking about this on Thursday,' she says, recovering herself. 'I don't *handle* disruption in my class.' A Freudian slip perhaps?

'Leo had a very tough week last week, which is why I'd especially think you would have told me,' I say. 'He's had a very rough time emotionally.'

She *rolls her eyes*. Again.

'You're saying he didn't have a tough week?' She knows about the diagnosis.

'*I don't think so*,' she drawls.

And this is when I start yelling.

'You don't THINK SO! He has just learned that he has Asperger's Syndrome! How dare you tell me that MY CHILD has not had an emotional week? WHAT DO YOU KNOW?'

I tell her that over the past week, I have seen him vomit, I have seen him cry like he hasn't cried in months. He has been physically sick with the stress of it.

'Don't you yell at me,' she says.

I step back.

'You know what?' I say. 'I *don't want to talk to you.*'

I turn to go. At the door, I swing around, lean into the classroom and I scream, really scream, at her.

'That is BULLSHIT! YOU ARE BULLSHIT!'

My chest hurts with the force of it.

I stalk through the schoolyard, past Ryan's mother, who is talking to a cluster of other parents. I feel like I'm having a nervous breakdown.

I still want to yell and scream.

* * * *

My feet take me to the school office, where I pace up and down in front of the empty deputy principal's office. A few students loll on the new plastic lounge chairs by the reception desk. The school secretary's glass window is empty, too. A young male teacher in a tracksuit is talking to a mother. I hear her say she is waiting for Eliza. I go to leave, then return. I pace in front of the empty glass window, then in front of the office. I am literally shaking with anger.

People are eyeing me cautiously, as though I'm shooting up or eating out of bins.

'Are you looking for someone?' asks the tracksuited teacher.

'Um, yes, but I think she's looking for her, too.' I wave at the mother nearby. 'I'd better go.'

'No, I'll get her,' he says hurriedly. 'Or maybe the principal?'

'Okay.'

I eye the open office door as I wait. Maybe I can slip in there where no-one can see me. Just in case I start crying.

The principal arrives and sweeps me into her more secluded office, nestled at the end of the hall. She gets me a glass of water. The deputy quickly joins her. I explain what has been happening, with Leo and Tom, Leo and the teacher, the teacher and me.

I tell them what I have just done, that I have shouted at her. Lawyer-like, I carefully apologise *for having yelled*. I ask them to pass on my apology *for having yelled*.

I say that I am appalled that anyone could say what she said to me. I tell them I want Leo to be listened to. That it is not okay for anyone to hit him, even if they are *just a Prep*. It is not okay for me not to have been told about it. I tell them that all I ever wanted was for the two boys to talk to each other and be told that what they did was inappropriate.

The two principals say all the right things. Well, almost. (They defend the teacher to a fault.)

'Of course no-one should say that, but she wouldn't have meant it. Not like that.'

'She's had lots of special-needs kids and knows exactly what she's doing.'

'She must not have known that he was hit that day, or *of course* she would have told you.'

They do acknowledge that times are tough, that they want to approach what is happening with Leo as a team. They say Leo is a wonderful child.

When I open the door, Leo and Conor are waiting in the corridor. Leo has a football under his arm. We walk together to the bike shed.

'Where *were* you?' asks Leo. 'What were you doing?'

I tell them that I got angry with their teacher, that I lost my temper and yelled at her. I tell them I shouldn't have done that and will need to apologise.

I figure it's not a bad lesson: anyone can lose their temper, but it's not right and you need to apologise if you do.

'So, did you sort it out with Tom?' I ask.

'Yep,' says Leo.

'He beat Leo up,' ventures Conor. 'He hurt him.'

'I know. I hear you were the only one who stood up for him and helped him. Thank you. You're a very good friend.'

'Tom lied at first,' says Conor. 'But eventually he had to tell the truth and admit it. He stood there and cried, in front of everyone.'

'Oh yeah,' I say, unsympathetic. 'Did he get told off?'

'Nah. The teacher was nice to him because he was crying. She was really mean to Leo.'

'Really?'

'Yup. She yelled at him.'

'What happened?' I ask.

'She told Tom to apologise and he wouldn't,' says Leo. 'And she wouldn't make him. So I said to her, *You're letting him get away with it because he's got a sweet and innocent little face.*'

'Oh dear.' I do remember saying something like that about Tom last week.

'Yes,' says Conor. 'Then she yelled at Leo to *GET OUT OF MY SIGHT!* And he hid under the table.'

'Oh.'

A typically Asperger's literal response. If she really does have experience working with special-needs children, wouldn't Kaye realise this?

Leo tells me that he's not allowed to play with Angus or Tom anymore.

'Oh, that's a good idea,' I say. 'Did your teacher say that?'

'No, Angus told me. Their parents have banned them.'

20. LOSING IT

'**How's Leo going?**' asks a work colleague, Sarah. I'm buying a book on my way home from proofing the newsletter. I like her a lot, but don't know her well. Most of our conversations are about what we're reading.

'He's good, thanks,' I manage.

'How's school? Does he like it?'

'Not really.'

'Oh, why? His teacher?'

'Yeah, I hate her.'

'Is she a yeller?'

'No, she's just a bitch.'

'Really?'

'Yeah. The other day I screamed at her. She told me Leo *wasn't* having an emotional week, even though he's just been diagnosed with Asperger's Syndrome!'

I glance up to catch Sarah looking back at me with the blank horror that tells me I've over-shared.

I pay her and hurry away.

* * * *

I visit Naomi, the psychologist who diagnosed Leo. It's both strange and somehow comforting being back in that office, where it all began. It's a relief to be able to talk about what's been happening to someone who understands, someone I don't need to explain Asperger's to.

We talk about how Leo is coping. But mostly, we talk about my 'issues' in dealing with his diagnosis. She listens sympathetically as I tell her about the incident with Leo's teacher. It's common, she says, for parents to have trouble with schools. I was right to stick up for him, right to insist he be taken seriously and have his situation dealt with. She says his reactions all make sense; that Asperger's people have a strong sense of social justice, and of course he'd be angry about the person who hit him not being punished. Of course he hid under the table when the teacher told him to get out of her sight. She laughs at this; so do I.

I tell her I want to move forward with the teacher and the school, that though I'm angry, I need to be able to work with them. I want to go back into the classroom. But I'm not sure how to move forward. I can't bear to face Leo's teacher, let alone start a conversation about what happened.

Naomi suggests I write a letter of apology: 'short, sharp and to the point'.

I deliver the letter to the teacher's desk the next day. It pretty much reads, 'Sorry for yelling, we have been through a very tough time as a family but that was no excuse. I hope we can continue working together for Leo's benefit.'

Friday morning, I go to school assembly, planning to go to the classroom and listen to kids read afterwards. I sit up the back with Lucy. While I move about the schoolyard in a rush, trying to avoid eye contact, she meanders, stopping to talk to everyone she passes, greeting them by name. She introduces me to a woman who has two sons on the autistic spectrum; they both had Leo's teacher, whom she loathed. When I tell her about how I lost my temper and yelled, she says, 'I'm sure you're not the only one. She had it coming!'

I hesitate outside Leo's classroom, gathering all my courage to go in. Leo is eager for me to return to classroom reading. He comes out to stand with me.

'Are you coming?' he says.

'I think so. I'm not sure if I'm welcome in the classroom.'

He pops his head around the door. 'Is my mum welcome in the classroom?' he calls, before I can stop him. Then he turns back to me. 'MUM!' he shouts, in a voice so loud that the parents sitting on benches nearby look up. 'SHE SAID YOU'RE WELCOME IN THE CLASSROOM! COME IN!'

Kaye is perfectly polite in the words she uses, though her tone is flinty, her eyes shards of ice. She tells me that she's changing the way we do reading. Instead of letting me call out the kids to come and read in my own order, as we've done all year, she now wants me to listen only to the kids with difficulty reading. She gives me a list of names. Of course, Leo, Mikhela and Bhanu are off my list.

'Thank you,' she says in a perfunctory manner as I finish with the last kid on her list. She doesn't look up as I walk out of the classroom.

I leave thinking it's such an unpleasant and degrading experience that I'll never come back. But I'm not there for her; I'm there because Leo likes it. Fuck her. I will not give her the satisfaction of giving up.

It's a mixed blessing, not having to get dressed or leave the house for work. I don't feel like wearing anything more dressy than jeans and a hoodie these days, so I don't. I'm comforted by wearing my ugg boots, so I wear them all over the neighbourhood. It's only when I have to catch a train to go somewhere that I bother with make-up, or wear shoes without sheepskin lining. I have almost all my conversations via email, eliminating the need for small-talk.

The downside? Cocooned in my house, wearing my comfortable clothes and typing most of my conversations, I lose the habit of social discourse.

'You get weird,' says Tony, 'when you go too long without leaving the house. You should catch up with your friends or something.' He means that I talk too much when he gets home; that I tell him about my work day in too much detail. I forget to censor myself.

So, I go to a work function. I'm nervous, given my recent experience in blabbing my innermost thoughts over the shop counter. And though I like most of my co-workers and enjoy my bantering email relationships with them, I realise how disconnected I am when we have functions like this, where everyone else is united by private jokes, what happened in the office that afternoon, or bonding over the computers breaking down again.

Kabita and I arrange to arrive at the same time; I stand with her in the cafe where wine and nibbles are being served before the night's presentation.

Someone asks if I want a sandwich. I politely demur.

'You didn't see them being made?' jokes Kabita.

I laugh. John, a new co-worker, raises an eyebrow.

'I have a thing about sandwiches,' I admit. 'I have to see them being made. Or make them myself. I can't eat unmelted butter. There's probably butter in those ones.'

'Is it a trust thing?' asks John. He says he knows someone who can't eat anything he doesn't see being prepared, or drink pre-mixed drinks.

'No. It's because I don't like soggy. At all. I have to make the sandwich in a special way; for instance, with lettuce on the outside, protecting, say, tomatoes from touching the bread. That way I know it's fresh, too.'

He makes another joke about his friend.

'Oh, that's nothing,' I say, buoyed by approximately three sips of wine. 'My dad went through a stage where he wouldn't eat anything that my mother didn't make.'

'Was *that* a trust thing?'

'Nah. He's just very fussy and said that she knew how to make food the way he liked it.'

'That must be a problem.'

'Oh, he sometimes ate out, at places he knew he liked. Just not often.'

'That sounds like a trust thing.'

'No. Once Mum left him ingredients to make a pizza when she went out; he made it and then threw it out because it didn't taste right. He made it himself!'

'So it was his way of getting her to do everything for him?'

'No. I don't think so.'

'So he washed his own clothes and stuff?'

'Not really, no. Once, when Mum was in hospital, he woke my little sister at 6 am to ask her how to use the washing machine.'

'Wow.'

'He looks after himself fine now.'

'What happened?'

'They separated.'

'Did he leave her or did she leave him?'

'Sort of both. I don't know. I guess they just grew apart. Or something.'

There is an awkward silence.

'I'm going to get another drink,' says John, who I have met exactly once before.

Kabita and I look at each other.

'I think I just scared him away,' I say. 'I have no idea why I just told him all that.'

We laugh and laugh.

* * * *

I go back to see Naomi. I tell her that I sent the letter to Leo's teacher, as she suggested; that I returned to listen to classroom reading. To my surprise, she is surprised. She congratulates me and tells me I'm a good mother. This is money well spent. But it's not why I'm here, not really.

Tentatively, I tell her that I've been reading Tony Attwood and thinking about all she's said, and I'm wondering whether I might be Asperger's too. I think the same way as Leo does; we can tag-team each other's stories, finish each other's sentences. We both have to work at making sense of other people. And like him, I tend to lose myself in the subjects I'm interested in, and find it hard to keep a grip on the rest of the world—appointment times, household tasks, even remembering to look in the mirror before I leave the house. This is part of the reason why so much of Leo's behaviour has always seemed normal to me.

I am afraid Naomi will laugh at me, that she'll tell me I'm over-analysing. I'm afraid she'll tell me I have a point.

She asks me a series of questions. What was I like as a child? Did I have trouble making friends? Did I play alone? Did I have special obsessions?

* * * *

I was the eldest of five children; I had nineteen cousins. I didn't need friends. I always had a tribe of kids to play with. And as the eldest, I was always in charge.

Like Leo, I was always obsessed with reading and writing. I read all the time, from a young age. I wrote too, making my own little books. I liked to play schools and teach my brothers and sisters. I would write stories about everyone I knew, and would read them aloud to them.

Mum says that I was quite upset after my own first day of school; I had thought I'd be teaching the other kids, like my parents, who were English teachers. I didn't expect to be a student.

I had a best friend who lived down the road from me, from kindergarten to Year Five. She was tall and big-boned; I was the shortest girl in the class, and tiny in every way. They called us Big Jo and Little Jo. She walked me to and from school; we played together on weekends and after school. Our families were friends. I remember having other friends, but they weren't terribly important.

When Jo and her family moved to Queensland when I was in Year Five, I was devastated. I cried myself to sleep at night. Another girl in my class adopted me; she became my new best friend. I don't remember choosing or questioning it. My memory is that I was just relieved to have a solution to what to do with myself without Jo. We were friends with two other girls; one of them was Chelsea. Three of us moved on to high school together.

Chelsea was quirky and smart and fun. Like me, she lived half in the real world, half in her imagination. She had chronic eczema: sores like splashes of raw meat crept up her arms and over her calves. In primary school, some of the boys used to call her *Chelsea fever*. They'd run screaming from her, pretending to be afraid of catching her rash. She would obligingly chase them; they were her friends. Chelsea had a younger sister with Down Syndrome and her father, a retired jazz musician, was old enough to be her grandfather. Her mum worked behind the bar at a local golf club. They lived in a tiny brick unit with an eat-in kitchen and a sliding door that divided Chelsea's bedroom from her sister's. Chelsea embraced being different, even flaunted it. She turned it to her advantage. She loved the Muppets, sang loudly on buses, talked about getting a green streak in her hair.

I learned how to be a teenager from watching her. She knew everything first, everything about how to be adult. In the primary school playground, she told us about prostitutes and bondage and what it was like to be drunk. She learned most of this from watching movies. At her house on weekends, we watched John Hughes movies and *Nightmare on Elm Street* and Diane Keaton in *Looking For Mr Goodbar.*

About a year into high school, when I was in Year Nine, I suddenly noticed social hierarchies and where I stood in them. I realised I was a nerd and that I didn't want to be. This was probably partly because I had a taste for the popular boys, who didn't go out with nerds. They didn't go out with me either, but I was keen to improve my chances.

I had started to notice clothes a few years earlier, in the final year of primary school. Mum chose and bought my clothes. She had her own preferred style, which was not the preferred style of my classmates. We lived in what would now be called a bogan suburb; my classmates wore tight jeans, miniskirts, flannelette shirts, lots of black. Mum said black didn't suit me; she thought tight clothes were slutty. She sent me to school in pinafores and skivvies. I was mostly oblivious, for a long time. I was more interested in comfort. I remember wearing gumboots with shorts one summer afternoon because I couldn't find my thongs and I couldn't be bothered lacing my sneakers.

Then one day, walking home from school, a girl asked me, 'Why do you wear your socks *like that?*' I looked down at my socks, which were pulled smoothly to my knees. Then I looked at her socks, which were scrunched to her ankles. Scanning the street, which was swarming with schoolkids, I saw that no-one else wore their socks like me. 'I don't know,' I said honestly. From then on, I thought about what I wore.

I deliberately did badly at school, alternating working hard with ignoring my work in favour of writing notes to my friends under the desk, or drawing cartoon stories about the boys we were in love with. I remember failing my first test and being relieved. I proudly told everyone, especially my secret crush of the time. He high-fived me, which didn't help.

My French teacher pulled me aside in the yard one day to give me a lecture. He said he'd been watching me, that I was ruining my life. He said I wasn't being myself, that I was just copying my friends, that I was better than them. I didn't want to be better than my friends. I wanted to *be* them. I was both annoyed and pleased by the teacher's approach; it was proof that I wasn't a nerd anymore.

The teacher changed from having been fond of me to hating me. He was especially incensed after I didn't hand in a classroom test I hadn't studied for. 'You sat there and did it,' he said, blocking my attempt to leave the classroom. 'Where is it? Give it to me.' I pulled it out of my bag and tore it into tiny pieces over the bin. Despite my efforts to be the opposite of a nerd, I actually liked to do well. If I couldn't do a piece of work to the highest standard, I preferred not to do it at all.

I never did badly in English, a subject I loved. Some people say studying literature and strip-mining it for meaning ruins the books they study forever. For me, it was the opposite. Even in the midst of my trying hard to be cool, or at least normal, I didn't stop raising my hand to answer questions on *Macbeth*, or David Malouf. I worked hard on my major project, a journal and comparative essay on a central theme in three texts. (I chose the existence of evil, using *Lord of the Flies*, *The Crucible* and *To Kill a Mockingbird*.) In the week leading up to the due date, I went to my English teacher's house one weekend and he helped me hone my essay.

Six weeks before our final exams, I decided I wanted to pass Year Twelve after all. This was partly because I had lost all my friends and had nothing else to do. And, I admit, because Mum's incredulous reaction to my statement that *everyone fails Year Twelve the first time around* made me reconsider. So I devised a study regime and threw myself into it, working after school, weekends, all through the school holidays. I read over all my notes and textbooks, wrote practice essays. The fact that I passed all my subjects, despite my terrible classwork, means I must have blitzed the exams. Mum was both baffled and thrilled. I got a perfect twenty (out of twenty) for Year Twelve English; it was by far my highest mark. I was the only one in the school to get a perfect score in the subject.

Naomi listens to all these things, these fragments of evidence of being different. She offers to give me an adult test for Asperger's. I accept.

Tony has taken to bringing what I now think of as 'the blue book', Tony Attwood's *Complete Guide to Asperger's Syndrome*, to bed. Slowly, he is engaging with the idea of Asperger's, finding out what it might mean rather than simply dismissing it as irrelevant, or shrinking from its potential to brand Leo as different—to press him into a mould defined by a textbook list of traits.

'You know, I think reading too much about this makes you think you have it,' he says, turning to me. He reads snippets aloud, about being solitary, about feeling anxiety in social situations, and asks me if I think he might be Asperger's.

'I don't know,' I say. 'Maybe. I don't think so.'

'Nah, neither do I.'

'Do you think I'm Asperger's?'

'Yes.'

'Really?' I am surprised at the certainty in his voice, and a little offended. 'Why?'

'Well, it would explain a bit,' he says. 'You know you're a little bit mad.'

'I'm *not* a bit mad.'

'Yes you are. Come on, you know you are.'

'No I don't.'

'Okay.'

I think I know what he means, though I pretend I don't, even to myself. He means that I talk too much, not with strangers but with people I'm familiar with. Specifically, with him. The alarmingly intense emotional reactions that scared him when we first began dating. And that I get obsessive about things I care about, like Leo, and work.

'There's nothing wrong with that, you know,' Tony says. 'Being a bit mad.'

'Yeah, I know.'

'I love you as you are. I'm just saying. You did *ask* me.'

'I know.' I kiss him on the cheek and burrow back into my book.

It is the annual concert for the school music program. Last year's concert inspired Leo to learn guitar after he watched a group of his classmates perform AC/DC's 'TNT' to a screaming crowd. (In fact, that concert inspired his love of AC/DC, too.)

'Mum, I think I prefer the classics to recent music,' he tells me solemnly on our way to the concert. 'I think AC/DC is better than Sneaky Sound System, after all.'

Leo sits near the front of the audience, between two friends. He cheers on the performers. He counsels Conor about stage fright, telling him he'll be *great once you get on the stage*. During his solo, 'Hit the Road Jack', Leo stands up from the chair he's been sitting on and steps towards the front of the stage, posing like a rock star. He skids to his knees as the solo concludes. During the group performance, he stands with Angus, the two of them singing with great gusto, swinging their hips. Leo hooks his arm around his neck and they beg me to take a photo. I do.

This is such a turnaround for a boy who has always been reluctant to join group activities and performances. I love watching him mix so easily with the other kids, with such reciprocal affection.

Maybe finding out about his Asperger's *has* been a positive thing. It gives us a new language to frame his challenges: with teachers, other parents, ourselves. A language centred on difference rather than naughtiness, overload rather than tantrums, needs (like appropriate teachers) rather than selfish desires for special treatment. And, of course, this understanding has put us on a path to addressing some of those challenges, helping us teach him how to behave appropriately in different situations. Perhaps this has filtered through to the way Leo sees himself? He certainly seems more confident lately, less stubborn about engaging with the world on his own narrow terms.

Leo is fond of donating money to buskers. We stop in at the supermarket on our way home from a Saturday afternoon in the city. As we approach the train tracks, Leo is distracted by a pair of shaggy-looking musicians sitting cross-legged on the triangle of grass beside the station. Acoustic guitars balance across their bent knees; a guitar case is open at their feet.

'Mum!' Leo grips my arm. 'We have to give them some money!'

'Oh, yes?'

'Their sister has been carried away by giant wasps!'

'*What?*'

'Their sister has been carried away by giant wasps and they need money to buy flyspray.'

'Where did you get *that* from?'

'They've got a sign.'

I look at his small, solemn face, his hair brushing over his eyebrows.

'And you think that's true?'

'Of *course*, Mum.'

'I'll tell you what,' I say, stopping to put down my shopping bags. 'You can give them some money if you ask them if it's true.'

'Okay!' He runs back through the dark, his shopping bag thumping against his leg. I watch him bend to drop the coins I've given him into the open guitar case, the boys smiling their thanks.

'Sorry Mum,' he says, re-joining me. 'I couldn't do it. If it is true, they're probably *really sad* about it. They probably don't *want* to talk about it.'

'Hmmmm. You *really* think this is true?'

'Why wouldn't it be?'

I consider the many, many reasons.

'Well ... they're being funny.'

'That's FUNNY?' He is horrified.

'Well ... giant wasps ... it's not very likely. Have you ever heard of anyone being carried away by a giant wasp? And the wasp would have to be pretty big. If it was that big, I don't think flyspray would be able to kill it.'

He is unmoved.

'If you found out they were making it up, would you be sorry we gave them money?'

'No.'

'What if I say that it was your money? Your pocket money?'

'Nope.'

'Oh.' I look at his serene countenance, puzzling over how children can surprise you.

Leo changes the subject, to football, and we cross the train lines, continuing our way home for dinner.

*

21. PARALLEL TRACKS

Naomi has asked me to talk to my parents about what I was like when I was little. Did I play on my own? Did I connect with other children? Was I was a fussy eater? Did I have sensory issues?

Mum is sceptical when I tell her why I'm asking. She agrees that Dad is probably Asperger's, but is defensive when I mention anyone else in our family in that context, including myself.

'Well, I don't know,' she says. 'I mean, yes, you played by yourself, until Simon came along. But so what? And then you played with your brothers and sisters, and your cousins. You organised them all into games.'

'You were always a picky eater, I guess. But then so was your father, so you probably just got that from him. You weren't as fussy as *he* is.'

'You didn't like scratchy jumpers. But no kid likes scratchy jumpers.'

She sounds almost offended, as if I'm suggesting there's something wrong with her child. Which I suppose I am. If you consider Asperger's to be a defect.

If you asked me if I think Leo is defective, I'd not only say no, I'd believe it, too. I like Leo exactly the way he is. I like the way he has strong opinions, the way he gets crazily passionate about the things he loves. I like that he reads and thinks; he questions and discusses everything. I like that he has an unconventional way of seeing the world.

He doesn't take anything at face value; he has to look at it from every angle and figure out what *he* thinks about it, rather than simply accept what he's taught. It can be exhausting, it can get him into trouble, but ultimately, it's an asset.

The one thing that breaks my heart is that he will always have to work hard to connect with other people; it will never be easy for him. I hate the idea that he will be anxious all his life, always questioning himself.

Like me.

When I think about myself being Asperger's, I feel like it *is* a defect. Like I have always had something wrong with me that I haven't known about; worse, that because I haven't known, there may be all kinds of things I *do* wrong that I don't even know about. Maybe that's why I need to know if it's true. So I can fix them.

Another part of me likes the idea of being Asperger's. It might explain why I have twelve years worth of taxes to do, because I panic every time I think about doing them. Why I am terrible at any kind of paperwork, why I leave jackets on trains, lock my keys in my house, forget that I am meeting people until they call to find out why I haven't turned up. Even why I have avoided learning to drive. It might mean that the excuse I tell myself—*I'm not good at the little things in life*—is grounded in scientific fact.

And I like the idea that I am the same as Leo. That we understand each other on a subterranean level; that our brains send out signals on parallel tracks.

Then again, if I'm Asperger's, maybe I don't know how to teach Leo what he needs to know to function in the world. Maybe my shortfalls will cement his. Maybe my make-do cooking and haphazard housekeeping skills, my losing battle to be organised on a daily basis, undermine my ability to be a proper mother.

And so it goes, round and round. It's impossible to know what I really think and feel, on any aspect of this subject.

The one thing I'm sure of is that I want to know.

* * * *

I don't ask Dad for his recollections of my childhood; I'm not sure why. Maybe because Mum's always been the keeper of pertinent facts about the family. (Dad finds it hard to even remember our birthdays and ages—not because he doesn't care, but because he can't.) Or maybe because I know what he'd say, the stories he'd tell. For instance, that I liked to play tennis sitting on a chair when I was little, with him reluctantly hitting the ball to me on my courtyard throne. He might also remind me of the way I changed my personality during my high school years. Dad and I share an interest in popular psychology—the way brain structure influences personality and character, how you can read people through their body language. (I borrowed Allan Pease's *Body Language* from the library again and again as a teenager; I would use it to study my crush of the time—for instance, watching the direction of his legs when he spoke to me.) Really, we were both in the business of decoding people.

One day, as we were amusing ourselves by assigning Myers-Briggs personality profiles to my brothers and sisters, Dad observed that he thought my profile had changed.

'You used to be an introvert, but you've taught yourself to be an extrovert,' he said. I was about nineteen at the time.

This was true; I had consciously, over the years, manufactured a persona that was jokey and opinionated, with a determinedly confident exterior. A barrier between the world and my uncertain self. Not entirely unlike Dad's constant stream of jokes and puns, their flow increasing when he's uncomfortable.

'Thanks,' I said to Dad, taking it as a compliment. I always hated being shy, being stuck for the right things to say.

Since then, I have relaxed more into who I really am, rather than who I think I should be. My two selves have merged, into one that is more authentic.

I am starting to wonder if this life's work of constructing a self, of analysing it and how others see it, might be relevant to this question of Asperger's. Or is that what goes on under the surface for everyone?

Naomi has considered the data from written questionnaires I've filled out, her interviews with me, the scraps of information I've collected from my parents and from Nana, who looked after me while Mum worked when I was small.

'Do you think you have Asperger's?' she asks me.

I consider. I have no idea.

'Yes?' I say.

'I think so,' she agrees.

I am stunned.

She tells me that I can pursue a formal diagnosis if I want, like we're doing for Leo. This would mean getting confirming opinions from two other professionals. She is not sure if I would get this confirmation, because I *present so well.* But she believes that the underlying anxiety I have about, well, everything, is a result of my continuing to intellectually process my every social interaction.

There is no reason for me to go down the formal path. I just wanted to know.

At home, Tony rushes to the hallway to greet me.

'Well?' he says.

I peel off my coat, shrugging out of one arm then the other; then I carefully hang my bag and coat on the brass hooks outside the entrance to the dining room. A cap falls to the floor. I bend to pick it up; replace it on the hook. Finally, I turn to face him.

'Positive or negative?'

I think for a moment. Which is it? I'm not sure how I feel. Of course, that's not what he's asking.

'Positive,' I say.

He folds me into his arms, murmurs reassuring words into my hair. I tell him some of the details of what Naomi said, then he returns to the dining-room table where he is writing a university assignment on his laptop. I lie on the couch, looking into the centre of the room, thinking about everything and nothing.

Leo wanders in, looking for food.

'Hey, guess what?' I say, brightly. 'I went to see Naomi today. I did the same tests as you and today she told me whether I'm Asperger's. And what do you think the answer is?'

'Yes?'

'That's right.' I high-five him. He nods and moves to put his head on Tony's shoulder.

'Do *you* have Asperger's?' he asks him.

'What? Why?'

Leo shrugs.

'Is it because he's part of our family?' I venture.

Leo nods. Tony laughs.

'Well, maybe,' he says.

Steven arrives at the open door.

'Can he come and play?' asks Roger.

'Sure.'

The boys disappear down the hallway, already laughing and shrieking.

I pick up the phone from the dining-room table. 'I want my Mum,' I say to no-one in particular. Tears gather behind my eyes as I speak the words.

Mum is in hospital. She went in yesterday for a minor operation. I know she's in hospital. But I dial her number anyway. 'You never know,' I tell Tony. 'She might be home. I might have it wrong. They might have let her out early.'

The phone rings out. I hang up as the machine clicks on.

The dogs break into a flurry of barking, their strangled cries overwhelming the high-pitched hum of boys' voices. Tony goes to the door, I go to the window.

Jordan is on the footpath, dancing on the spot with excitement. I dash past the open front door and duck into our bedroom, slamming the door behind me. Jordan's voice grows louder as he enters the house with Tony and Margaret. I lie on my bed and watch the ceiling, listening to them talk, wondering how long I can hide in here without being rude.

Leo and Steven are getting louder too. Their footsteps pound the wooden floorboards.

'MUM! MU-U-UUM!'

As I don't answer, their voices fill my ears, getting bolder and louder by the moment.

I'm now officially rude.

In the hallway, I find the boys clutching fans of Yu-Gi-Oh cards.

'Can you photocopy these?' asks Leo.

'You said once a week!' says Steven. 'It's been a week.'

Last week, I helped them photocopy some of each other's favourite cards using our photocopier, teaching them how to make them into new trading cards. They were so delighted by the discovery that I had to allocate a limit to how many they could make at once, so they don't use up all the coloured ink in the photocopier.

This was three days ago.

'You can do it on Friday,' I tell them. 'Don't ask me before then!'

They groan and scatter back to Leo's bedroom.

'I'm staying here!' announces Jordan, behind me.

'Yes, you are.'

'HA!' he shouts. 'HA! Ha-HA!' He wiggles maniacally, shimmying his hips and waggling his head like a Bollywood film star, then disappears in the same direction as the boys.

I manage to chat with Margaret as if nothing has happened to me today. She has brought a gift for Leo, for doing so well at school. I call him in to receive it.

He eyes the telltale silver-wrapped square as she talks. He looks as if he'd like to eat it.

'It's a CD!' he exhales, before he even touches the gift. When he unwraps it to find *AC/DC's Greatest Hits*, he launches himself backward onto the floor, his head hitting the polished wood.

'THANK YOU!' he shouts, rocketing to his feet. 'OH MY GOD!'

He shoots across the room to the stereo. The three boys kick off their shoes and leap about the living area in their socks. Leo leans in and turns the volume up as far as he dares, though not quite all the way.

He shoots a sideway glance at Jordan. 'I'm going to put on "Problem Child",' he says.

Luckily, Jordan is oblivious to the implied insult. Leo watches smugly, enjoying his private joke as Jordan rocks back and forth to the music, smiling beatifically.

After Margaret leaves, I go back to my room to lie on my bed.

22. JINGLE BELL ROCK

The sun is hot, but I wear long black pants anyway, and pack a jacket along with our make-do picnic of muesli bars, bread-and-butter sandwiches (with ham cling-wrapped separately) and Mount Franklin bottles filled with juice and water. I bring a book, just in case, and a stack of Yu-Gi-Oh magazines for Leo.

As we load my bike basket with supplies, footsteps sound across the back fence.

'STEVEN!' shouts Leo. 'STEVEN! I'm afraid I can't play with you tonight.' There is a kind of triumph in his voice. 'I have Carols in the Park and I'm singing in the choir. SORRY!'

'THAT'S OKAY,' comes the reply from next door. 'I have my school's Christmas concert anyway. Santa is coming.'

The ride feels easier than I'd imagined, probably because this year Leo is riding his own bike rather than sitting heavily on the back of mine. He shouts conversationally above the traffic as we cycle along the footpath of busy Somerville Road, but I can't make sense of it. I shout back lots of 'uh huh', interspersed with instructions on when to stop and where to turn.

I smooth the patchwork rug across the grass in front of the stage. A woman walks by barefoot, nursing a can of beer. I watch her polished toenails pass. Another trots officiously across the park, wrapped in a

Christmas apron and carrying a paper cup branded with a coffee logo. I pick up my purse and follow her trail to a coffee wagon. It's next to a Yarraville Cellars tent; I buy a bottle of Margaret River sparkling and two plastic wineglasses. Back on the quilt, I am secure in the knowledge that company is on its way. Tonight, I will not be conspicuously out of place.

In the meantime, I sprawl with my book. Wham's 'Last Christmas' crackles from the loudspeakers; the lyrics jam incongruously in my head with the description I am reading of an elderly Egyptian aristocrat preparing for his lover. Leo returns from the playground and lies at my feet with a magazine. Lucy is now officially late.

The Christmas-aproned mother stops at our rug and bends down close. 'Hi. Raffle ticket? Go on!'

I count out a dollar from the silver coins in my purse and write Leo's name on the ticket. In return, we get a printed booklet with the words of all the carols (and the logos of all the sponsors). Leo digs a biro out of my bag and busies himself circling the songs he likes best. 'Silent Night' is in; 'Rudolph' is out. He is sad that 'Jingle Bell Rock', his favourite, is not there.

On stage, the man in the red T-shirt speaks into a microphone at ten-minute intervals, welcoming us. He reminds us not to forget that Yarraville Cellars, the coffee van, the ice-cream van and the Scouts' sausage sizzle are all here, all with goods for sale.

I scan the park for Lucy and Conor, and instead meet a familiar gaze from the blanket directly behind us: an ex-boyfriend. It was a long time ago that we dated—four years ago, to be exact—and since then, I've married and he's moved in with his girlfriend, a writer whom I'm friendly with. I hire them both to write reviews and articles for me. In fact, we happen to have been emailing earlier today about a book review. But somehow, it's still awkward.

'Hi.'

'Hi.'

We stiltedly talk about today's email and the fact that his son's primary school choir is performing tonight, too. His children go to a school not far from ours. The schools are traditional rivals but come together to stage this carols night together once a year. It hadn't crossed my mind that they would be here. A beautiful, pigtailed girl joins him on the blanket. She is as tall and slender as a *Dolly* model.

'Hey. You remember Jo, don't you?' he says. She squints at me, unsure. He gestures at Leo, his head in a Yu-Gi-Oh magazine.

'You remember Leo?'

A shadow of recognition passes over her face. She nods slightly and smiles at me. I say a cheery hello.

We met just once, during the short time I dated her father, soon after her parents had tentatively separated. She and her brother had fish and chips at my house and were floored (and kind of spooked) by then four-year-old Leo's excited stream of chatter. I think she liked me. I gave her some sparkly bangles and a girls' comic from the giveaway basket at my work. She showed them to her mother, who then interrogated my ex about who I was and why I was giving gifts to his daughter.

Ah yes, *that's* why this is awkward.

Every once in a while, a girl from Leo's class wanders by and says hello. Leo smiles and greets them, then returns to his magazine. The girls run shrieking around the park, weaving in and out of the increasingly dense patchwork of rugs between the stage and the cake stalls.

'Why don't you play with those girls?' I ask. 'They're your friends.'

He shakes his head. The division between boys and girls is widening.

I'm now longing for Lucy to arrive. I'm surrounded by talk and laughter; not for the first time, I'm reminded of high school and cliques—and not belonging to one. Maybe this is why I love books so much. With a book in your hand, you don't look alone; you look busy.

Leo stands in the middle of the playground, licking an ice-cream cone and observing the chaos around him, still stubbornly solitary.

We've been at the park for over an hour when I hear Lucy greeting a chain of parents on her way to our rug.

'Sorry I'm late!' she says brightly.

'It's fine,' I say, and even though I've been inwardly cursing her, it suddenly is. 'Want a drink?'

I realise I probably could have been talking to some of these parents too, if I'd made an effort. I've exchanged pleasantries outside the classroom, even chatted with some of them at a parents' fundraising dance I went to with Lucy a few months ago. But something about this setting triggers a defence mechanism I find hard to shut off. I can't quite banish the memories of last year's Carols—of Leo and me, together alone.

Conor crashes onto the rug beside us wearing a cottonwool beard and a Santa hat with a bell. Leo joins him and together they disappear into the playground. At last.

Mark arrives just as I'm pouring wine for Lucy and me. Camera in hand, he sits between us. Feeling better already, I offer him my glass. He sips and passes it back.

'You'd better not have any diseases or anything,' I say.

The kids from the other school file onto the stage, identically dressed in school uniforms and Santa hats.

'They'll probably kick our arses at this, too,' mutters Lucy, as they launch into the first of three carols. I'm amazed at how up she is with these inter-school rivalries—and that she cares about them. Then I'm amazed that I'm not.

The kids close with 'Jingle Bells' as Mark and I squabble about which of us has more school uniform shirts at their house and *where they can all be* if neither of us has any.

Then they file off the stage and our kids take their place, wearing an assortment of red and green clothing. Some of the girls wear their favourite dresses instead. Leo stands, back straight and chin tilted to the sky, in the front row. He sings loudly, solemnly, with gusto. Most kids hold their songbooks in their hands but his is at his feet, held in place by his sneakers. He squints at his feet during the lesser-known carol, eventually giving up and reading the songbook of the girl next to him. Conor is a few rows back. He occasionally leaps up, his red Santa hat poking above the heads in front of him.

The deputy principal appears at my side, standing between Mark and me.

'Look at him,' she says. 'He's come so far. You must be proud.'

'He said he wanted to join the choir because they needed more boys and he felt it was his duty,' I tell her. She laughs.

As they finish, I push my way to the front of the stage and open my arms for Leo to leap into. Mark is right behind me. A keening, wailing noise cuts through the air, interrupting us mid-congratulations. The sound seems to be coming closer. It's a fire-engine, sirens blazing.

A man dressed in red, with black boots and a belly-deep white beard, is hanging from it, waving.

'SANTAAAAAA!'

The kids swarm towards the engine, Leo at the front of the shrieking pack. I run, barefoot, burrs pricking the balls of my feet. An anarchic line—more of a vaguely organised swarm—is forming behind Santa's plastic chair. It's the rule of the strongest, as the kids squash forward. I shout at them to all take three steps back to give the ones at the front breathing space, then intervene to sort out a couple of the obvious skirmishes. *'Back of the line! Give her some room! Your big sister was in front of you a moment ago, why are* you *there now?'*

'Wow,' says Leo. 'My mum, the policeman of the line, huh? Who would have thought it? She should be a footy umpire!'

Ten minutes into the queue, Leo has his lolly bag from Santa and we're making our way back to the quilt. Mark is going home. I've spent all my money on sausages and ice-cream (and wine) so I ask if he'll buy me a packet of chips. He agrees. On the walk to the wine tent, we talk about how pleased we are with Leo's progress, how great it is to see him getting involved in things like the choir. I tell him what a difference I can see compared to last year, when Leo wanted to join in but couldn't. When he played alone and longed to sing on the stage.

'It's been good, I think. Finding out about the Asperger's. Hard, but good,' says Mark.

I agree.

'And what about for you?' he says. 'Finding out about your Asperger's? Has it helped you to work some things out, about things that are hard for you?'

I really don't want to have this conversation. I feel like he's creating a division, between people who have problems getting on in the world— Leo and me—and those who know what they're doing, like him. It's as if me being Asperger's is the answer to all the behaviour he sees as 'wrong' on my part.

I steer him off the topic.

Back on the quilt, Leo is reading his Yu-Gi-Oh magazine again, eating lolly snakes and half watching the band sing jazzy Christmas songs. Lucy and I eat the lime-flavoured chips and drink most of the wine before Leo asks to leave. We cycle home in the fading light, shouting conversation as we go. As we idle at the traffic lights at the top of our street, I notice a golden peach sunset bleeding into grey-lined clouds behind us.

Tony is waiting in the lounge room when we get home.

'How was it?'

'Great,' says Leo. 'Can I have a drink? I'm thirsty.'

'He was wonderful. He sang beautifully. We were so proud. And I was the policeman of the line. For Santa. Leo couldn't believe it!'

'Yeah, I was embarrassed. I couldn't believe that everyone knew I was your son. It was humiliating.'

'Oh.' I am hurt, but try to mask it with annoyance. 'Well, maybe I won't come and listen to your class read tomorrow, then. If I'm so *embarrassing.*'

'NO, Mum!' He throws himself to the ground and hugs my ankles, pinning me to the middle of the hallway. 'NO!'

'But I thought I was embarrassing.'

'Not in the classroom, Mum. *Then* you're actually being *helpful.*'

23. A FAMILY CHRISTMAS

I catch the train to Adelaide; it takes all day, nearly twelve hours. I sit in the dining car at one of the four tables, eating food I've packed for the journey and watching the landscape out the window. It is mostly brown: dry creek beds, paddocks with sun-browned grass and spindly sheep, long stretches of nothing. An hour out of Adelaide, the dried-out country turns to bush: small towns embedded in eucalypt forests.

Mum picks me up from the station. At her house, in one of the guest bedrooms, I lie on a floral quilt all day and read a fat biography of Martha Gellhorn. At intervals, I move into the backyard and sit on the lounge swing that overlooks an abandoned quarry. We're at the edge of the world; sitting there, all I can see are trees and slopes of brown grass, houses in the far distance. I luxuriate in the silence.

We have a tennis picnic near my sisters' flat, with my brothers and Dad, and those of Dad's brothers and sisters who still live in Adelaide.

I play a bit of tennis, but mostly sit on a rug with my brothers and sisters near the courts, eating bits of food—biscuits baked by Nana, crackers, grapes—and slowly drinking a plastic glass of wine. I stretch out my sneakers on the rug and frown at the holes in the canvas where my socks are visible underneath.

'You need new shoes, sis,' teases my brother Nick. 'What's with the holes?'

'I love these shoes,' I say, whining a little. 'I don't want to get rid of them. I want to keep them as long as I can.'

'Pink?' he says.

'I like my pink shoes.'

He laughs. 'How old are you?'

I stick my tongue out at him.

'So, Jo,' says Nick, when we are briefly alone, the others having scattered to play tennis or fetch more food and drink. 'What's with this Asperger's thing? What exactly is it?'

I look up sharply, then tell him what it is, what the signs are.

'Do you think I have it?' he asks, as if he's been thinking about it.

'I don't know,' I say. 'Maybe.'

Later, at Liz and Sarah's flat, I tell Sarah about our conversation and collapse into sobs. I can't stop crying.

'What's wrong?' she asks. 'I don't get it.'

'I feel so guilty,' I manage, eventually. 'It breaks my heart.'

'Why?'

'Because I should have taken better care of him.'

When Nick finished Year Twelve, he moved to Melbourne with my friend Jason.

It was Jason I moved to Melbourne with soon after my twenty-first birthday—the move was his idea. He only lasted a fortnight; I stayed. Jason rented a cheap house in the Adelaide Hills and Nick stayed with him every weekend. They had a dartboard in the hallway that they shot with an air rifle and spent all night on the phone to talkback radio, winding up the hosts with invented characters like 'old man annoyed with skateboard hooligans'.

When Jason changed his mind again and moved back to Melbourne, he convinced Nick to move with him when he finished his school year. I was living with Mark by then; Jason was sleeping on our couch. Mark said Nick could live with us if I really wanted him to, but Jason had to go.

Nick moved to Melbourne at the end of his school year. Jason got him a job as a kitchen hand at the shopping centre cafe where he was a chef; they both moved in with the head chef, who turned out to be a gambling addict. The head chef began to lose a lot of money. A pretty young waitress from Queensland started working with them; Jason and the head chef fell for her. She fell for Nick. Jason and the head chef fell into depressions, which they were both prone to. Nick began coming to my house in tears.

I didn't invite him to move in with us.

Mark and I decided to amicably split up; I decided to return to Adelaide. I found out I was pregnant with Leo.

Nick was offered a chef's apprenticeship by his boss, but he didn't want to stay in Melbourne without me.

'It's not your fault,' says Sarah. '*You* didn't ask Nick to move to Melbourne.'

'Still,' I say. 'He was miserable and he was seventeen years old and I didn't help him.'

'You were there for him.'

'Not enough.'

'Nick is fine,' Sarah says. 'He's happy with his life.'

'We were so close,' I say. 'I feel like we don't know each other anymore.'

I feel like I hardly know any of my family anymore. They're the closest people to me in the world, but the years apart mean we've grown and changed in each other's absence. A few short visits a year is hardly enough to fill in the gaps.

Tony arrives on Christmas Eve, just in time for a barbecue at Dad's house where my brothers and sisters and I exchange presents. Nick gives me a pair of pink Converse sneakers.

We stay at Dad's for the six days Tony is in Adelaide, in Dad's new spare room. He's converted it from a study; there is now a couch bed and a lamp.

Tony has driven with the dogs, who tumble, barking, from the front seat as he opens the door. Dad doesn't like dogs, or any animals really, but he does his best not to mind their presence, even when Doug digs under the back fence and escapes into his neighbour's yard.

On Christmas Day, Dad goes to his sister's house for lunch. Mum picks us up and drives us to her sister Kathy's, in the Adelaide Hills. I wear a strapless red-and-white floral dress Simon gave me the night before, with a straw hat over two plaits that brush my bare shoulders.

Most of my Christmases have been spent with this group. All of my mum's family—her five brothers and sisters, my cousins—flew to Melbourne, then drove to coastal Aireys Inlet, for my wedding.

A few faces are missing, some of them lost to divorce. One of my sisters calls to say she's too hungover to leave the house; she spends the day throwing up in her toilet instead. Last year, Nick missed my birthday barbecue for the same reason.

'Where's Sasha?' I ask Kathy.

'Sasha has been dead for *five years*,' she says, slowly, as if to an idiot. She waves at a framed photo on the wall. 'There she is.'

Everyone laughs.

'I'm sorry,' I say, 'I meant *Cody*, not Sasha.' Cody is the dog she adopted from my mum earlier in the year; a kelpie Mum had adopted from my sister after she moved out of home and into her flat. 'I don't know why I said Sasha!'

'Oh, Cody's running around out there somewhere.' Kathy gestures at the bush beyond her back deck. 'She'll turn up eventually.'

I don't even know why I asked. I was just making conversation.

I reintroduce Tony to my relatives as they arrive; he's only met them a few times, usually in a fog of faces and voices like this, where they're hard to distinguish from one another. Incredibly, I keep messing up the introductions. Again and again, it goes something like, 'Tony, this is Graeme, I mean David, I mean Nick, I mean *Michael*. You remember my Uncle Michael.'

It's not that I don't know; I have known these people since I was born, or since they were. The words just won't come out like they're supposed to.

Even with the people I am most comfortable with in the world, I am no longer certain of who I am, or how to act.

The cousins gather outside after the meal has been eaten. The boys are looking at the motorbikes in the shed. On the back deck, my mother and aunts are talking about Kathy's renovation plans for the house, about what kind of kitchen she will have and why she's decided not to put in a pool. I'm standing on a stump in a patch of dirt that is earmarked for a vegetable garden.

My favourite cousin, Ali, has arrived late, after her lunch shift at her dad's house. We used to spend part of each school holidays together as kids; we'd hang out while our dads (high school best friends) played tennis. She moved to Melbourne for a year, into a sharehouse on my street; she would sometimes stop to say hi in the mornings on her way to the train station. On Saturday nights we would eat pasta and watch *Parkinson* together on my couch. She was my bridesmaid, along with my sisters. Jason was showily besotted with her; he called her *lovely Ali*. She found it hilarious.

We talk about *Entourage* and *Veronica Mars*; she has downloaded the latest seasons and promises to bring them over on a USB for me to copy. We talk about her partner and her job and my job and Tony.

'So, I hear Leo has been diagnosed with … Asperger's Syndrome?' says Ali. 'How are you going with that?'

'Oh, fine,' I say. 'Okay. You know.'

She nods.

'What does it *mean*?' she asks.

I give her a textbook summary.

Ali is Leo's godmother. I have a photograph of two-year-old Leo eating chips out of her mouth.

One Christmas when we were kids, Ali and I picked almonds off Nana's tree in the backyard, shelled them with bricks, then chewed them up and spat them in each other's faces. We got into trouble for fighting; I don't think we knew whether we were fighting or playing.

'Have you told Leo?' she asks. I nod. 'How did he take it?'

'He was pretty freaked out, but now I think he's used to it. Like us, I guess.'

* * * *

Mum drives me to pick up Leo; Rachel's parents live in the Adelaide Hills, not far away from Kathy's house. Leo runs to the front door wearing a superhero mask, roaring with sugar and adrenaline. He invites us into the house to see his Christmas toys and Mum follows him before I can come up with a reason why I don't want to. She makes small talk with Rachel's mother while Mark and I exchange *How was your Christmas Day?*

And then we drive back to Kathy's house, where Leo opens his presents and we finish our day drinking the last of the wine in the evening sun.

Mum's sister Debbie invites us over to swim in her backyard pool; she had it put in soon before her kids moved out of home and she doesn't feel like it gets used enough. She tells us we're doing her a favour.

Mum and Debbie sit under an umbrella by the side of the pool, hose in hand to squirt Debbie's dog when it barks. It's a small dog so it barks a lot, just like ours do. It also likes to jump on the boogie board and go spinning across the water. While it barks. Leo predictably finds this hilarious.

Ali arrives with the promised USB. After I copy the files to my laptop, we sit in the spa, wearing straw hats and sunglasses, and talk. Debbie and Nana move into the pool, leaving Mum sitting alone under the umbrella. She doesn't seem to mind, but continues shouting her conversation across the water, pausing occasionally to squirt the dog. Leo intermittently shouts, 'LOOK AT ME!' and jumps into the water.

'So, I've been diagnosed as Asperger's too,' I tell Ali, the words strange in my mouth. I haven't really told anyone, apart from Tony and my parents, my brothers and sisters.

'What?' she says. 'Really?' She looks dubious. 'But you're *really* social. You're not shy.'

'Well, I am,' I say. 'I just hide it well.'

'Right,' she says, eyeing me suspiciously, as if I might be someone new.

As teenagers, after we'd both left high school, Ali and I hung out with the same group of friends. We went to nightclubs together and drank ourselves into oblivion; she was better at knowing when to stop than I was.

'I *am* shy,' I insist. 'I analyse everything after I'm out of a social situation; you know, what I said, what other people said, what they meant, what they really think of me. It's kind of exhausting.'

'Mmmm, it sounds like it.'

It's not comfortable to talk about how you're uncomfortable talking to people. Or to tell someone you're talking to that you mine your every conversation for hidden meaning after it's finished.

We change the subject.

I am starting to realise that I used to get very drunk on a regular basis because it dissolved my inhibitions. Magically, I could socialise without thinking. All my self-doubt, all the internal prompts that quizzed me like a vigilant schoolteacher about whether I was performing well, melted away like ice in spirits. As my brain turned to liquid, my conversation would flow. Later, I wouldn't remember the precise details of what I'd said and done, apart from stray phrases and feelings. Mostly, I remembered laughter.

I stopped getting drunk, at all, a few years ago, after I realised that inhibitions can be valuable. Specifically, after I got very drunk at a party for a publication I'd just started freelancing for and threw up on the carpet, then spent the rest of the night in a toilet cubicle. From which I emerged just as the party had wound down to four remaining people, including the editor, who saw me come out from the toilets and asked, 'Is that where you've been all night?' Luckily, the editor thought it was hilarious and it didn't stop him taking me seriously as a writer. But I knew I was lucky.

I can count on my fingers the number of times I've had more than two drinks at a time since then, at a work function anyway.

I was shocked when Tony expressed relief when I stopped drinking— and not just because it made it easier for him not to drink (and thus not to be cripplingly ill the following day). He said I was annoying when I was drunk, that it was exhausting looking after me when I inevitably ended the night throwing up behind a shed or in an alley.

'But that's how we got together,' I said. 'We were drunk every night for the first month of our relationship.'

He shrugged. Somehow, he'd liked me anyway; not because of my drunken charm (or what I'd imagined was charm) but despite it. Just the way I later learned he'd liked me *despite* my quirky fashion sense, like my habit of wearing red stockings with a red vinyl jacket and red hat, and my collection of silver clothing.

At Mum's house, Leo and I play Monopoly all day, sprawled on our stomachs on the cool tiles. The television plays in the background; it always does here. I make us grilled cheese on toast for lunch, which we eat on plates surrounded by our real estate cards. Leo gulps from a tall glass of lime cordial which Mum refills when it's empty. He gets upset when he realises how badly I'm beating him; I let him win, but slowly and only just.

Leo and I catch the bus to the tourist beach suburb of Glenelg. We go alone, just the two of us. The bus passes through the city and then the airport; it takes one and a half hours. We spread our towels on the sand under a perfect blue sky.

I miss Adelaide skies during fickle Melbourne summers; the skies of my childhood, as consistent as a child's drawing, with their cloudless paintbox blue. Almost every day hot enough to swim—I used to wear my bathers under my clothes, every summer day, so I'd be prepared. Here, I do it again—or at least, I keep my bathers in my backpack along with a pair of board shorts and clean underwear for Leo.

We queue for dinner in a Jetty Road fish and chip shop, dripping wet. A towel is wrapped around my waist; seawater spills from Leo's shorts onto the linoleum floor, puddling at his feet. It doesn't matter; we are surrounded by teenage girls in bikini tops and denim cut-offs, kids in their underwear, shirtless men in board shorts.

We take our paper parcel to the sand and eat on our towels before leaving our scraps for the seagulls as we return to the water. Leo digs a hole and we garland it with a border of shells and rocks, collecting them from the lip of the tide. He runs around it in circles, whooping, then into the waves. He collects more shells and rocks to drop into the hole. We are still circling from the water to the sand and back again as the sun sinks, an orange glow melting into dark water.

The sky is black as we walk to the bus-stop. Leo falls asleep on my shoulder somewhere between the airport and the city. Later, I have to wake him so we can walk home.

'Oh, Jo-*annne*,' sighs Mum, as she opens the front door to us. It's just after 10 pm.

PART THREE

24. HAVING YOUR SAY

Leo and Conor trickle out of their classroom, deep in conversation.

'It's good for the economy!' huffs Conor, scuffing his black lace-ups deep into the gravel. 'We need it!'

'I don't know,' frowns Leo. 'It doesn't sound right. Mum, what do you think?'

They both turn to look at me as I pick tiny stones out of my open-toed Birkenstocks.

'We-ell … it's not very good for the environment.'

They're talking about the government's plan to artificially deepen Port Phillip Bay, to improve access to Melbourne's ports for industrial shipping.

'Aha!' Leo mounts his bike, buckling his helmet under his chin with a snap. 'I thought so! I'm against anything that's against the environment!'

'Well, I'm *for* anything that makes more money.'

'Money's not *everything*, Conor,' sniffs Leo, a little self-importantly. 'Right, Mum?'

'Mmmm.'

And Leo pedals off, winding perilously close to a mother and daughter on the footpath ahead and disappearing from sight. Conor, who has forgotten to bring his bike to school for the third week in a row, climbs onto the cushion behind me and holds onto my waist.

At home, as we suck fruit juice iceblocks under the ceiling fan, the boys restart their conversation, batting their arguments back and forth.

'What if the WHOLE WORLD was going to be polluted but you'd make more money?' spits Leo.

'Well, I'd pollute the world then,' says Conor.

'Okay guys,' I sigh, peeling myself off the couch and backing down the hallway towards the sanctuary of my study. 'Conor, you're winning anyway. They're *doing* it.'

'Yes!' He punches the air.

'Oh-hhhhh!' Leo clenches his fists at his side. I sink into my desk chair and shut the door on them.

Leo and Conor delight in having opposing tastes. They seem to pick sides on purpose in order to argue about things. Or, as in this case, they transform vaguely held views into iron oppositions, fiercely fought. Conor likes U2 while Leo loves AC/DC. Conor barracks for Geelong; Leo is a newly minted North Melbourne supporter now that his favourite player Chris Judd has left the West Coast Eagles.

After dinner, dressed in his pyjamas and ready for bed, Leo copies Japanese manga figures from his Yu-Gi-Oh cards, telling Tony about his day. He puts down his red pencil and looks me in the eye.

'I'm so angry!' he says. 'I want to *do something*. What can I do?'

'I don't know.'

'I want to do something,' he repeats. The steel in his voice twists my conscience. I shouldn't dismiss him so casually.

'Well, let me see. What could you do? I guess you could start a petition.'

'What's that?'

'You write down what you want and what you're angry about and you collect signatures and take them to the Parliament asking them to change what they're doing. Anyone can do that.'

'I'll do it! What do I need?'

'Um … a clipboard. And some paper and a pen. I could do something for you on the computer if you're serious?'

'I am.'

* * * *

Here is what Leo wrote at the start of his petition:

> *I am very angry about the dredging!! John Brumby should know better!!! The environment is <u>way</u> more important than money! I mean, <u>who</u> wants to be a millionaire <u>and</u> a bad country for looking after the environment? The dredging threatens the bay and the creatures that live in it. The bay belongs to the sea creatures, not the government.*

I was careful not to feed him any words, though I did coach him on the *kind of* thing to write: What is this about? Why don't you want it to happen? Why should people care? What will the effects be?

On Saturday morning, we decide to collect some signatures on Yarraville's main shopping strip. Leo carries the clipboard. It's nearly forty degrees Celsius; my plan is a quick tour up and down the street and then the beach. I pack a bag with towels, sunscreen and spare board shorts for Leo. I'm wearing a straw cowboy hat and a sundress over bathers. But Leo doesn't want to go to the beach; he is set on his task. Instead, we canvas every business, stop every passer-by. Leo does the talking; I give him tips on how to approach people and how to make sure he treads the line between pushy and polite.

At the bottleshop, the man behind the counter, his greying hair brushing the shoulders of his lizard-infested shirt, steps out from his potato-chip-lined enclosure to shake Leo's hand. He calls goodbye as we pass the axolotl tank in the open doorway. The woman in the New Age shop is so impressed that she lets Leo take an amethyst stone he admires, refusing to let me pay for it. 'Keep up the good work!' She asks her teenage daughter if she'll sign Leo's petition. 'I don't know anything about it,' she says. 'But I'll sign it.' On the footpath, Leo turns to me, beaming. 'Mum, she's a TEENAGER and she doesn't even know anything about it, and I'm only EIGHT and I do.'

At the video store, the owner who regularly combs the shelves for Leo's favourite *Pokemon* DVDs is wary. 'Mmm, I don't know what I think about the dredging,' he says. He calls to an older woman inspecting a Jennifer Aniston film nearby. A silk scarf puffs at her neck; her hair is a stiff curve of white blonde that brackets her chin. 'What do you think about the dredging of the bay?' he says.

She gives a cross sigh before answering in polished tones that complement her clothes.

'Well, all the fuss is ridiculous. We obviously need it to happen. People should get over it.'

The owner looks relieved: now he can both stick with his convictions and obey the maxim that the customer is always right. 'Absolutely, couldn't agree more.'

Leo looks at them both in bemused horror.

'Okay, thanks,' I say and lead Leo and his clipboard back into the midday sun.

'Why didn't you *say* something?' he demands, once we're safely outside. 'Why didn't you *tell* them?'

'Sometimes,' I say, ashamed, 'when you know you won't change someone's mind, there's no point.'

We arrive home flushed and sticky, sucking on lemon Solos through pink straws. Leo has collected over thirty signatures.

On the Monday after our weekend of signature-gathering, Conor and Leo burst out of the portable classroom, shouting over each other in their excitement.

'Mum, look at all my signatures!'

'Look at MINE!'

Leo has filled an extra page with childish pencilled-in names, spilling over the lines in an unsteady rainbow of colours. Conor has a sheet of paper with his own plaintive message, 'Support the dredging,' and a brown texta-ed grid that includes a column marked 'reason for decision'. He, too, has a collection of signatures. Some of the names appear magnanimously on both petitions—both for and against the dredging—including some I recognise as belonging to teachers.

'Can we collect more signatures?' asks Conor. 'Now? Can you take us down the street?'

I know it's awful, but I don't want to take them down the street. I especially don't want to take Conor around with his petition, with which I don't agree. This is supposed to be about teaching the kids to stand up for their beliefs, to encourage them to have a say. But while I think it's great that Conor is having a say, I don't want to be an active part of helping him gather signatures. It's part embarrassment, part conviction. I decide on a neutral solution, and suggest the boys might like to set up on the footpath and approach passers-by to sign their petitions.

We erect a card table from the shed and folding chairs, with tall glasses of lemonade for the boys. I sit on the porch behind a screen of trees and bushes to watch. The minutes pass and no-one comes. They get bored and climb the tree that shades the table; forgetting their mission, they lose themselves in jokes and banter. Then a couple of girls in school uniforms approach from the direction of the train station. The boys drop from the branches onto the footpath, grasping at their clipboards in a flurry of competition. Conor is the first to run at the girls, asking, 'Will you sign my petition?' Leo comes from behind, arguing, 'No, sign mine! His is for the dredging, mine is against it!' The bemused girls sign both before walking on.

Over the next hour or so, a pattern forms. Roughly every twenty minutes, a smattering of commuters pass and are greeted by a joint assault. Every so often, I call out from over my book for them to remember their manners. While some people stride past with curt nods or that flick of the hand you give to those who are trying to sell you something, most are affable enough, some are admiring. Some have an opinion and will sign one or the other petition in accordance with their views. Others sign both. In between sales pitches, Leo and Conor spend most of their time up the tree.

When Lucy arrives to pick up Conor, she is greeted by shouts from the tree and pleas for signatures from both boys. She is kind-hearted— more than I am—and she agreeably signs both. I mix us gin and tonics, garnished with slices of lemon, and we sit back on the porch and drink them while I tell her about the afternoon.

The boys count the extra signatures they've collected.

'You've got more,' grumbles Conor, and Leo beams.

'It's because I'm right.'

'I think it's because yours looks better, because your mum typed it up for you in Microsoft Word,' says Conor, frowning critically at his brown texta-ed page. He turns to me.

'Can you type mine up, too?'

'You're about to go home,' I say. 'And I have to start dinner soon. Sorry.'

* * * *

Neither Tony nor I thought much about the bay-dredging issue before Leo's petition. In fact, to my shame, I have written about the issue from the other side, in my past life working for a PR agency: championing a client's involvement in 'the channel-deepening project'. This week, Tony sent off an angry letter to *The Age*. Both of us have taken the petition to work and asked our co-workers to sign it.

I like that Leo is leading us on this. It reflects the way we're trying to bring him up, to care about the world around him. He's obediently scornful about the Nestlé products we boycott, on the grounds of babies being addicted to expensive formula in third-world countries. (Though he delights in eating surreptitious Eskimo Pies while at his dad's house.) And he scoffs that McDonald's is junk. I've heard him telling classmates that you don't need to eat it *when you can just go in and buy the Happy Meals toy separately.* (Our compromise for when he really, really wants the toy they're offering.)

I want to help Leo take this as far as he can, to leave him with a sense of achievement and encourage him to do more things like this. So I write a media release about his petition which I circulate in the lead-up to a local rally organised by the Maribyrnong Truck Action Group. The local focus—on the effects of an increase in truck traffic to the area—is different to Leo's concerns about the damage to the bay itself, but it's the same cause. By now, Leo has nearly 120 signatures. I hope he might get his photo in one of the two local papers: something he can cut out and keep as a souvenir.

Kabita and Mel, another girl from the bookshop, invite me for Friday drinks. We go to a little bar off an alley, near the shop. It is dim and cave-like, all polished wood and bare cement. We sit at a tiny table and order a bottle of red wine to share. Kabita tells stories about the authors she works with in her day job as an editor. She looks tired; working six days a week will do that to a person.

'I thought you didn't drink wine anymore?' she says.

'I don't, not really. I just thought … what the hell.'

'That's it!' laughs Mel. 'Drink up!' Mel is the opposite of Kabita: she is loud where Kabita is quiet, reckless where Kabita is considered. They seem to appreciate each other's differences, but the glue of their friendship is the fact that they both grew up in Singapore. The talk ranges everywhere, but often circles back to it.

'So, where are you at with Leo?' asks Kabita.

I tell them about my day, writing and sending media releases about Leo's petition. Mel hoots with laughter. 'No way!' she says. 'You *wrote a press release* about your son?'

'Well, yeah,' I say.

Kabita is laughing too. 'That's Jo for you!' she says.

'That's me!' I join in, rolling my eyes and pulling a face. 'I *know* it's ridiculous …' Even though I have only just realised how strange it seems. 'But I really want to encourage him, when he's actually interested in making a difference in the world.'

'With a press release!' says Mel.

'I think it's nice,' says Kabita kindly. 'He'll love it if he gets his picture in the paper.'

'It's awesome,' says Mel, 'but it's also kind of hilarious.'

* * * *

We wake to heavy rain on the morning of the rally. I've written a note explaining why Leo will be late to school. Leo, Tony and I ride our bikes through the rain and chain them up under the cover of a service station on the corner of Francis Street and Somerville Road, where a surprisingly large gathering of locals have stopped the traffic. There are other kids in school uniform, shorts and bare legs emerging from raincoats and plastic ponchos. Most of the messages on the home-made placards are anti-trucks. When the speech finishes, the umbrellas and hooded raincoats scatter, fleeing the road and the spitting skies for the shelter of the service station.

Leo brings his petition from under his raincoat and begins to approach people to sign it. One of them is a reporter from the local paper, who asks if he's the Leo from the press release. She asks to borrow a giant placard ('Dredging = More Trucks') from a nearby protestor, then poses him at the intersection, holding the placard in one hand and his clipboard in the other. More reporters and photographers approach. That night, he'll be on ABC and Channel Nine news. A *Herald Sun* reporter interviews me while waiting his turn to talk to Leo. He asks why we're against the dredging of the bay. When I talk about environmental damage to the bay itself, he prompts me with a question along the lines of, 'Are you here because you're concerned about the increased truck traffic to the area and the associated health risks?' I say no.

Roger next door is a truck driver. In our first house in the inner-west, we also lived next door to a truck driver, who'd pointed out that these neighbourhoods, situated between the river port and the city, have always been truck thoroughfares. It's the make-up of residents that has changed, more than the truck traffic. And we all use goods transported by trucks every day. My view is that the truck situation is more complex than the way these protesters present it; I have sympathies with both sides.

One of the locals who signs Leo's petition is June, the electoral officer for our local Greens senator, Colleen Hartland, who is at the forefront of these local protests. June brings Colleen to meet us; they suggest Colleen takes Leo's petition to Parliament for him.

What follows is a front-page story on Leo in the local paper, complete with enormous photograph, which is pinned up in his classroom and forms the basis for a class discussion of the issues raised by the dredging of the bay. His actions are mentioned at a whole-school assembly and he's the next recipient of the weekly class award.

I am quoted in the *Herald Sun* as saying that I am concerned about the associated health risks of increased truck traffic to the Yarraville area.

And then June emails me, with the idea of a class trip to Parliament to hear Colleen present the petition.

Gathering at Yarraville station, the children are seized by the excitement of being outdoors and on their way to the outside world at a time when they'd usually be on their way to school. On the platform, they squeal and roar in mock terror as trains sweep past, blowing back our hair and drowning out conversation. In the carriage, they squint out the windows at the tunnels, shouting out the blue-striped names of the stations. *FLAGSTAFF! MELBOURNE CENTRAL!* They marvel at the height of the escalators at Parliament station, their uniformed bodies shooting past the ranks of sober suits and briefcases in a breathless race to the top.

As we snake onto Collins Street in single file, the *Big Issue* vendor sings a song just for us, threading his words together in an improvised ode to schoolkids. On the other side of the road, on the stone steps to Parliament House—backdrop to a thousand wedding photos—Mark waits beside a newspaper photographer and June. Leo lets go of my hand and breaks away to hug his dad tight. I hang back, even as I secretly long to snatch him back to my side.

June is obviously relieved by our arrival. She arranges the class in rows, urging them to sit for the photographer. They obediently drop to the steps, descending like dominoes. The children arrange their faces in tight smiles as the photographer dances back and forth before them. He drops to his knee in front of Leo, focusing on his frown, his pursed lips and raised two-finger rock salute. ('It was a serious occasion,' Leo will explain later. 'I'm not supposed to be happy—I'm angry!')

The photographer waltzes Leo off for a solo shot, instructing him to gaze ahead down Collins Street. His father and I watch from a few steps behind as Leo, with an imposing pillar as backdrop, glares into the gathering clouds, raising his rock salute again. The shutter clicks in quick succession and he is released. We usher him to the back of the line for security clearance.

A gangly boy-man with a thicket of ash-blond hair and a mauve shirt tucked into trousers has followed us. He carries a spiral-bound notebook and wears a plastic pass around his neck. I assume he is another electoral staffer, but he turns out to be the journalist from the local paper.

As we shuffle towards the twin gates of the metal detectors and strip ourselves of jewellery, watches and mobile phones, a hand touches my arm. It is Tony with the petition—which I'd left on the kitchen table this morning—still clipped to its yellow plastic board. 'My hero!' I half joke, crushing his stiff suit jacket in a grateful hug. We chat amiably with June.

'Excuse me.' It is Conor, tapping on her arm. 'Excuse me. Hey, excuse me!'

She smiles down at him. 'Hi there.'

'Excuse me, but I did a petition too. Can mine be read out?'

She looks at him, alarmed. 'You did?'

'Yes, I'm FOR the dredging of the bay.'

'Ohhhh.' Recognition flickers across her face. 'That's right. I heard there was another kid who was getting a petition on the other side.' She tells Conor that she'll find out if there's something she can do about his petition, too. 'We're against the dredging, of course, but it's still great that you got involved. The journalist from the local paper is here and he'll want to talk to you. It's important that he gets *both* sides of the story.'

'Okay!' Conor fairly skips through the metal detectors and past the uniformed security guards, his small face glowing. 'I'm going to be in the paper!' he trills, to no-one in particular. 'I'm going to be in the paper!'

June addresses us in the tiled lobby, filling us in on the rules: *be very quiet; no clapping or booing*. Led by her and the teacher, we pour upstairs and round corners, streaming through the dim corridors. The further we go, the more subdued the kids grow, until finally we are in the upper rows of the gallery, edging onto velvety carpeted pews and looking down on our Greens senator, Colleen Hartland. She talks in a barely punctuated stream to an audience of suited fellow senators who chat among themselves, stare into the distance, read over documents in their laps: anything but listen to what is being said. Nobody looks at us; we could be ghosts. The children watch politely, their faces fixed in puzzlement, their hands and feet twitching in boredom. Now Colleen is talking about 'Leo Watkins' and the petition, mangling his surname. Tony and I exchange looks. 'Hmmm, yes, this really is *all about* Leo, isn't it?' he deadpans. 'Good of her to get his name right.' She tells her distracted audience that they can meet Leo at an upcoming rally in April. Tony looks at me again. 'Will Leo be there?' It's the first I've heard of it.

Colleen meets us outside a few minutes after her speech, as we gather once again on Parliament steps. The kids are arranged into rows, retrieving their stiff smiles to pose for more pictures, this time with Colleen.

'Do you have any questions about what happened in there?' she asks.

'Why do they all talk on top of each other like that?'

'Ah. Yes. Good question.' She concurs that it was pretty rude and that they should all know better. 'You all have better manners than that.'

Then she reiterates that they must all call each other 'Mr' and 'Ms' and that if they use anyone's first name in the chamber, they will be thrown out. So: real manners are ignored, but formalities that don't really matter must be adhered to. Colleen talks some more about the processes of government and the rules of Parliament. We all perform the act of listening, kids and adults alike, our good manners on display.

* * * *

At the close of Colleen's speech, June appears with another Greens senator and a primary school student she introduces as being from the other side of the bay. She, too, is eight years old and has collected a petition against the dredging, signed by her schoolmates. Tahlia is blonde, with glasses and an immaculate school uniform: navy blazer and skirt, knee-high white socks under polished Mary Janes. She and Leo look at each other. She is embarrassed but open-faced, ready to be friendly. Leo frowns back at her, clearly wishing she would just go away.

'Leo, this is Tahlia,' says June. 'She wrote a petition, too.' Leo mutely looks at his feet. One of his socks is tan, the other dark brown. The laces of his sneakers have unspooled and trail on the cement. The two children pose together, with the two senators, for a photograph we're told will be displayed on the Greens website. Leo frowns at the camera; Tahlia beams politely.

The journalist crouches to Conor, who sits on the concrete steps. He is awkward with the kids, as if not quite sure how to talk to them. On the other side of the children, who are still grouped into rows, Mark poses with his arm around Leo's shoulder as June captures their image on her own small camera.

Then it's time for Leo's interview.

'So Leo, why did you do this petition?' asks the journalist, pen poised above his spiral notepad.

'Because I was angry with Conor. I wanted to beat Conor and show him he was wrong.'

The gathered grown-ups laugh, the journalist included.

'I thought you were best friends?' he says.

'We are.'

'You guys have sleepovers and go swimming together and stuff; is that right?' Leo looks away, towards Collins Street. 'That's what Conor told me,' the journalist continues, doubt creeping into his voice. Leo is no longer listening.

'That's right,' I tell him. 'They're friends, but they have a very competitive friendship.'

'Right.'

He tries again.

'So, Leo, what do you want to be when you grow up?'

I know immediately what he is fishing for. I also know he won't get it.

'A rock star.'

More laughter. The journalist looks disappointed. Then he nods to himself. '*Ohhhh*. That's why you were doing the rock star salute. In the photographs.'

'Yep. But, you know, I'm not going to be a *polluting* rock star. I'm going to be the kind of rock star who *doesn't* contribute to global warming. I am *against* global warming.'

'Ah. I see.'

Leo looks pleased with himself.

'So, Leo,' says the journalist. 'If you could say one thing to John Brumby, what would it be?'

'Well …' Leo begins, pausing dramatically. 'I was talking to my friend Steven about this the other day—he lives next door to me—and what we decided would be *really good* was this: make John Brumby buy a house and live right on the bay and *then* because of global warming and the dredging, a BIG TIDAL WAVE will come *right through* his window and onto his HOUSE and he'll be like …' Leo rolls his eyes, clutches his throat and gargles dryly, his body crumpling under an imaginary weight. He straightens triumphantly. 'And THEN he'll be sorry he didn't stop the dredging!'

The journalist closes his notebook and drops it to his side. He hasn't used his pen at all.

'Excuse me,' says Leo, looking at him sharply.

'Yes?'

'Is Conor going to be in the paper too?'

'Yes, he will. You both will.'

'Hmmm. I know what will happen,' Leo growls, his face like thunder. 'Conor will *push* me aside and *elbow* me out of the picture.'

June and Colleen ask Leo what he'd like them to do with the petition. He looks at them blankly.

'Would you like us to send a letter to all these people here?' June taps the clipboard, with its 171 signatures. 'To tell them that the petition was read in Parliament?'

'Okay.' He pauses, before surprising us with his vehemence. 'I'm *angry*. I'm angry with that judge who let the dredging go ahead. I haven't stopped the dredging. It didn't work.'

We explain that he's had his say, that if enough people show that they care about issues like this, eventually the government will have to listen. That sometimes these things can take years, but it's always worth having your say. He is unconvinced.

25. CALL ME BOOMER

Leo and Tony have been training for the new football season for weeks. Most afternoons when Leo finishes school, they retreat to the backyard or go to the oval to practise their kicking and marking.

The hole in the native bush in front of the side fence, the one that perfectly aligned with the trajectory of the average football kick, has grown. The bush is now more hole than branches.

Leo and I lie at opposite ends of the couch, a fleecy red blanket pulled up to our shoulders, our legs side-by-side underneath. From above, we are one two-headed, four-armed creature. A manuscript balances on my knees; Leo is reading a Japanese manga novel. The kitchen is dark behind us; so is the sky behind the red-and-orange-striped curtains at the lounge-room window. I love these curtains—I chose the fabric and Mum sewed them for me. They were the one bright element in the dour two-bedroom flat Leo and I lived in when he was a baby. To me, they look like a sunset. Tony thinks they're ugly, but grudgingly allowed me to put them up.

'Mum, listen!' says Leo. 'This guy says *absolutely* after everything. Listen, it's hilarious!'

'Ha!' I say, without looking up or listening. 'Hilarious!'

And we return to silence.

A symphony of barks breaks the mood, followed by footsteps on the boards of the verandah and a fumbling in the lock. Tony appears in the doorway, dogs leaping at his knees. The aroma of grilled meat fills the room as Tony sits down, unwraps a burger and turns on the television.

It's footy season.

'I'm going for the Dogs!' says Leo, abandoning his book.

'Why?'

'Because I want to win footy tipping and they're number two.'

'You're betraying Essendon for that?' Tony shakes his head. Essendon is Tony's team.

Leo rests his head on Tony's shoulder, stretching his legs over mine.

'Can I have something to eat?'

'You can have an apple.'

'Okay.'

I stand to get it.

'But do you want to go to bed? You've got Auskick in the morning, maybe you should be fresh for that.'

'Okay.'

Tony and I raise our eyebrows at one another.

'Wow, that was very mature,' says Tony.

I feel Leo's presence beside the bed before I open my eyes. The bedside clock says 6 am. I pull him under the quilt for a morning hug.

Two hours later, he's watching cartoons on the couch, dressed in shorts and a yellow skivvy, a boot kicking a football drawn across his chest in permanent texta. The box of Orangatangos is on the bench beside an empty bowl. Leo convinced me to buy the sugary organic cereal yesterday, against my better judgement, by arguing that it donates money to saving orangutans with the proceeds of every box.

He is electric with excitement, or a sugar high, or both.

'You'll need to wear a jumper, Leo,' I say. 'It's cold outside.' Moisture is beaded on the kitchen window.

'I'm not Leo,' he says. 'It's Boomer.'

Leo's former football hero, Chris Judd, has defected from the West Coast Eagles to Carlton this year. Leo doesn't want to support the Eagles without Judd and feels too betrayed to follow him to Carlton. So he's chosen a new football team (North Melbourne) and a new hero, Nathan 'Boomer' Harvey. He's been telling us for weeks that we should call him Boomer.

'Sorry, I forgot,' I say, 'You'll need to wear a jumper, Boomer.'

During the drills, Leo jumps and yowls, pulling faces, chanting, tackling his friends around the waist. He trades menacing shoves with Jack, the kid who has everything, including sporting ability. Every time Leo flubs the ball—which is often—Jack taunts him. I don't hear the words, but I hear the tones and see their faces. The shoves and scowls escalate in intensity, but burn out quickly, like lightning flashes.

Standing on the sidelines, I look down and notice that my fists are clenched.

On the other side of the drills, Vanessa's husband moves closer to the game. He watches Leo as intensely as we do, his arms folded tight.

'Shall we stand closer to him?' asks Tony.

'No! I might say something I'd regret.'

'Yeah, me too.'

I hug him. He smiles back, weakly; he doesn't like public displays of affection.

'Those two are the kinds of parents who think they're perfect and everyone else is wrong,' he continues.

Lucy arrives at our side, paper coffee cup in hand. She snorts in agreement. 'There's a word for that,' she says darkly.

'What is it?'

'Oh, it'll come to me.' She sips at her cup. 'Oh, this is crap,' she grimaces.

We watch the boys: Leo's shoving, Jack's taunting, Conor's running, the hugs and tackles that are impossible to tell from fighting—at least, for me.

'I've got it!' Lucy says.

'What is it?'

'*Wholesome.* You know, those parents who think they have it all worked out. I know someone like that. We're friends, but we have opposite values.'

'Like what?'

'Like … like, she didn't want to send her kids to our school because she didn't want them mixing with all the African children.'

'Are you joking?'

'No! And I went over there the other day and she had all these private school catalogues on the kitchen table and she was writing down the pros and cons of them all. Private primary schools.'

I lose myself in the conversation while Tony pointedly concentrates on the drills.

As he leaves for work, Mark arrives. The game begins.

Leo does prove hungry for the ball—he chases it tenaciously around the field and manages to get hold of it quite a few times. Not having touched the ball is his most frequent post-game complaint, so this is a good sign.

He also wrestles players to the ground in too-rough tackles; he screams in frustration when these players are awarded free kicks as a result. He yells and cries when Conor, who is on the opposing team, kicks a goal. In fact, he runs off the field, to shout and cry on the fringe of the oval. I watch helplessly as Vanessa's husband leads him back to the game.

Then Jack calls him an idiot for dropping a mark. Leo shoves Jack to the ground with a flash of intensity and kicks him. Jack lies on the grass, bawling and clutching his knee.

I rush onto the field. Both boys are crying; Leo stands over Jack with unrepentant eyes.

At the end of the game, the coach asks me what Leo's deal is. I tell him that Leo has Asperger's Syndrome, which means he has trouble controlling his emotions—and knowing where the line is when it comes to tackling. I explain that he has trouble coping with losing, or in fact with not doing things perfectly. I tell him that Leo and Jack had been needling each other all morning. I tell him that this is, of course, totally unacceptable.

The coach and I talk to Leo together. We tell him that he needs to speak to the coaches if there is a problem, not resort to violence.

'Right,' sobs Leo. 'So I should be a dobber?'

'If someone was bothering you in the classroom, would you push them to the ground or would you tell the teacher?'

'Tell the teacher.'

'Okay, then. The coach is your teacher.'

On the way home, we talk about attitude and positivity and teams and sportsmanship. I tell him I am embarrassed and ashamed by his behaviour, though generally I am very proud of him; he is the best thing in my life.

'Aren't you glad Tony wasn't here to see this?' I say.

The defiance leaks from his face.

'Don't tell him!' he says. 'Please!'

'I'll see. You have a chance to make a fresh start next week. It's the first game Tony will watch. Does he need to coach you on attitude instead of footy skills this week?'

Leo considers. 'Maybe I need both.'

I have started doing weekly book reviews for Triple R's breakfast program. Once a week, I get up at 6 am and catch the train in the dark. It's light when I change for a tram to East Brunswick in the city.

Monday night used to be TV night; I'd watch *Desperate Housewives* followed by *Brothers and Sisters* followed by *30 Rock*. Tony would sequester himself in the study, browsing the internet, then go early to bed.

Now Tony watches football shows on Monday nights; I sit on my bed or in the study, madly cribbing the book I'm reviewing the next morning. I skim-read the book again, then I take notes, then I divide the notes into four or five talking points. Then I rehearse possible conversations, pacing around the bedroom or the study, talking to myself.

This usually takes about four or five hours.

Then I go to bed.

Somehow, I do okay on the air. I enjoy myself, for the ten minutes my segment lasts. Afterwards on the tram home, I run through it again in my head, combing my performance for errors. On the occasions where I make a stupid comment or fumble my words or create a moment of dead air, it takes the rest of the day to recover.

Nikki calls after my first show to congratulate me; she is shocked when I dissolve into panicked sobs.

'But you were great,' she says.

I point out my errors.

'God, no one would have *noticed*,' she says. 'Honestly, I promise, I thought you were great.'

'I don't know if I can do this again,' I tell her. 'I feel so humiliated.'

But I do it again, every week.

'You don't have to do so much preparation,' Tony tells me as I shut myself away each Monday night.

'Yes, I do.'

'You just have to chat, that's all. Just say whatever comes into your head.'

'I know. But if I don't do this, nothing will *come into* my head. Trust me.'

He shrugs, kisses me and returns to the television.

Tony listens most mornings while he and Leo are eating breakfast. I ring him from the tram to hear his verdict. He tells the truth. Some mornings his words carry me through the rest of the day; others, they plunge me into despair.

But I love that I can trust him; I don't have to mine his words for meaning.

* * * *

I'm leaving to go to a work meeting, then I'm running an evening book club in the city. I style my hair and put on make-up, with a dress and zippered boots.

'Hey,' says Tony, as I check that I've packed my purse, keys and a book for the train. 'Leo, look at your Mum.'

Leo looks up from his comic. He laughs. 'Heh heh, yeah.'

'What?' I say. He shakes his head, giggling.

'No really, what?'

Tony makes a meaningful face at him.

'It's just that your bum looks *really* big in that dress.'

I return to the bedroom and change.

'Don't listen to him!' calls Tony from the lounge room. 'You look fine!'

'I hate *fine*!' I yell back. '*Fine is code for you could look worse.*'

I hear them talking as I exchange the dress for jeans and a top.

'Leo, *never* do that,' Tony says. 'Really. You should never say that to a woman.'

'Why?'

'They don't like it.'

After the meeting, before the book club, I go to the Borders across the road from my bookshop, scanning the street to make sure no-one sees me go in.

The General Psychology shelves are packed with books with titles like *Scarred* and *Shattered*; sad-faced children stare out from pale covers. I feel sick looking at them, like I've glimpsed something private, something obscene. It's a kind of grief porn.

I raid the shelves and get out of that aisle as quickly as I can, settling myself in an armchair with my pile. The books are all on Asperger's Syndrome: a couple of memoirs, some Tony Attwood books that supplement The Book, including *Girls and Asperger's Syndrome*. This is what I'm really interested in. I'm not here for Leo, not really. I'm here for myself.

I sat in a corner of my bookshop with this title recently, looking for clues. One of my colleagues found me and started talking. Who starts a conversation with a colleague browsing the Psychology section? I quickly replaced the book.

Girls with Asperger's Syndrome are good at role-play. They are consummate observers of people, of human behaviour. Their obsessions, or 'interests', are often different from those of boys with Asperger's. They might be interested in horses, or films, or fiction. At school, they often adopt the mannerisms and habits of a chosen female friend, to fit in. They don't tend to act out, as boys with Asperger's do. Instead, they turn their anxieties inwards, on themselves. They withdraw.

I make an appointment to see Naomi again.

'Good,' says Tony.

Tony changes his Saturday shift to a later one so he can come to Auskick.

Leo wakes us with a question. 'Tony, if I have a good attitude but play badly this week, will you still be proud of me?'

He bounces the ball on the footpath as we walk to the oval, tossing it in the air and catching it, running ahead of us so he can *get there faster*.

It begins well. He chases the ball, he hugs a teammate who scores a goal, he participates in teamwork rather than focusing on trying to score. Then he lets out a wail when the other team scores a goal. He cries over an umpire's call.

Tony has to physically restrain me from walking onto the field and pulling him off.

'He has to learn that he's part of a team,' Tony says. 'He can't let his teammates down by coming off the ground in the middle of a game.'

'But his teammates would be better off if he came off the field for five minutes to cool down; if he came back positive and focused.'

'You can't control everything,' says Tony. 'You're not in charge here, just let him be.'

And then Leo hits a teammate who accidentally kicks a goal for the other team; he is sent off the field.

'Is there anything you can do?' asks Ryan's mum. 'Anyone you can ask for advice?'

I am burning with shame.

'I could maybe ask his psychologist,' I say, trying to sound calm. 'But I think I have a fair idea of what to do. It's just about repetition. He'll get it eventually.'

'I guess you probably know what to do by instinct,' she says, sounding unsure.

I'm not sure either.

Leo sobs; he says he never wants to go to Auskick again. He doesn't even want his customary end-of-game hotdog.

'Sure you do, mate,' says Tony. 'Come on, have a hotdog and you'll feel better.'

'No. I can't. I don't deserve one.'

'Leo, I've had about enough,' I explode. 'Tony is being very nice to you, but I'm about to tell you to *cut the crap*. If you want a hotdog, have one. But I'm not going to offer again and I'm not going to give you one later.'

Leo pauses, midway through stepping through the hole in the fence that separates the oval from the skate ramp. He turns and heads for the hotdog table.

A ponytailed mum in jeans and a hoodie, tongs in one hand, takes Leo's two dollars. She looks at his football jumper.

'Did you see the game last night?' she asks.

He shakes his head.

'Did you know our team lost?'

He nods.

She passes him his hotdog, a pale, limp sausage nestled wetly in a bun, crumbs gathering on its skin.

'Were you upset?'

He shrugs.

'I was gutted!' she says.

'I tipped Carlton,' says Leo. She laughs.

'Because they've got Chris Judd now,' I explain.

'Ohhhh yeah,' she says, suddenly serious. 'I cried for *two hours* when he left the Eagles.'

I try to look sympathetic.

Conor is sitting outside the classroom, blond head resting on raised knees, sobbing into the gap between his arms. It's a theatrical kind of sob: loud, throaty and curiously dry.

'Ooh hoo hoo, OOH hoo HOO ...'

'Hey Conor,' I say, as Leo drops to sit beside him. 'What's up, mate?'

His head snaps up; his face is contorted in mourning.

'My dad was leaving my soccer gear out for me,' he wails, 'on the front verandah. And my mum's forgotten to get it and it will be there all day, and it will be *sto-lennnn*.' And he begins to sob again.

'It's there now?' I ask. He nods. 'I'll go get it for you, okay? No need to cry.'

'Thanks.' A smile replaces the sobs, like a rainbow after a summer storm. His dad lives opposite the school oval; it's an easy favour.

Then I notice the rubbery sleeve of a rashie emerging from Conor's school shirt.

'Oh no.'

'What?' says Conor, panicked. 'WHAT?'

'Nothing,' I say. 'It's just that I've forgotten Leo's swimming things.' I look hopefully at Leo, willing him to say, *No, I've packed them Mum.* Of course, it doesn't happen. He just smiles serenely back at me.

'Leo will have to stay behind in the classroom today while we go swimming then,' says Conor.

'No, I'll go home and get it.'

'But you'll get my soccer gear first?'

'Yep, don't worry.'

All the way home, I curse myself for forgetting the swimming gear.

Back at the school, I arrive out of breath, just in time to see the end of a parent's talk to the class about his career in robotics. Leo's hand stays in the air throughout; he has two questions during question time.

Then I work with the kids on reading comprehension activities for an hour, helping them learn for a national standards test tomorrow. I'm with the kids who have literacy issues: feisty, confident Marianne; painfully shy Ivy, who winces when it's her turn to read aloud; and overweight, softly spoken Jennifer, who tries hard and smiles a lot. She often says hello when she sees me in the schoolyard. We read through the passages, then talk about how to approach the questions and where to look for answers in the text. It's rewarding, watching them figure out how to do it.

'Leo! Leo! Let me see!'

I look up to see him at his desk, surrounded by kids, their heads bent over a piece of paper. All lesson, Leo has been moving from table to table, conducting a poll on an AFL game being played this weekend: Victoria versus the Dream Team. He moves to his teacher, Peter.

'Who do you think will win?' I hear him ask.

Peter considers. 'Hmmm,' he says. 'Well, I'm from Albury, so I'll have to go with the Dream Team.'

I leave feeling good.

At home, I'm dying for a coffee and breakfast. And a shower. Fresh clothes. I sit at my desk and check my emails; press the glowing button on the answering machine. An email pops up from the PR agency I am freelancing for, asking me to brainstorm titles for a report I've edited. Nicola wants me to call her. The rambling message on the machine is from Mark, something about not having a car and not being able to drive us somewhere.

I call Nicola back. She wants me to brainstorm on the spot. There is a long blank pause over the phone line. I promise to call or email her my ideas in five minutes.

Then I replay Mark's message and listen to it properly. It's about Leo's paediatrician appointment, in just over an hour's time. On the other side of the city.

Fuck fuck fuck.

I ring Mark.

'I forgot,' I tell him. 'I'm so sorry. I knew about it, I remembered, I did, I've just had a really hectic morning. And now he's at swimming.'

Mark gets very angry. I don't blame him. But I swing back anyway.

'Don't yell at me! It's not like *you* don't fuck up *all the time*!'

'Okay,' he says, surprising me. 'But this is a three-hundred-dollar appointment. It took months for us to get it. It's the final step in confirming his diagnosis. And it's too late to cancel.'

'But … he's at swimming. What do I do?'

'I suggest you catch a cab.'

'But he's at Maribyrnong. And we have to go to St Kilda Road. It'll cost me a hundred dollars.'

'I don't see any alternative,' says Mark crisply.

Neither do I. I call the cab.

And realise I haven't called Nicola back. I call and tell her that I have three lame suggestions, but no time to think up anything better. She asks me to email them through, which I do. Then I swap my hoodie for a cardigan, my tracksuit pants for jeans, and throw a jacket and a pile of books into a bag for Leo.

I jog past the turnstiles of the swim centre, through the canteen with its plastic chairs and tables and past the parents talking on benches, just inside the tropical atmosphere of the pool area. Children are massed along the sides of the pools in groups, still dry. Some of them stand by the benches, their swimming bags or towels in hand. The cement is dangerously damp under my soles.

'Leo?' I call, desperate to get to him before he hits the water. 'LEO!'

I peer at the small, half-dressed bodies, scanning for his face, but without my glasses all their features blur together.

'Hello.' It's Peter. Surprise registers in his eyes, but only mildly.

'Where's Leo?' I ask.

He waves over the blue tile of water to an island of land where kids line up on the side of the water, only their legs submerged.

'I have to get him!' I say. 'I have to take him to the doctor! I forgot!'

'Okay.'

And I run again, aware that I should not be running, that I am setting a terrible example for the kids (and that I might slip and fall on my arse). But I'm in danger of missing an important, three-hundred-dollar appointment, a cab is idling in the carpark with its meter running, and if I can get Leo while he's still dry I'll save myself a good ten minutes.

'LEO!' I shout as I run. 'LEO, NO! NOOOO!'

On the other side of the pool, the line of children slides into the water and thrashes across its width, their small bodies gloriously slick.

'You can't do that!' A female lifeguard advances towards me, waving her arms sternly. 'You can't run in here!'

It's too late anyway.

Leo looks back mid-stroke, hearing me argue with his coach about whether or not I can take him away. He bats at the water, making his slow way back to me.

'MUM! What are you doing here?'

'Hurry, Leo! Quick! You have to go! I forgot you have a doctor's appointment!'

I reach down and pull him out of the water. 'There's a taxi waiting outside.'

He is bright with the adventure of it.

The sports teacher is openly laughing as we rush past towards the change-rooms.

'He won't be back today,' I call to Peter as we pass. He nods affably, waves goodbye to Leo.

'Really?' says Leo. 'Really? I get the afternoon off school?'

'Really,' I say. There is no way I'm going back there today.

'HOORAY!'

'Now, can you get in and out of that change-room faster than you've ever moved before? Be like the wind?'

'Yes, Mum. I will! You can count on me.'

The cab driver colludes with us, checking the street directory for the quickest possible route, speeding a little, changing lanes to shave vital seconds off our travel time. Leo sits barefoot, his hair dripping onto the seat, rivers of water dribbling down his cheeks and neck, damp patches leaking through his school shirt. I grab his towel and rub it over his head. He speaks from under it.

'Mum, do you have any books for me to read?'

'Yes! Yes I do.' I pull them from the bag.

He reads contentedly for the rest of the ride.

We arrive at the clinic five minutes before the appointment. I feel like a superhero. Mark greets us amiably in the reception area, as if nothing has happened.

The paediatrician keeps us waiting for twenty minutes.

She asks Leo what he thinks Asperger's means.

'Um ... sometimes I think it's like a disease, like there's something wrong with me. But ...'

'It actually means you're terrifically smart and good at certain things—and you're really passionate about the things you're interested in,' the paediatrican says.

'YES!' I say. 'Yes, that's exactly what we tell him.'

'Is there anyone else in your family who has Asperger's?' she asks him.

'Yes, in my family,' I interrupt. 'My dad and probably my brother.'

Leo looks at me. 'You do too, don't you Mum?' he says.

'Yes,' I say, feeling my smile stretch artificially wide. 'Yes, yes I do.'

I feel exposed and somewhat ashamed, then ashamed of my shame. Obviously I don't really believe what I tell him, that Asperger's is a positive thing and there's nothing wrong with it.

She continues to question Leo. He seems to quite enjoy himself. She asks about his interests, his family, his school. And, joy of joys, she asks him to tell her all about Pokemon, welcoming his expansions into the different subsets. I can't help but check my watch, anxious that we are wasting precious time.

'Are you smart?'

'Yes.'

'What are you smart at, at school?'

'Well, maths and reading. I think especially maths because I'm doing Grade Five maths sheets and I'm only in Grade Three. And another kid, he's in Grade Four and he's doing Grade Seven maths sheets. I think only Grade Fours are allowed to do them because I'm *sure* that I could do it too.'

'What's in your bedroom?'

'Japanese manga. Other books, like Andy Griffiths and Mark Jennings. Um, football cards. *Obviously* Yu-Gi-Oh cards and Pokemon cards. And *obviously* a bed.'

'Obviously,' she says, with a wry smile.

The paediatrician confirms the diagnosis. She gives us instructions on how to register with Centrelink to get a small fortnightly carer's allowance. We might like to use it to send him on holiday camps with other Asperger's kids, or to social skills training groups. Mark says these are good ideas, things we should look into. I privately recoil. I don't want to send Leo to a group for special kids, kids who don't fit in.

I've accepted the label of Asperger's Syndrome so long as I can shape it my way: different, not defective. A certain kind of personality, not a disease. The kinds of interventions the paediatrician mentions have the ring of segregation about them. They sound like treatment.

I want him to learn how to get along in the world, not just find a pocket in the world where he can get along.

26. ALL ABOUT ATTITUDE

The Auskick coach has been thinking about how to organise around Leo's issues; he assigns him to a smaller group with younger kids. For once, Leo lives up to his rhetoric about being the best player on the field—he kicks eight goals and the ball barely leaves his hands.

'Of course, the *real* test will come when things don't go so well,' says the coach.

I'm careful to praise Leo's *attitude* rather than his success.

'I know, Mum,' he says, with a touch of weariness.

Tony starts as assistant coach next week.

Steven comes running into the bathroom. I'm putting a band-aid on Conor's finger; Leo bumped it while they were playing football. Conor is sniffling.

'We can't play in the backyard anymore,' Steven announces. 'Leo did a poo and it stinks.'

'WHAT?'

Leo is sitting on the swings, laughing. He falls quiet as I open the back door.

'It's *disgusting*,' says Steven. I can't smell anything.

'OOH HOO HOO,' comes a noise from inside the house. 'My FINGER HURTS.'

'CONOR, YOU'RE FINE!' I yell through the open doorway. 'Leo, what have you done?'

'I needed to go to the toilet … and I didn't have time to get there … so I pooed under that tree.' He points to a thick bed of fallen leaves and laughs again, looking at Steven, waiting for him to join in.

'Did you see him?' I ask Steven.

'No,' he says. 'I was in the cubby. But he told me when I came out.'

'Leo, this is … *such* bad behaviour,' I say.

I point out that it would have taken the same amount of time for him to go inside to the toilet as it did to cross the yard and poo under the tree.

'Well, yes,' he says. 'But don't you *know* that song?'

'Yes,' I sigh. 'I know that song.'

* * * *

After Leo's fifth birthday party, just weeks after Tony had moved in with Leo and me, we all walked to a nearby pub for lunch.

'Tell me a story,' said Leo, who loves hearing stories about our childhoods.

Tony told a story about when he was four years old, and developed anxiety issues around going to the toilet, hamming up the tale and making Leo laugh by saying *poo* a lot. He'd been prescribed laxatives that tasted like chocolate, he said, so one day he binged on them behind his parents' backs. The climax of the story was him desperately needing to poo but still not wanting to use the toilet, so he pooed in the backyard. Leo whooped.

'Ah, *Leo*,' said Tony, leaning back in his chair with an air of hard-won wisdom. 'You haven't *lived* until you've done an open-air poo.'

Soon after we got home, Tony came to me, barely able to speak through his laughter. 'Look at this,' he eventually choked out, guiding me through the kitchen and into the backyard. Leo had come straight home and pooed on the bricks of the back verandah.

I didn't laugh, at least not then; I scolded Tony for encouraging him, as did Margaret when Tony retold the story during a family lunch the following weekend. (Tony's older brother Jamie thought it was hilarious.)

Tony made up a little song, which he and Leo still like to sing, to the tune of 'When I was Seventeen': 'When I was four years old, I did a poo in the backyard. / It was a very big poo, and I was four years old …'

✱ ✱ ✱ ✱

'It's just a song,' I say now. 'You are not supposed to *do* it.'

He giggles. Steven does not laugh. Conor appears at the doorway, having given up on someone coming to find and comfort him.

'What's happening?' he asks.

'I pooed in the backyard!' says Leo hopefully.

'Aw, that is *gross*,' Conor says.

I want to hug him. 'You can clean that up yourself,' I say.

'What?' Leo finally looks alarmed.

'You made the mess, you clean it up.' I bring him a roll of paper towel from the kitchen. His friends go inside. As he disappears under the tree and dabs at the leaves, I lecture him. 'How old are you now?'

'Eight.'

'How much older is that than four?'

'A lot.'

I tell him that if his dad wasn't picking him up tonight, I'd send him to bed at a four-year-old's bedtime of six o'clock.

There is a noise at the side gate. It is Lucy. As I'm talking to her about her day, my afternoon, Leo wanders to the plate of crackers on the outdoor table, picks one up and takes a bite.

'No!' I say. 'Put that down—*not* back on the plate—and go inside and *wash your hands*.' He puts the cracker on the table. 'Yuck!' I call after him as he slams the screen door behind him.

Lucy picks up the cracker and bites into it.

'No!' I say again, snatching it from her hand. 'You don't want to eat that.'

She looks offended.

'Leo pooed in the backyard and hasn't washed his hands.'

Now she looks pissed off. 'I wish you hadn't *told* me that.'

'I'm sorry, I just didn't want you to think I was being rude.'

'Hey, what happened?' She picks up Conor's bandaged finger and gives it a kiss.

I tell her about the football incident, that he's been *very distressed* by it. 'But he's fine,' I say.

She envelops him in a hug. 'Oh, my poor darling,' she says, raising her eyebrows at me over his head. 'There, there.'

Conor wanders inside to get his bag and jumper. Lucy tells me that she's about to drag Conor along to a work meeting, the second in two weeks.

'WAH!' comes a noise from inside the house. 'Ohhh, WAH. WAH!'

It's Conor.

'Oh dear,' says Lucy.

'Yeah, it's been one of those afternoons.'

If I were a nice person, I would offer to keep Conor while she goes to her meeting. It's just a couple of hours. But I can't face it today. Instead, I follow her through the house and wave them goodbye from the front verandah. I send Steven home. Then I yell at Leo, hoping to scare him out of doing this again.

That's when he tells me that he made it up—that he only pretended to poo—to make his friends laugh.

'But they didn't laugh, did they?' I say. This explains why the backyard doesn't smell, despite Steven's insistence that it does.

'No.'

'I hope you've learned your lesson.' I am relieved that he didn't really do it, but also bewildered as to why he'd make up such a thing.

When Mark arrives to pick up Leo up, I am crawling through the leaves under the tree, sniffing the ground, just to make sure.

'That's little boys for you,' Mark shrugs, after hearing my story. 'Oh, Leo.'

'Did you hear that?' I say, unable to resist. 'Dad said that's what LITTLE boys do, Leo. You're eight, for God's sakes.'

Naomi starts me on a program of cognitive behaviour therapy, with homework exercises and a textbook. It's about finding the false assumptions behind some of the things that make me anxious, then addressing them with logic.

We talk about my panic over not having heard back from an editor after submitting a story. *What reasons could there be?* He doesn't like it. He's not going to publish it, after all. He's busy. *Which one is logically most likely?* He's busy. *What could you do to find out?* Ask if he's received it.

'You say this is your second story for this person?' she says.

'Yep.'

'Well, doesn't that mean it's unlikely that he doesn't like your work? If he didn't like your work, he wouldn't have hired you again.'

'You'd think so, but no,' I say. 'I figure, the first time, they're trying you out. A second assignment is good, it means they liked you, but it *might* be because you fluked it the first time. The third assignment is when you can start to relax.'

'Really?' she says. I like that she doesn't dismiss me; that she considers my logic and accepts it if it makes sense.

Of course, I don't ever entirely relax, not even after the fifth or tenth assignment. But it gets easier. And this applied logic I'm learning, this pattern of sense that I can lay over the competing buzz of self-doubt, is something I begin to internalise.

Self-doubt is not great for the psyche, but I suspect, when tamed to a manageable level, it is good for the work. There's an advantage to never being satisfied that what you've done is good enough.

Naomi is shocked when I tell her I'm doing weekly radio segments. 'But isn't that incredibly stressful?' she asks.

'Yes,' I say. 'It is.'

It's kind of a relief to have someone acknowledge it, rather than tell me I'm being silly and there's nothing to worry about.

Still, the next week's program I'm more stressed than I've ever been. The night before, I end up pacing the study, panicking.

I'm going to talk about one of my favourite authors, Jon Ronson, and I'm worried I won't do him justice as I don't have time to re-read all his books.

Tony comes in as I am pulling at the skin on my cheeks, groaning. He looks at me with real alarm.

'You'll be fine,' he says. 'You've read his books loads of times. You've *interviewed* him.'

'Still …' I say. 'The words just aren't coming out. I'm stuck.'

'Maybe you shouldn't do this anymore,' he says, drawing me into a hug.

* * * *

Leo tells me, rather grandly, that he plans to treat me *like a queen* for Mother's Day. 'You deserve it!'

'Why, thank you,' I respond.

We are passing through the Myer cosmetics department; his phrase makes me think of all those smarmy ads with the models assuring you that *you're worth* buying expensive face cream or scientifically advanced mascara.

Cycling home from school on Thursday, he calls back along the footpath over the wind and traffic noise, 'For Mother's Day, Mum, I'm not going to get you anything. I'm going to donate money for breast cancer instead!'

Something about his tone is suspicious, hovering between generosity and punishment. He's just asked me if he can make his own lunches from now on; I've said no, suspecting he wants to pack them with sugar and salt. I imagine chip sandwiches, no fruit, chocolate as his snack.

'That's lovely, how nice,' I say.

There is silence from the bike ahead.

'We-ell, actually … I'm going to pretend Mother's Day doesn't even *exist*.'

'That's fine,' I call smoothly. 'Because I was planning to do exactly the same thing about your birthday.'

'My BIRTHDAY?'

'Yup.'

'This year?'

'Uh huh.'

'Oh. I'm only joking, you know, Mum.'

That night, Tony and I are on the couch watching Gordon Ramsay and eating take-away noodles. I tell him about Leo's breast cancer plan.

'He *told* you?' he says.

'What do you mean? You mean he didn't make it up to piss me off?'

'No. Something about donating to breast cancer came on television the other night. You were sitting between us. We looked at each other and we nodded.'

'So he *was* doing it to be nice. At least, at first.'

* * * *

On Sunday morning, I am woken by a hug.

'Happy Mother's Day, your Majesty. Would you like breakfast?'

'Um, maybe later.'

I think every mother feels conflicted about Mother's Day breakfasts: one the one hand, it's very thoughtful. On the other, you usually end up eating concoctions or combinations you'd never usually consider eating—especially for breakfast—with a smile plastered on your face. As well as Vegemite crackers with an apple ('I'm not allowed to use the toaster'), I've had hot chocolate with marshmallows ('I don't know how to make coffee'), a muesli bar.

My presents are chocolate almonds (my favourite vice) and cupcakes from the school's Mother's Day stall. He has made me a book about Ben 10, his favourite cartoon. Best of all, I get a card with a Mother's Day poem:

Mother's Day is like, a day for yo mama
So don't give her no drama
Let her wear pyjamas
While this day is mama o'rama

Yo!
MAMA'S DAY

We eat breakfast at a cafe down the road, at Tony's suggestion. I order poached eggs, sautéed potatoes and roast tomato; Leo has a crumpet with honey. Tony and I split the weekend papers; Leo reads the latest issue of the AFL kids' magazine. We try to draw him out but get about three sentences out of him. We give up. I feel compelled to make the effort, but I secretly like this quiet companionship of readers, the three of us together alone.

Nikki's partner George, a fellow freelancer, is eating at a table across the cafe, his laptop on a chair beside him. I duck my head, hoping he won't see me. We were at the same party last night; I am still wearing the same dress. The dress I was wearing when he dropped me at my front door at 1 am.

In the old days, being seen in the same dress I wore to a party the night before meant I *got lucky*. Or got really, really trashed. I still remember trying to sneak in to work the day after the Christmas party when Tony and I got together, wearing the slinky black dress and knee-high boots that everyone had seen me wear the night before.

Today, the day-old dress means that after George dropped me home, I fell asleep on the couch watching *Veronica Mars* on my laptop until 3.30 am. That when I woke two hours later and crawled into bed, I couldn't be bothered peeling off my dress. And I was so tired when I got up that I decided—*what the hell*—I'd shower and change after breakfast.

'Hi,' says George, coming over. 'How are *you* this morning?'

'Great.' I quickly change the subject. 'Working on a Sunday? Really?'

He tries to make conversation with Leo but gets about three sentences out of him, too.

In the afternoon, we take Leo and Steven to the movies to see *Iron Man*. It has something for everyone: Robert Downey Jr for me, comic book characters for the kids, action for Tony. The boys are so excited that they run along the footpath, shouting, startling the shoppers.

'Guys! This is a *Mother's Day* outing!' I remind them. 'Please make this fun for *me*.'

They slow to a kind of half-walk, half-skip.

The candy bar has run out of choc-tops and the ATM has run out of money. I sulk over my popcorn.

Angus, Tom and their dad are in front of us in the line for tickets. The boys see each other; they grab each others' arms and squeal, jumping up and down on the spot. Their dad, Tony and I nod coolly at each other, exchanging bright, careful *hello*s. In the cinema, we sit directly behind Angus and Tom. Their dad pulls pieces of fruit from a backpack; he hands them each an apple, then methodically peels a banana and bites into it.

'Steven, you're eating all the popcorn!' whines Leo, his voice loud in the dark.

'Well, *you're* drinking all the raspberry lemonade!'

Stupidly, we have bought them one large drink and one large popcorn to share.

'Shut *up*, boys!' I hiss. 'Share!'

The night ends with Leo and me, alone, eating Cambodian fried rice in front of the television. Tony is in the city; he and his brother are taking Margaret out to dinner. I'm here with my child, but I feel curiously alone. If Tony were the father of my child, he wouldn't be organising dinner for his mum; he'd be organising it for me. It reminds me of a Mother's Day early in our relationship, in the break-up-get-back-together days, when I cried because he was going to spend Mother's Day with his mum and I would be alone with my three-year-old.

I admire single mothers, but I didn't like being one.

Maybe it would be different, easier, if I lived in Adelaide. When you grow up with four brothers and sisters and nineteen cousins, it's hard to accept that two people might be a family.

27. LOVE OUR WAY

'**No offence, Mum.** I really like this house and it's really fun … but I miss Quentin.'

Mark is overseas, so it's been nearly three weeks since Leo has seen his little brother. He wants me to invite his stepmother to Auskick this week, to ask if she'll bring Quentin to see him.

Rachel has never come to Auskick, though Quentin usually comes once a fortnight with Mark. They live on the other side of the West Gate Bridge; I doubt she'll come all this way.

But to my surprise, she emails to say that she'll be there if the weather is fine. (Quentin has a cold.) Saturday morning is crisp but radiant: a golden haze bathes the world in a cold glow.

I like the fantasy of a *Love My Way* kind of blended family. Dinner at each other's houses and joint family celebrations. The characters in the television series babysit for each other; the stepmother and the real mother occasionally meet for coffee. Sure, there's the occasional barbed comment, but essentially they're one big family in which all the people who have to see each other on a regular basis feel comfortable with each other, invested in each other's happiness.

We're pretty good, as far as these things go. Other split-custody parents often tell me they're envious, that Mark and I are the ideal separated couple. We talk on the phone all the time, about how Leo is going at school, how much sugar he's having, what forms are due in (or overdue) at the school. We easily swap days or rearrange our schedules to accommodate Mark's overseas trips, my visits to Adelaide, work meetings or social engagements.

But we're not the fantasy.

* * * *

Nikki is also coming to watch Leo play this morning. She emailed last night to ask about his team colours.

There are no team colours, I write back. *But they do wear red or black bibs. His team is North Melbourne. They're blue and white.*

I spot her as I climb through the hole in the cyclone wire fence to the oval. Her neck is swaddled in an enormous blue-and-white scarf over a navy knit top. She is buttoned into a 1960s-style knitted coat, white with navy pinstripes. It skirts her hips in a jaunty A-line. She is scanning the field from behind giant prescription sunglasses. She is a vision of childlessness in a sea of tracksuits, padded parkas and misshapen woollies. She is even wearing lipstick. When she sees me, she responds with the energetic wave of a morning person.

'Nice colours,' is the first thing I say. 'I'm impressed.'

She gives a little half-twirl.

'Coffee?' I ask, after pointing out Tony and Leo on the oval.

'Any good?'

'We-ell. It's okay. Not bad. It's pretty good for coffee you can buy in the carpark of a kid's footy game.'

'I can only do one coffee a day.'

'Skip it.'

She follows me across the bitumen fringe of the oval and past the parents huddled around the card table where they will later sell two-dollar hotdogs and alarmingly coloured 'fruit' drinks. There is no line in front of the small van parked in the oval's driveway, which holds a coffee machine, some jars of marshmallows and cartons of milk, and stacks of Styrofoam cups. A small boy takes my money as I place my order for a latte with his apron-clad mother.

'Wow,' says Nikki. 'Fancy.'

We sit on a bench facing the oval, where we can see Tony and Leo practising footy drills in the far distance. I unwrap a muesli bar from my bag: breakfast. (Nikki, of course, ate a proper breakfast in her kitchen this morning.) We exhale gossip in heady clouds: people we work with, people we used to work with, our partners. We talk in the uninterrupted flow of freelancers on day release. It's exhilarating, having conversations like this at a kids' event. Worlds are colliding and I like it.

Leo spots us and sprints across the oval. 'Hi, Nikki! Mum, I need water!'

I hand him the Auskick bottle he left by the front door this morning, forgotten at the last minute. He gulps at it, hands it back and disappears.

Nikki and I jump the fence and follow him across the oval to stand at the edge of the training drills: rows of small figures, most of them in official AFL jumpers and shorts, stand facing each other across the grass. The coaches and their helpers, including Tony, stand in the centre. The lines wriggle back and forth, side to side, as the boys shove and wrestle each other. Headlocks, grabbing at torsos, skipping and dodging. Leo is one of the wrestlers, his face intent. It's just fun right now, but my stomach twists at the possibility of it all.

'I hate the way boys do this,' I tell Nikki. 'I can't watch him. By the way, Rachel is coming today. She's bringing Quentin.'

'Really?'

That's when we see her, standing just outside the fence of the oval, head spinning in search of a familiar face. She is easy to spot: a smooth blonde curtain of hair falling over a sensible black woollen coat; a marshmallow blob of puffy parka and oversized beanie wobbling beside her at knee-height.

'We should wave, right?' I say. 'We should go and bring her over here?'

'Yes,' says Nikki. 'We should.'

The marshmallow is clutching a fist-sized green ball. He is beaming from beneath wisps of orange hair that have escaped over his forehead. He staggers determinedly towards the oval, towards the boys and their balls. More specifically, he staggers towards the nearest bright yellow football and bends to pick it up. It is bigger than his head, the size of his torso. He drops it and kicks it along the ground, then follows with a beatific smile. I have seen him do this before, but it still staggers me.

Leo, at this age, had more interest in a football than he did in a bug or a leaf—that is, some but not much. He certainly had no idea what to do with it.

'I remember when Leo was five,' I say. 'His teacher told me I needed to teach him ball skills. I used to kick the footy with him in the driveway after school and he'd be practically in tears. I used to bribe him, saying that after one more kick he could go back inside to his books and comics.'

Nikki laughs. I look over at Leo now, chasing the ball with the fierce, unyielding devotion that usually drives him to tears of frustration at least once a game.

Rachel, Nikki and I settle into a rhythm of small-talk, mostly about working from home, which we all do.

'How's it going with Mark working from home now?' I ask.

'Well, he hasn't been here much.' Pause. 'But he's ... I guess you must have heard about his new Mac Air laptop?'

'Yep.'

'He loves his toys,' says Rachel. 'Anyway, the week before he left he spent all this time playing with the computer and trying to get all the Macs talking to each other and I was in the lounge room, working, and the network was going down because he was playing with it.' She sighs. 'So, I'm getting more work done now he's gone. But it's been long enough. I'm ready for him to come home now.'

Quentin is tunnelling into her chest, his little arms diving into her armpits. 'Muuuummy!' he wails. She holds him close.

'It's his cold. He's a bit clingy,' she says. 'I had to take him to the toilet with me this morning. I had to sit him on my lap.'

'Wow. That sounds awful.'

It's conversations like this that convince me I don't want another child—the idea of rewinding to those labour-intensive days of early childhood leaves me cold. And then there's my conviction that the child would be Asperger's—or maybe even full-blown autistic. What if the child *wasn't* autistic at all? Would I know how to mother such a child—a 'normal' child?

Quentin totters across the oval again as we talk. He stands, transfixed, between the goalposts, while a flock of boys swoops back and forth in his direction. Rachel runs to rescue him. While she's gone, I start telling Nikki about my week spent fighting with Australia Post about my missing parcels.

'Oh, I hate that,' says Rachel, returning. 'I'm always having to chase missing parcels.'

'They told me I should get everyone to send everything registered mail; that's their solution.'

'You can't do that,' says Rachel. 'That's ridiculous.'

'I know.' I sigh. 'Tony won't let me talk to Australia Post anymore. After I swore at them.'

'What did you say?' asks Rachel.

'Oh, I told them to go fuck themselves.'

'What?' says Nikki. We all laugh.

'Yeah, she was about to hang up on me. I'd just threatened to call *A Current Affair* on her.'

Both Nikki and Rachel are looking at me in disbelief.

'I know … I don't know why I said that.'

I decide not to tell them that after I swore, a small voice piped up from across the room and a small head bobbed above the couch and said, 'MUM!'

'I know darling,' I said. 'I know it was naughty of me. I said it after they hung up but it was so naughty of me.'

'You said it after they hung up, huh?'

'Yep.'

'That's two dollars in the swear jar, Mum.'

We don't have a swear jar.

I've revealed bad behaviour to the other half of Leo's family, though only part of it. But we're all laughing, we all hate Australia Post and we're all exclaiming over Quentin's ball skills and cheering for Leo when he gets the ball.

This is going just fine.

I mention that I am cooking meals more often.

'Why?' asks Nikki.

'She's becoming a *grown-up*!' says Rachel.

I don't answer. We move on, quickly.

It's the final moments of the game. Leo gets the ball in a daring semi-tackle. He runs towards the goalposts, aims and kicks. It's a goal! The three of us cheer and call his name. He runs in a circle on the field, his own tiny victory lap. He directs princely nods at his teammates, acknowledging their admiration even before they give it. The boys gather in a tight circle, then scatter. Leo runs towards us. The game is over.

He runs, smiling, in a straight line. He is going to hug someone. He bends and embraces his baby brother in a running tackle, picking him up and running towards us. Quentin's arms flail at right angles from under his embrace; his legs dangle as if bracing for a fall. His orange head nestles in Leo's chest. Leo puts him down and smiles into his face, their eyes just centimetres apart.

'Did you see me kick a goal at siren?' he asks us.

'Yeah!' says Nikki. 'We all cheered your name. Didn't you hear us?'

'No! Did you? Thanks! Thanks for coming, Nikki. Thanks for bringing Quentin, Rachel.'

And the brothers are off, following Tony across the oval to kick the football one last time.

'I have to be at work soon,' says Nikki. 'If we're going to get that coffee …'

'Yeah, I'm going to get a coffee too,' says Rachel.

Nikki and I look at each other.

'Why don't you join us?' says Nikki.

'Yes, go on,' I echo.

'Um … okay, sure.'

And so we end the morning squeezed around a laminated table built for four—Nikki, Rachel, Quentin, Leo, Tony and me—eating muffins and sipping hot drinks, continuing a polite conversation that is beginning to strain at the seams, but manages not to tear.

Maybe we're not so far from *Love My Way*, after all.

28. FAKING IT

A publisher invites me to an industry awards night to make up the numbers on their table. When my bookshop colleagues go to book launches or dinners, they travel as a pack, organising things by conversations across the shared office space. Because I'm not there, they often forget to invite me. Most of the time, this suits me. I get to stay home in my jeans and cardigans, guilt-free. But on the day the invitation comes, I like the idea of getting out of my own headspace. Besides, I'm wildly flattered. So I say yes.

Two days before the event, an old employer, Stephanie, calls to say she's coming to town for the awards dinner, and would I like to be her date? I tell her I'm already going.

'Why did they ask *you*?' she says.

'I don't know.' I imagine that they have decided to offer me a book contract, based on … my book reviews? A hunch that I could write a really good book?

We arrange to meet for drinks beforehand.

On the day of the event, my manager calls to ask if I want to join the bookshop table. 'I'm sorry it's such short notice,' she says. 'We thought we'd already invited you, but I just realised we forgot.'

I explain that I'm already spoken for.

'Oh good,' she says. 'We'll see you there.' And then her tone becomes breezy. '*So*, why are you going with *them*?'

'I don't know.' Maybe they want to offer me a job!

The awards dinner is held at an underground ballroom on Collins Street. Stephanie and I are photographed at the door as we walk the red carpet of the crowded lobby, where publishing folk mob under the metres-high ceilings and lit golden walls, quaffing free champagne. I hadn't expected so many people; half the publishing industry is here. And I can't believe there's actually a red carpet.

Inside the cavern-like ballroom, we sit beneath candle-studded chandeliers that droop like stalactites. The room is dim, each table its own haven of light amid the baroque gloom. I sit between an author whose book I have favourably reviewed who is up for an award, and a publicist in a strappy gown of a pale silvery-blue. On the other side of her sits a renowned crime author. Another publicist, in a black satin dress, introduces me to the publisher who comments warmly on my coverage of their books. *Ah, that's why I'm here.* Secretly, I knew this all along. But it was fun to fantasise. Looking around, I am starting to feel self-conscious in my grey woollen tunic dress and purple stockings. I am dressed for lunch in a cafe, not dinner in a ballroom.

Talking to the author I've reviewed is easy. She tells me that my review of her book was her favourite and I allow myself to be flattered, though I know I shouldn't be. We talk creative writing courses (I am thinking of taking one, she teaches in one), mutual friends and books we've read. *This is easy*, I think. *I'm doing fine.*

At the end of the ceremony, before dessert, most of the table leaves to mingle with the rest of the room. I could go and find Stephanie or my work colleagues, but I'm struck with a shyness that pins me to my seat. Once I move, I'm obliged to start a conversation somewhere. Sitting here, it's less obvious if I'm alone. This leaves just the crime writer, one empty seat away, and me. He nods laconically in my direction. I can't think of anything to say, but now that eye contact has been exchanged, it seems awkward not to say something.

We talk, haltingly, about working from home; the thing we have in common. About sleeping in, working late at night.

'So-o-o, did you drag yourself out of bed to come to this?' I ask.

He looks evenly back at me. 'Well, I didn't drag myself out of *bed*,' he says. 'I dragged myself off the *couch*.'

The unspoken fact that this event began at 6 pm, that this would entail an extraordinary amount of time for a person to sleep in, hovers between us. I vaguely realise that I have either a) insulted him, b) revealed how stupid I am, or c) both.

'There was nothing on TV anyway,' he continues, battling on. He takes a drink. 'But there's never much on TV.'

'Yeah,' I say, 'but I like *House*.'

'Oh dear.'

'Alright then.' I madly rummage inside my mental bag of scraps for something more highbrow to admit to. 'I like *Insight* on SBS.'

'Even worse,' he says, arching an eyebrow.

'I give up,' I mock-huff, genuinely exhausted. 'You don't like my trash *or* my highbrow choices.'

He likes *Skins*.

It is raining. A fine mist falls outside the lounge-room window; a hypnotic rhythm plays on the roof above. I am curled on the couch, wrapped in a poncho, eating pear and chocolate tart with a fork and reading the new David Sedaris. This is work, sort of. Children's voices sound on the footpath. *That's odd.* I look out the window to see the turquoise and navy uniform of the primary school down the road. *They must have been let out early*, I think. More voices, this time a chorus of them, rising and falling as they hurry along the footpath and through the rain. I leap up and check the time on my computer in the study.

It is 3.40 pm.

I stare at the time for a whole minute, until it changes to 3.41 pm. I was supposed to pick up Leo ten minutes ago; supposed to leave the house half an hour ago.

I try calling the school, to ask them to send a message to Leo that I'll be late. Engaged. After Care, in case he's gone there. Engaged. Call Lucy, in case she's in the yard. It goes to voicemail.

I swear, bang the phone on the desk. Try the school again. Swear again.

Outside, my bike is standing in the rain. So is my helmet, upturned and pooled with water. I wipe the bike seat with a towel and back into my parka sleeves. Riding along the footpath (I'm not going to risk the road with no helmet), I barrel past the turquoise and navy school kids, scattering them in my wake. One of my ugg boots is tucked inside my jeans leg; the other jeans leg rides above my boot, just below my knee. It's raining hard; I squint into it as I ride, ducking my head as if to shrink from the onslaught.

A block of black-clad teenagers, high-schoolers, advances towards me. As I swerve to the grass to avoid them, they mumble at me in the kind of shouted aside you're clearly meant to overhear.

'She's CRAZY, man!'

'Fuck off!' I call over my shoulder.

As I cycle through Cruikshank Park, I pass Jack and his dad, who waves at me with a grin.

'Oh-ho!' he calls. 'You're late!'

At the school gate, I jump off and walk the bike through the mud of the playground. Outside After Care, under the tin-roof verandah, some kids are huddled over a foosball table, shouting and laughing. One of them is Jai from Leo's class. He glances up at me, mid-play.

'Hey,' he says. 'Leo is …'

And then Leo bowls into my waist.

'I'm *so* sorry,' I say.

'What happened? Were you working?'

'Um, yes. Sort of. I was reading this book and I lost track of time.'

'Oh,' he says serenely. 'It must have been pretty good, huh?' He goes to get his bag.

'Hello.' Bhanu appears at my side. 'What happened to you?'

'I can't tell you. It's too embarrassing.'

'Go on,' she pleads. 'Please!'

Her mouth forms a round *O* as she hears that I lost track of time because I was reading a book.

'Don't worry about it,' she says. 'Last year, in daylight savings, my mum forgot to change the clocks and she was an *hour* late.'

'Were you worried?'

'Nah, I was bored. I had to wait in the office.' I look at Leo, who is leaping around the soccer table, cheering Jai on. When Jai's team gets a goal, Leo hugs him, or attempts a high-five. Jai is only half paying attention; he doesn't seem to mind.

Bhanu pats my arm. 'Don't worry,' she advises. 'It happens *all the time.*'

Over dinner, I tell Tony about my encounter with the school kids.

'You swore at kids?'

'Yeah.'

'Good one.' He shakes his head.

'They were *high-school* kids.'

'Hmmm. What did they say to you?'

'They called me crazy.'

'What were you doing?'

'Just riding down the footpath. I guess I had my head down because of the rain. But I was about to swerve around them.'

'Well, you probably did look crazy.'

'Because I had my head down while I was riding?'

'No. You look crazy when you ride your bike sometimes.'

'Just normally?'

'Yeah. You put your head really close to the handlebars. Like this.' He demonstrates. I punch him, not too hard.

The literary editor of a major newspaper replies to my email pitching him a book review. He says, 'Yes, please' and gives me a word count.

I scream when I read the email.

Tony looks up from his computer screen, concerned. 'Good or bad?' he asks.

'Good!'

I have been pitching to this editor, on and off, for years; we have recently met.

I ring Kabita and scream. We make plans to go out for a celebratory lunch.

We venture out in the dark to collect our fish-and-chips dinner, Leo and me. He plays with a torch in the laundry as I lace my sneakers. He flicks it on and off like a disco ball, shines it into my eyes, then laughs as I flinch. He shines it into his own eyes. And into mine again. I snatch the torch away and set it firmly on the washing machine.

'But it's dark outside,' he protests.

'We don't need a torch. There are street lamps.'

But I'm wrong; there are no street lamps here, at Aireys Inlet. As we leave the lights of Margaret's beach house and step into the driveway, we are swallowed by an eerie blackness. True darkness. We walk with our arms outstretched, feeling our way forward.

'Keep to the right!' I warn. 'Away from the dirt pile!'

I hear him veering to the left. The dirt pile in the driveway, topsoil waiting for Margaret to shovel it onto the garden, holds an inexorable attraction. In the daylight, when we're watching him, he creeps around the edge of it, his sneakers kissing its muddy plains. I yank his arm.

As we reach the road it's still dark, but we can see again. Our way is lit by the windows of the houses we pass. I tip my head back idly and gasp at the view. 'Leo, look!'

It's like static fireworks. Trails of glittering dust streak the ceiling of the enveloping darkness. These are real stars, not the isolated, faint pinpricks of light we see at home. I explain to Leo that normally we can't see these stars because they're drowned out by streetlights.

'I know, Mum.'

We walk to the main road with our heads tipped to the heavens.

Tony and I got married here, in Margaret and Edwina's backyard. Tony went to bed early, unwell, while the wedding guests were still dancing in the driveway, which had been transformed into a bar for the occasion, wooden boards laid over the gravel. I stayed until late, under the pretext that it would be rude for us *both* to abandon our guests, many of them from Adelaide. But really, I was being selfish. It was, perhaps, my diva moment.

All day, everyone had remarked on what a *calm bride* I had been. I only used a hairdresser because my sisters had hired one. My cousin Ali improvised bridesmaids' bouquets out of flowers picked from Margaret's garden because I didn't think it was necessary. My sister Liz did my make-up, Mum sewed my dress and we didn't hire a photographer but decided to rely on family and friends' photos. The day before the wedding, I sat on a beach with a book all afternoon; I got married with sunburned shoulders, halterneck bather-straps etched in relief on my skin.

After my sister Sarah had disappeared with one of Tony's friends and long after Margaret and Edwina had gone upstairs to bed, the remaining guests turned off the music and moved the party up the road to the local pub. I had changed from my wedding dress, with its voluminous tulle skirt, into a filmy bronze silk dress: transforming from The Bride into one of the party.

Some guests, on their way back to their hotels or rented houses, drove us to the pub in carloads. There was one of my brothers, a handful of my cousins, my friend Adam. And my Uncle Michael, who was drunker than the rest of us, alternating between telling filthy stories about John Howard and worrying that his mother had seen him smoking. ('Your Nana will *kill* me!')

In the pub, my drunken relatives struck up conversations with the locals, telling them that it was my wedding night and I was the bride.

'You're not,' said one twentysomething boy in a surf T-shirt and jeans. 'Where's your wedding dress?'

'Left it at home.'

'Then where's the groom?'

'He's in bed.'

Michael asked our opinion on whether a woman he'd been talking to was into him.

'We never see you like this, Michael,' laughed Simon. 'You're usually so quiet.'

'I've got five sisters!' he snorted. 'Wouldn't you be quiet, too?'

Then someone reported that the surfer boy and his mate were convincing my youngest cousin to go to the beach with them, alone. Michael snapped into sobriety; Simon worked himself up into aggrieved gallantry.

'Her mother would *kill* me!' said Michael, shaking his head. 'I'm her uncle. I'm supposed to be looking after her. I think I'm in charge.'

'That's how girls get date raped,' murmured Simon darkly.

We assured Michael that he had done his job well. My young cousin, who was still in high school, whispered that everyone was treating her *like a baby*.

'I'm old enough to look after myself,' she said. 'I would have been *fine.*'

It was midnight; the bartender announced the pub was closing. We walked across the carpark in a loose pack, all of us drunk and none of us driving, and started down the Great Ocean Road, shocked at the plunge into a rural blackness so thick that we were blind to each other; we dissolved into disembodied voices in the night. Somehow, we got home unharmed, despite the revelation by the occasional car headlight that we had strayed onto the road.

The group split again; Simon, Michael, Adam and I retired to the house next door to Margaret's, where Simon was staying. Adam and Michael raided the driveway bar while Simon and I sat upstairs on the deck, gazing in the direction of my wedding debris.

My missing sister appeared below us.

After one final drink, I left the party and, arms stretched to feel for unseen obstacles, went through the dark to the house across the road where Tony was sleeping. He woke up as I came in.

Two days later, when my family returned to Adelaide, I cried. It had been wonderful to have everyone in my life together in one place, for just a few days.

Now I am sitting on the balcony, eating Vegemite toast and sipping plunger coffee. I have borrowed Margaret's robe; it swims about my ankles and threatens to swallow my arms. The pants leg of my purple polka-dot pyjamas protrudes from the hem. I am basking in the sunlight that flashes on and off all day here, alternating with shrouded grey skies and light curtains of rain. Tony and Leo stand at my side, looking out at the lighthouse in the distance, the postcard view marred only by the blocky mansion that seems, from this angle, to climb from its base.

Cockatoos swarm the branches of the tree next door. The whole of Aireys Inlet smells of smoke. It is the aroma of wood fires burning in every house.

We are squatting on the fringe of the beach in the rain, dogs wandering at our feet, sniffing around the toilet block just metres away. Doug's lead dangles from his collar. I am distracted, helping Leo wedge his wet, sandy feet into sneakers. No-one is around. And then somebody is.

A tall man in a navy beanie. Broad shoulders, blond hair just visible, an outdoors tan even in winter. He nods at us; I nod too, then turn back to urge Leo's heel into his shoe. An eruption of barking and scuffling rends the air, just over my shoulder. The man is kicking the dogs off his leg. Doug tumbles in one direction; Snuffy—who never bites or even growls, only jumps on any human being nearby as if they're a potential best friend—goes flying in the other direction. He's not just kicking them off; he's aiming at them and kicking them. Hard. There are terrible, piercing squeals, as if a car has hit them.

Leo and I gape as the man strides over and leans into us, shouting and swearing. The dogs run to us and sit still, barking. I am mortified, but don't know what to think. As I gather my jumbled thoughts, he draws back his leg and delivers a hard kick to Doug's guts, with the force of a footballer aiming for the other end of the field. There is a sickening thud as his foot connects with the dog's underside and Doug flies across the sand, literally twisting in the air before he lands, dazed, on the grass.

'You could apologise!' he yells. 'Your fucking dog fucking bit me!'

'Well, I would have,' I find myself saying. 'I am sorry, but you shouldn't have done that. I would say sorry if you hadn't just kicked the dog like that.'

'Well, he can't bite me! You're going to pay for this. There's an eight-hundred-dollar fine. I could report you.'

'Fine, do it,' I say.

Leo dissolves into tears as the man runs towards Snuffy. Before he reaches her, Leo grabs her, burying his face in her damp, gritty fur.

'She's a good dog!' he shouts. 'She didn't deserve that! How could you kick her? She's a good dog!'

The man stalks off. Leo sobs into Snuffy's neck as he strokes her.

'She doesn't deserve it!' he cries. 'She loves everyone! She just doesn't deserve it.'

I hug him and hug the dog, even pulling Doug back towards us. I pat him too, even though I know this started with him barking at the man, the man kicking at him, then Doug biting him.

I can actually understand the man's first kick—a reaction to shock. But the second, calculated revenge kick was just wrong.

When Leo is composed enough to move again, we get up and head for home, the dogs' leads firm in my hand. The man appears again further down the road, beside a glossy four-wheel drive.

'Right!' he says, stomping up to us. 'I want your name and number.' I see that he is holding paper and a pen.

'No.' I keep walking, holding Leo's hand tight.

'So, you know you're wrong!'

'I could report *you* to the RSPCA for kicking the dog like that. He doesn't seem well.'

'Fine, give me your name and I'll see you in court. We'll see who wins.'

Leo turns to him and clenches his fists. 'Well, it won't be YOU!' he yells. I take his hand and lead him away, ignoring the shouts at our backs.

'I wonder what just happened back there,' I muse, half to myself.

'You know how they say dogs know if someone is a nice person or not?' says Leo.

'Mmmm?'

'Well …'

Leo rushes into the house ahead of me, calling out. The dogs chase at his heels.

'Tony, TONY!'

'Hey,' Tony looks up from his book. 'What's up?'

We tell him the story in a duet of righteous panic, talking over the ends of each other's sentences.

'That's IT!' says Tony, lacing his sneakers. 'I'm going to find him.' He pats Leo's arm. 'But you did the right thing not to give him our details; we don't want someone like that knowing where we live. He didn't follow you home, did he?'

We shut the dogs in the laundry and return to the scene of the crime, half walking, half running. From the balcony Leo watches us leave. The man and his car are gone; I'm secretly relieved.

Back at the house, we gather on the couch in a tangle of dogs and arms and legs. We decide to leave later, after dinner perhaps, or even in the morning. For now, Tony re-lights the fire, Leo pulls Snuffy onto his lap and we sit a little longer.

29. MADNESS AT THE MCG

We walk from Flinders Street station to the MCG, along the river. Bare-limbed European trees are stark against the bleak sky; the Yarra is a serene sheet of grey glass. A Ferris wheel with candy-coloured seats stands empty by the river, alongside a doughnut van and a roundabout.

We cross the bridge over the tennis centre. Breathy voices whisper and chant at our knees, didgeridoo music swirling behind the song. The disembodied voices, Indigenous storytellers, are emanating from loudspeakers built into the bridge. It feels literally haunted by those who came before us, singing over the sodden green tennis courts below.

'I don't like this,' I say, stopping in the middle of the bridge. 'It feels like a bad omen.'

Tony laughs.

It's MCG day for Auskick; Tony, as an assistant coach, will be working with the kids on the oval. Last year, the game ended with Leo wandering a corner of the vast oval, blinded by howling tears, snot running into his open mouth. Punching himself repeatedly in the head, growling, 'I suck at this! I'm no good!'

But last year, we didn't know he had Asperger's. Last year, we hadn't briefed the coaches on his behavioural issues or convinced them that his tantrums were due to something other than overindulgent parenting.

'MUM! TONY!' Leo bowls us over with a flying hug. I look at his legs, pale and purple-tinged. He is wearing navy cotton school shorts with a khaki padded parka.

'Have you got my lucky skivvy? Look at my footy shorts!'

'They're … great.'

I have a thing about Leo wearing shorts in the cold, but decide to let this one through to the keeper. After all, he's not the only one in footy shorts (if the only one in school shorts). He's going to be running around soon, anyway.

Tony hands Leo his lucky skivvy and his football boots. The lucky skivvy is yolk-coloured, with a number one drawn on the back with a permanent texta and a leg kicking a football on the chest. The mythic game where Leo kicked seven goals, he was wearing this skivvy, he told Tony on the phone this morning—so it is lucky and must be worn to the G.

I am in favour of any lucky charm.

I watch him in his yellow skivvy, navy knee-length shorts and white socks pulled to the knees, playing a ferocious game of handball with Tony outside the curved concrete wall of the stadium. His hair brushes his eyebrows in an outgrown mop top. He is surrounded by kids in top-of-the-range official AFL gear and smart, camera-ready combed hair. He doesn't care. Neither do I, not really.

A carrot-topped marshmallow totters past, throwing a small red ball at the MCG wall. He barrels into the concrete and turns back again, as if on autopilot. A blonde woman snatches his ball while he's not looking and slips it into her pocket. The blonde woman looks up. It's Rachel. We exchange wary smiles and she looks away again, following the marshmallow into the crowd as he heads for the yellow Auskick football passing between Tony and Leo. Mark ambles over with his own ball, which he holds out to Quentin.

'Hey,' says Rachel. 'I'm just going to get coffee from the van. You want one?'

I don't really, having already had one on the way here, but I appreciate the gesture. 'Sure. Thanks.' I fumble in my overstuffed bag.

'Nah, I'll get it. Don't worry about it.' And the crowd swallows her up.

✴ ✴ ✴ ✴

Kids and parents enter the MCG in separate lines. Leo squirms with excitement in the line beside us. We offer parting encouragements. 'Have fun!' 'You'll be great!' 'Remember to have a positive attitude!'

We sit in the bottom of the stands, just metres from where Leo is training: Tony, me, Mark, Rachel and Quentin. Tony stands on his seat, his eyes hopefully on the oval.

'What are you doing?' I hiss. 'Sit down next to me.'

'I'm looking to see where the security guards are, to see if I can sneak onto the ground.'

He was told, just before we filed into the G, that he can't participate today, after all. It's coaches only: no assistants.

'Right.' I leave him to it and look around glumly. 'I don't think we can ever have another child,' I say.

'Why?'

'I don't think I can bear the idea of having to make friends with parents. You know, starting at the beginning again.'

Tony doesn't reply. He is intent on the fun he is missing out on.

We move closer to the action, leaving Mark, Rachel and Quentin behind as we settle directly in front of Leo's team. The drills are going well. Leo is joking around with the kids in his line. They take turns jumping on each other's backs, grabbing for imaginary balls, shouting to each other. It looks like there is real interaction going on. Last year, it was Leo crash-landing endless jokes against a wall of bemused indifference.

I climb over to the front row and lean over the barrier to the oval, camera raised. Through the lens, the small figure that is Leo stops, looks straight at me and waves. They are handing out red and black bibs. The game is starting.

It is sadly, predictably, awful. Tony, Mark, Rachel and I negotiate the maze of seating to follow the leaping figures on the field, shouting encouragement across the ground.

'You can do it!'

'Get in there!'

'Good on you, Leo!'

'Remember your attitude!'

This last one is me.

We marvel at his ragdoll doggedness, the way he throws himself in front of the ball at every chance, however slim. Physically, he is remarkably hardy; forever flung to the ground, picked up and flung forward again. But it doesn't take too many setbacks before the first tears come; once he cracks, he is soon broken.

The referee, who isn't usually with this group of kids and doesn't really know them, shouts for Leo to *get in there and tackle*. So he launches himself at a kid and takes him down like a bowling pin. And gets a penalty. Because they're not really allowed to tackle; the coach didn't mean it literally, he meant *knock the ball out of his hands*. But Leo didn't know that.

He passes the ball to a teammate near the goal and the teammate kicks it through the posts. Leo had expected him to kick it back to him so he could take the goal.

He charges a teammate who kicks a wide ball to him, stopping just short of thumping him.

'NO!' I shout. 'LEO, NO! DON'T DO IT!'

'You can't get upset,' says Tony. 'It won't help him.'

I nod despairingly, watching him drag his feet across the field, pinned by the weight of his own melancholy.

At the end of the game, he bleeds towards us, howling his frustration. 'This is the worst game ever! It's the worst day of my life!'

His coach tries to comfort him, as he has throughout the game, but now that there's no next step to push him forward to, he has come completely undone.

'Come for your team photo, mate,' urges the coach.

'No, I don't want to.'

'It's to remember the day by.'

'I don't want to remember this day. I never want to remember this day.'

Leo stands to the side of the gathered children—the whole of the Footscray/Yarraville Auskick, smiling for the cameras wielded on the other side of the oval fence. Everyone is waiting for Leo's tantrum to end.

'My feet are pinned to the ground,' he wails, holding his body determinedly still, his arms rigid by his side, his fists balled. The coach scoops him up in his big arms and carries him over to the group where he stands him back on his feet.

Tony, Mark, Rachel and I cheer and whoop. We call out that he's played a good game. Last year, we greeted this behaviour with stern admonitions. I'm still not sure which approach we should be taking. I want to leap over the fence and smack him; I want to fold him in my arms and comfort him; I want to weep with humiliation and defeat.

Leo plants himself apart from the group, sidestepping a good metre or two away from the rest. His arms crossed, he scowls back at us.

Tony and Mark leap over the maze of seats to meet Leo as he leaves the oval. Rachel and I stand looking at each other. For a moment, we don't talk; but it's not awkward, not really. We are joined in this moment.

'He said he doesn't want to remember this day, but he'll remember it now,' she says. 'And the pictures will tell the story.'

'Yep.' I sigh. 'I wish I could pay the psychologist to come here, watch a game and give me notes afterwards on how to handle this.'

We both laugh.

'I wonder what it must be like for you,' begins Rachel, a little un-certainly. 'Do you understand what's going through his head, what he's thinking …? You must understand the way he thinks.'

It's the first time that she has ever acknowledged that I have Asperger's too and one of the most personal conversations we've ever had. Or that I've had with anyone outside my family, really.

'Yes,' I say, after a pause. 'I do, to some extent. I understand the thinking behind it. But I don't know what to do about it or what to say or how to help him.'

'I hate team sports myself; I'm terrible at them,' says Rachel. 'So I would never be in a situation like that anyway.'

'Yeah, me too.'

We slowly ascend the stadium steps together, bonded by caring about what just happened, by having to deal with the fallout. And by hating team sports.

At the top of the steps, the boys rejoin us and we leave the MCG together: Leo's family. Rachel and I walk a few paces behind the men and boys. They pause at the ice-cream van.

'I think one of those would make me feel better,' Leo tells his dad, with a weariness that is only part affected. Mark buys him a chocolate-coated soft-serve cone with coloured sprinkles. I watch him bite through the hard surface, losing himself in his sugary consolation.

'Hmmm,' I say. 'I'm glad it's you and not me today.'

* * * *

It is Thursday, three days before Leo's birthday. Mark rings me at 4 pm to tell me that Leo would like to bring cupcakes to class tomorrow. 'So, can you make some this evening?'

'No,' I say. 'I can't.'

'Oh.' He sounds shocked. 'Well, what if I make them and drop them to you tonight when I drop him off?'

'Sure.'

'Oh.' He pauses. 'Okay. But I thought I'd give you the chance to do it, you know, because it's your thing. You do it every year.'

'He's in Year Three now,' I say. 'They don't do that anymore. I'm not baking him cakes to take to school every birthday *for his whole life.*'

'But … he wants them. He's asked about it.'

'Well, he should have asked earlier. I have work to do tonight. I just can't.'

I am chairing a writers' festival session tomorrow.

Last year, the first time I chaired a session, I lay awake for hours the night before. When I woke, at 5 am, my whole body had frozen, as if in terror. Every time I tried to move a limb, my body went into spasms of pain that shot up my spine and attacked the nape of my neck. *I guess I can't do it*, I thought to myself. *I guess I'll just have to call in and tell them I can't move, or sit up. I'll just have to give someone my notes to use.* And with that thought, I fell asleep. When I woke, my body ached but the paralysis was gone. I did the event, squeezing drops of supposedly calm-inducing Rescue Remedy onto my tongue in a toilet cubicle beforehand. I did not freeze onstage or forget my lines.

This year, I attended a workshop on chairing delivered by an ABC radio presenter, who assured me I was actually quite good at it. I waited until the end of the day and followed him after everyone had left; I asked him for tips on battling stage fright.

'But you don't have stage fright,' he said.

'I do, actually. When I'm doing this for real.'

He gave me an exercise to physically relax the body (with the theory that the mind will follow). He went deliberately limp, slumped his shoulders and wriggled his limbs, resembling an octopus who'd taken a hit of morphine.

'It works,' he assured me. 'Just go somewhere where no-one can see you. Like a toilet cubicle.'

I have Rescue Remedy in my handbag (though I know it's a placebo, I'm trying to pretend I don't) and have practised the radio presenter's tip. Tonight, I plan to read over my notes and practise reading my questions and introduction aloud so they'll sound natural tomorrow.

There is no time for cakes in my schedule.

I meet Mark's car on Swanston Street, below the blue fairy lights of the Arts Centre. Leo slithers out of the car feet first as his father passes two bulging supermarket bags through the open door, tied in a filmy white bow.

'Here are the cakes and the icing,' he calls. 'It's all there. All you have to do is ice them!'

'I don't have time. I told you that.'

'The icing is made! It'll take you no time at all.'

'I have work to do.'

We glare at each other as I close the door and step back onto the footpath, pulling Leo with me. He chases the car along Swanston Street at a leisurely jog, easily keeping pace with the crawling traffic; he taps on the car window and pulls faces.

'Bye Dad, bye Dad!' he chants, skipping against the tide of suited office workers and groomed theatregoers.

'You could get yourself run over,' I snap, and pull him towards the gates of Flinders Street station.

I tell Leo that I can't ice the cakes, that I have a big talk to prepare for, that he can't ask for things at the last minute, that I *told* his dad I couldn't do it. My stomach whirls with resentment. I'm picking up Leo as a favour: Mark's car needs to go to the mechanic, and he doesn't want to take him to school on public transport tomorrow.

As Leo serenely accepts his fate, that he will be taking naked cakes to school tomorrow, I realise that I will, of course, ice the damn things.

'You *are* a good mother,' hums Tony, watching from the couch as I untie the bags and wrestle with the plastic containers of icing: one gluey-white, the other iridescent blue. North Melbourne colours. I dip a tentative finger into the blue and lick it, recoiling at the chemical assault on my tongue. I cross the room and extend a blue-tipped finger to Tony. He squints at it.

'What?'

'Taste it.'

'No.'

'It's disgusting.'

'Yeah, I know it will be. It's bloody bright blue, for God's sake.'

I scrape the knife across each cake as quickly as I can. At 9 pm, I'm ready to start work.

The next morning is also Crazy Hair Day. I smother Leo's hair in surf wax and tease it upright. He looks like a sandy-haired Robert Smith, in school uniform.

'I look SO crazy!' he shouts at his reflection. 'I will DEFINITELY win the prize for craziest hair! Yeah!'

He poses on the rim of the bath, pouting at his reflection and plucking at the strings of an imaginary guitar.

We take the long way to school, so we can buy coloured hairspray on the way. Just one can remains on the pharmacy shelves; it's orange.

'There must be a school sports day or something,' apologises the assistant.

'It's Crazy Hair Day,' beams Leo.

'Ahhhh,' she smiles. 'Well, your hair certainly *is* crazy.'

'I know,' he says. 'It's my birthday, too.'

'What lovely cakes,' she says, nodding at his plastic-wrapped tray as she hands me my change.

'Yeah, all the kids always love my mum's cakes,' he says. 'She makes the *best* cakes!'

Weirdly, I am touched even as I remind him that his dad actually made them.

In the carpark, Snuffy watches, wide-eyed, as Leo dips his head and I attack it with a hissing mist of fluorescent orange. His ear is streaked with colour; so are my hands. I spit on a tissue and wipe at his ear. My hands remain stubbornly bright.

Leo bounds along Somerville Road and its growling chorus of trucks and cars. He practises leaping, in a kind of flying crouch, landing with his feet wide apart, his tongue protruding in a defiant pink arrow.

'RAAAAAAAR!'

It's an unconscious perversion of the Maori haka.

Uniformed kids emerge from a cross-street, their hair wound with coloured pipe cleaners. He leaps at them with a battle cry: 'RAAAAAAAR!'

'Oh, hello Leo,' laughs their dad. He looks at the cakes. 'Is it your birthday?'

'Yes! It is!' He turns to me, suddenly serious. 'Can you come to assembly today?'

'Sorry darling, I can't. I have to give a talk today.'

'Please? They'll give me my birthday card. I'm going to achieve my dream today—to get up on a stage in front of people looking like *this*.'

'I'm so sorry darling, but I just can't. I have to be in the city at midday and before that I have to have a shower and wash my hair and change into nice clothes.' I appeal to his finely developed sense of logic and humour. 'I can't get up on a stage in front of people like this, can I?' I gesture at my jeans and sneakers, my hoodie and greasy ponytail.

'Sure you could,' he says.

We're at the school gate. I hug him tight and wave him off as he leaps into the schoolyard, tongue flickering, tray of cakes held aloft.

'Mum, you're the most organised person I know,' says Leo, as we rush down the street to catch the train.

'What did you say?' I'm sure I must have heard him wrong. But he repeats it.

It is his birthday party; we are meeting his friends at Yarraville station then catching the train to the MCG where we'll watch Leo's beloved North Melbourne play Port Adelaide. Port Adelaide is doing badly this year, so we're confident that he'll witness a win.

I ponder what Leo can possibly mean about me being organised. Maybe it's because Tony is still at home, pacing the bathroom, having shooed us out the door and told us he'll meet us at the station. Or maybe it's the six packages of 'party' food in my backpack: six lamingtons, six small packets of salt-and-vinegar chips, six fruit boxes and six mini packets of Barbecue Shapes. I picked them up in a rush-and-grab visit to the supermarket between this morning's Auskick trophy presentation and the dash to the station, and divided them at the counter while supervising Leo's change into warm outdoor clothes. It was, in fact, horrendously bad organisation. But who am I to disabuse him?

'You're so *good* to take all these boys to the football,' says one of the other mums as she farewells her boy.

'Oh, it's nothing,' I say modestly. This is obviously one of those times when I get brownie points for doing something that is, in fact, the easy option—far easier than organising a home birthday party, with games, baked goods, decorations, party bags and a house to clean up afterwards.

Steven is excited and nervous about being on a train; his mum has told him that trains are full of drug addicts and homeless people and he should be very careful. Of course, she also believes that he's in danger of being abducted if he climbs the tree on our footpath with Leo, or walks to our house by himself.

Leo loudly points out a puddle of dried vomit on the floor as we step onto the train, confirming all of Steven's misgivings.

'That's the problem with public transport sometimes,' Leo says, with the weary air of an expert. 'It can be *disgusting.*'

The party goes okay—the boys all seem to get along and they are thrilled with the hot chips and *Footy Record* (with pens) we distribute once they settle in the stands. Jai, the oldest party guest, shouts on the train and touches every tree and public artwork on the walk to the MCG, but he is quickly absorbed in the game and his *Footy Record* once we arrive.

Against all expectations, Leo's team is thrashed. He and Steven both cry. Leo makes up a mournful song, which he sings like a funeral dirge: *Happy Doomsday to ME, Happy Doomsday to meeeee.* He tells me he hates

North Melbourne and that this is the worst birthday he's ever had. 'Why did you have to bring me here?'

'Because you asked us to,' I say, losing my patience fast. 'Fine, we'll never come back here. I hate football anyway.'

'No!'

Outside the stadium, on the grass before the footbridge that leads us back to Flinders Street station, Tony instigates a football game. I sit under a tree and watch.

When we leave, Leo is happy again, the game inside the stadium forgotten. Steven, too, has moved on. They're the same joking, slightly hyperactive band of boys they were when we met at Yarraville station.

It's only after we've dropped Leo at his dad's house the following evening, the day of his birthday, that I realise: not only have I not baked him anything for his birthday this year, I didn't give him a birthday cake. There were no candles, no 'Happy Birthday' song. I'd wanted to take him out for birthday lunch but he wasn't keen, preferring to stay home and play in his room with Steven. Instead, I walked down the road and bought them cheese and bacon rolls and cinnamon finger buns from Baker's Delight, which I served to them on a plate as they sat on the carpet, surrounded by Lego.

'Wow!' Leo had said as he spotted the finger bun. 'You're the best, Mum!'

I replay those words over and over in my head, trying to tell myself that he was perfectly happy with a cinnamon finger bun instead of a birthday cake.

The next morning, I ring Mark and casually ask whether Leo had a birthday cake at his house.

'Of course,' he says. 'It was a big chocolate one, with sparklers, and we all sang 'Happy Birthday'. He loved it. We had a *lovely* evening.'

I'm relieved Leo didn't miss out. But to my shame, it doesn't make me feel any better.

Wednesday morning. Ten past nine. The trill of my mobile phone wakes me. Even as I press the small green button to answer, I know it will be Mark, and remember that we have a 9 am appointment with Leo's speech therapist at the school. I am already ten minutes late.

I pull on yesterday's clothes, discarded at the end of the bed. Ten minutes later, I'm stumbling into the front office, pushing greasy hair from my eyes. The school secretary watches me down the length of her nose as I approach the glass window that separates her desk from the lobby. I ask for the deputy. She visibly weighs whether or not to answer.

'I'm supposed to be in a meeting with her,' I add, and she relents with a hiss like a deflating tyre.

'Dunno. Maybe in the staff room?'

I make a breathless phone call to Mark.

'I can hear you from where we're sitting,' he says smoothly. 'We're in the room next to you.'

Mark is on one side of a chipboard table strewn with documents, a pleasant-looking woman facing him. Eliza is not here. I am relieved, as if she's my teacher and I've escaped a scolding. Looking closer at the documents, I realise they are the Tony Attwood Asperger's workbooks.

Mark nods at me as I slide in next to the speech therapist. He continues leafing through them, pointing out the work he and Leo have done. Then he shows her his Happy Scrapbook, where he has encouraged Leo to paste pictures of things that make him happy. (Predictably, mostly footballers.) My creeping shame is in inverse proportion to the pride that puffs Mark's chest.

'Do you have these?' asks the therapist.

'Yes.'

'Do you do them with him?'

'No. Not yet.'

She smiles and nods.

'We were going to start doing them together, Mark and I. At the same time.' I give Mark a hard look across the table. As he turns the pages and Leo's childish handwriting swims from them, I realise, with horror, that I am leaking tears. I brush them aside as I strain to read the words, hungry for this access to my son's inner thoughts and feelings. (Why haven't I been doing this?) Despite my best efforts, pressing my fingertips to my lower eyelids, I am looking through a flimsy, wavering curtain of tears: now openly, silently, crying.

'I'm sorry,' I mutter, pushing back my chair and edging past the therapist, out of this cube-like room barely big enough to contain the three of us. Past the school secretary in her glass enclosure to the end of the hallway, where the choices are the principal's office or the sick room. I choose the sick room, where I stand at the small white sink, two empty single beds to my left, and sob into my cupped hands, the empty hallway at my back.

I know that I am being selfish, that I am crying for myself, pitying myself for being a bad mother. I know, too, this emotion coursing through my body is humiliation: tart and unforgiving. When I manage to stop the tears, I wipe my face and return to the little room, looking straight ahead as if nothing is wrong.

'We sit down at breakfast and at dinner and we talk about our days,' Mark is saying. 'I say, *What are you going to do today*? And we each talk about it in turn. And then at dinner I say, *Tell me one thing about your day*.' He beams as the therapist nods her approval.

'That's very good,' she says.

I am silent. Leo and I talk on our way to school; as we walk home; in the hallway as I watch him put on his socks; in the kitchen, where I cook his cheesy scrambled eggs for breakfast while he half reads a comic. He tells me about what happened at school and I give him advice, help him sift and analyse. I praise and critique. But I do not have any particular ritual, let alone twice daily, of discussing the day's events.

'Is something wrong?' Mark asks as we leave the office.

'No,' I say. 'Why would you think that?'

'No reason.'

I go home, shower, dress, eat and get a couple of hours' work done before it's time to cross town for my appointment with Naomi.

I tell her about my morning, just as an example of the kind of silly thing that's upsetting me at the moment, obviously because I'm overtired. I try to gloss it over, to move on to something else, but I begin to cry again before I can finish the sentence. Of course, if something makes you cry, if you can't quite let it go, a psychologist will tend to want to talk about it. I explain that I felt ambushed, that I hadn't realised it would be a show-and-tell. 'Not that there's anything wrong with that,' I add.

'Did you say the session was supposed to be so you could hear what she's doing with Leo?'

'Uh … yes.'

'So why was he going through the books and telling her what he does?'

'I don't know.'

'Why do you feel bad that you're not doing them?'

'Because it means I'm being selfish and lazy.'

'Why do you think you have to do them? He's doing them.'

'Because you told me to.'

'What?'

'You told me to. You said we should do them together, at the same time.'

Naomi says it would be good if Leo and I did the workbooks together, but it's fine for him to just do them with Mark, too. She tells me not to be so hard on myself. Then she asks how Leo is going. I tell her about what happened at the MCG with his Auskick group. I tell her that we're trying, but Auskick is not going great.

'It sounds like he could do with some emotional management therapy,' she says. 'Fortnightly. Tell them to focus on anger management.'

I berate myself on the tram home. Why would I think I need therapy, but not think of it for Leo?

At home, I lie back on the couch, feeling as if movement is too much effort, as if weights are tied to my limbs. I cry until my eyes feel like they have been hollowed out. I indulge in my oldest fantasy, that I am hospitalised for exhaustion. Time out from life. From responsibility. From being me.

'You're not selfish,' says Tony, coming in from the study. 'You always put everyone else first, especially Leo. Don't be so hard on yourself.'

My tears descend, from despair to self-pity to relief.

30. WHEN THE DOG BITES

It's the kind of awakening that makes you realise you did get to sleep after all. You gradually realise you're conscious, which in turn makes you realise you must have been unconscious at *some* point, though your memories of the night before consist of staring at the red eye of the digital clock by the bed.

I squeeze my eyes shut and try to eke out another half-hour of sleep before it's time to get up for Auskick. But the same wall of thoughts that kept me from sleep last night has sprung up again.

On the couch, Mum is buried under a quilt, only her hair visible: brown with a bolt of silver at her hairline. Tony and Leo are at the breakfast table, eating rice porridge and crumpets respectively. The dogs patter around the living area, their toenails clicking on the floorboards.

I kiss Leo hello and cut two slices of bread from the loaf on the counter. Tony puts his bowl in the sink.

The doorbell rings. I race into the bathroom, pulling the sliding door behind me. Tony is peering into the mirror over the sink, adjusting his hair. He looks at me for a moment before leaving to answer the door. I hear murmured conversation, lowered voices, small-boy yelps.

'How was he?' I whisper as Tony rejoins me, giving his hair a final dab.

'He's here,' he says over his shoulder as he moves out into the hallway. 'That's a good start.'

'Who's here?' asks Leo, bouncing on the carpet outside the closed door.

✳ ✳ ✳ ✳

Yesterday, Doug bit Steven in the face, just centimetres from his eye.

We were sitting in the lounge room together, watching television. Leo and Steven sat on the floor, talking, idly stroking the dogs. Doug is especially snappy with Steven, seemingly because he lives next door. It's a territorial thing. Yesterday, Steven was patting Doug almost absent-mindedly, as he lay on his back, paws in the air, apparently serene. Until he wasn't.

It was all over in an inexplicable instant—a flurry of barking and a snap. No-one could tell what had gone wrong.

Tony took the dogs away, to the laundry. I ushered a shocked Steven into the bathroom where I bathed his face with a washcloth and applied a band-aid.

'Are you okay?' I asked.

He shook his head. Tears, loosened at my question, began to slide down his cheeks. I kept him there as long as I could—a minute or two— before he asked to go home.

I asked Tony to take him. 'I can't face his parents,' I said. 'They'll be so angry. *I'd* be so angry.'

I've wanted to get rid of this dog—who ran away, snapped at children who came over, barked at friends and strangers alike and had bitten people in parks and on beaches—for years.

'I'm not having a dog who bites children,' I said. 'It's not fair to Leo, or to them.'

'I don't want a dog who bites my friends,' said Leo. 'I hate him.'

Tony agreed, quietly furious; ashamed. 'A dog is for life,' he said.

✳ ✳ ✳ ✳

The wind grows colder as Mum and I walk down the road towards the oval, climbing the path past the skate ramp, towards the hole in the wire fence. I duck and stand, holding up the wire for Mum to climb under.

'I hope you remember soon that I am getting older,' she says, as she straightens her back.

'Nah, you've got another ten years. Or more. Look at *your* mother!' Nana was still tap-dancing, performing in travelling revues at nursing homes in fish-net tights, when she was in her sixties. When Nana stopped at her own mother's nursing home, Grandma would stand in the aisle, holding tight to her walking frame, to shout 'THAT'S MY DAUGHTER!' and wolf whistle.

'Hmmph,' says Mum.

We queue for coffee and carry our styrofoam cups to the edge of the oval, where we sit on a bench and squint across the chalky expanse of sky to where the boys are forming lines and starting their drills. The wind sends a spreading chill through my body, settling in my toes and marbling my hands, even as the coffee warms my palms.

Steven's father appears behind the goalposts, drinking from a silver thermos and sucking grimly on a cigarette. I try to catch his eye, then try not to. Mum demonstrates how penguins take turns shielding each other from the wind, hunching like a bird in front of me.

'Look Jo!' she says, deliberately cheerful. 'I'm a penguin! See?' I think about the mark on Steven's cheek and watch warily as Leo pushes out his shoulders in his first sulk of the match, disturbingly early.

Mum tries to distract me with stories about supervising football matches at the high school where she teaches, while Leo's behaviour descends from bad to worse. I watch him throw himself on his stomach onto the grass; wander the oval crying; punch an opposing player in the arm; rail at the sky, giving himself up to the rhythm of his wailing. Finally, he drags himself towards us, face red and eyes swimming, shouting that he doesn't want to do Auskick anymore, not ever again. He wants to go home.

I am glaring into the wind and the grey day I have emerged into, from the sleep I don't remember having. I have a dog that bites children in the face and a child who has tantrums on the field and punches people. This is Steven's very first day of Auskick and his father is across the oval, watching our family's atrocious, antisocial behaviour yet again.

'I don't want to EXIST!' wails Leo and I snap back at him, like a rubber band suddenly let go: 'Neither do I.'

This is Mum's second day of long service leave; she is visiting before she leaves for a round-the-world trip, her first time overseas since she moved here from America, aged twelve. She watches sadly, abandoning her stoic cheer, as I grab Leo by the arm and pull him after me under the rails bordering the oval, hissing that I am ashamed of his behaviour; that he is a bad sport and I will happily take him home. Tears and snot run into his mouth.

Tony calls from the oval as we stand by the hole in the fence: me on the street side, Leo still on the football ground.

'Leo!' he yells. 'Come here!'

I let him go. As Tony holds him by the shoulders and talks him down from his hysteria, the team shed their red and black bibs, dispersing to kick a shower of footballs towards the goals in a celebratory frenzy.

Vanessa's husband climbs through the hole in the fence, his two sons behind him. He smiles, too brightly, as he passes. 'Terrible weather we're having.'

'Yes,' I say, as the boys look at me with interest. 'Yes, it is.'

I wave at Lucy, further down the hill, where she is chatting with a cluster of parents by the canteen. But she doesn't see, or pretends not to. When I climb back down the hill to join my boys, she is gone.

'Hi,' says Roger. We chat awkwardly about the game and how much Steven seemed to enjoy it, before his voice drops an octave. 'I was angry as all hell yesterday,' he says. 'When I saw how close it got to his eye. But, as I was saying to Tony, we don't want to make you get rid of your dog. Maybe you should get him a muzzle?'

'Oh no! We want to get rid of him! I can't have the risk of … I feel sick about what happened.' Tears rise in my throat. 'I'm so sorry.'

Steven asks for a second hotdog and Roger gives him the money. We move quickly to another subject.

The coach pulls me aside after Tony has kissed me goodbye and left for a scheduled qigong session.

'Are you alright?' he begins, his hand comfortingly on my arm. I nod. We talk about what he said to Leo, what I'll say to Leo. I admit that I lost it back there, too. I tell him that we're getting Leo emotional management therapy.

'I told him that he's my star player,' says the coach, 'that I rely on him. When he gets down, he's getting the team down. I told him they rely on him for morale.'

There are no words for my appreciation.

We all walk home together—me, Mum, Leo, Steven, Roger. The boys run and skip ahead, stomping their spiked football boots into the pavement. As we reach our side-by-side front gates, Steven asks if Leo can come over to play. Roger says yes, without hesitation. Leo comes home first, to change his shoes and socks. I apologise, telling him that though his behaviour was bad, so was mine.

'I only slept a couple of hours last night.'

He wraps me in a hug, his body a warm blanket around my chest and shoulders. 'Mum, you should go inside and have a nap now. Really!'

And he skittles off the front porch and across the footpath, leaving Mum and me to watch from the doorway.

Tony rings his best friend, Carlo, to talk about what has happened. He takes the phone into the study and shuts the door. When he comes out, his eyes are red.

A few hours later, Carlo calls. Tony speaks to him briefly, then hands me the phone.

'He wants to talk to you,' he says.

'What do you think you're doing, making Tony get rid of his dog?' says Carlo.

'He bit a child on the face.'

'So?'

'What do you mean, *so*?'

'So, you can't just give up on him. It's not his fault.'

'You know Doug,' I say. 'You know the problems we've had. This is the last straw.'

'You can't just get rid of a dog when it doesn't suit you anymore.'

'Carlo, he bit Leo's best friend, *on the face*. I can't have a dog here that bites children.'

'Well, you need to teach him. What did the kid do to him, anyway?'

'Nothing. He was patting him.'

'He must have done something.'

'Carlo, why don't you take him if you care so much?'

'You know I can't. We have cats. And we're moving to London.'

'Well, then.'

'I would *love* to have Doug,' he says. 'I wish I could.'

I hand Tony the phone, wordlessly, before I start yelling.

'How dare he call and tell me what to do with *our* dog in *our* house?' I say, when Tony has finished talking to him. 'It's none of his business.'

'He had an opinion,' Tony says primly. 'He had a right to share it.'

'No, he did not.'

My mum tells Tony how sorry she is, but that of course the dog needs to go because you can't have a dog biting people, especially kids. Tony says nothing, just listens silently and leaves the room as soon as he can.

Tony's mum tells me how sad it is for Tony to have to get rid of his dog, how a dog is for life, but of course she understands in this instance. She says that Tony will have to get another dog, of course. I say nothing; I just listen and change the subject as quickly as I can.

Carlo's wife, Jane, was once in an argument with a mutual friend over the relative value of animals and people. Jane and Carlo, who have several cats and do volunteer work for animal-rights organisations, were both on the side of animals. They said all the troubles in the world are caused by people.

'What if you had to make a choice?' said the friend. 'What if someone gave you a gun and you had to shoot a baby or a puppy? Who would you shoot?'

'The baby,' said Jane, without hesitation.

Tony finds Doug a home. On his last night with us, Tony sits him on his lap on the couch, patting and whispering to him. When he comes home, alone, he doesn't want to talk.

The next day, we get a phone call. Doug has escaped from his new house and chased someone down the street.

Tony finds him a new home, with an obese couple on a disability pension. Every day, they send Tony emails about how marvellous Doug is. They cook him meat for dinner, introduce him to the neighbours, dote on him. After less than two weeks, they call to demand we take him back. He bit the postman and growls at their neighbours. They are frightened of him.

Afraid we'll be stuck with the dog forever, I tell Tony we can't take him back into this house. Tony picks up Doug from the obese couple and drives him straight to a shelter where, according to their website, they guarantee to find the dogs a home.

This time, there is no possibility of coming back. This time, Tony doesn't chase down a progress report. I think he's too afraid of what he might find out.

It takes some weeks before the household is back to normal. Tony grieves; I feel guilty. I am guilty because I made him send his dog away, but also because I am not sad at all. I feel as if a weight has been lifted.

31. NEW FRIENDS

I first properly met Jai at Leo's MCG birthday party. He was the kid who touched every statue or sign we passed on the walk from Flinders Street station. I thought he was annoying—a naughty kid. But when Leo asks if he can come over after school, I say yes.

Jai is a popular kid; Leo is a little awed by his friendship. I can hear it in the way he easily defers to him. They kick the football in the backyard while I work at my laptop on the dining-room table. I hear them through the open back door. Jai doesn't take advantage of Leo's deference. He murmurs encouragement—*good kick, better luck next go*—in amongst bawdy jokes and swear words. I feel bad for judging him so quickly.

Jai's mum, Kerri, comes to pick him up, with his little brother Matt in tow. She is earthy, voluptuous, in a plunging floral dress over leggings and boots. Her hair falls down her back in long, static waves; her voice and laughter fill the hallway as she follows me through the house. Matt trails into the backyard after his brother.

Kerri tells me, after just a few sentences of politely traded small-talk, that Jai has been diagnosed with ADHD; he is on Ritalin. This, I realise, is behind his compulsive touching and constant movement. She watches me carefully as I digest the information. She is obviously used to judgement, both spoken and silent. She tells me that without the Ritalin, Jai wouldn't sit through his classes. He's called to the school office over the PA to take it twice a day, she says.

'He's a danger to himself if he doesn't. The other day, he didn't take it in the morning and in the afternoon I caught him about to jump off the roof.'

I find myself telling her about Leo's Asperger's Syndrome. She puts down her handbag and sits at the table.

'It's so annoying,' I say, 'when people tell you they don't believe in labelling children. That it's all a fad.'

'Yes!' says Kerri. 'It's so insulting. Like you're making it all up.'

Those people are well-meaning; they think they're reassuring you. They say things like, *Yes, don't all the kids have that these days?* Or, *Everyone's on the spectrum, really, aren't they?* Then they laugh, in an offhand way that suggests you can stop worrying now, because it's all an invention, just another example of overzealous labelling by the medical profession. As if you've never considered that before. As if *it can't be true* isn't your own first thought.

It doesn't make you feel better; it makes you feel worse. It suggests that any challenges you have are not authentic. That you're a fraud, making up excuses for poor parenting. (And in Kerri's case, that you're drugging your kid for your own convenience.)

We're so engrossed in our conversation that we don't notice when Jai wanders in.

'What does Leo have?' he asks. 'Asperger's Syndrome? What's that?'

My stomach clenches. I may not want others to dismiss Leo's 'label' as irrelevant, but I don't want to share it with his school friends either. Kids can be cruel about what they don't understand.

'It means Leo's brain works differently,' I say, my voice artificially bright. 'It's nothing, really. It's just about the way he thinks.'

'Does he have to take medication?' Jai asks. It's then that I hear the hope in his voice. The relief, as if he's stumbled upon a kind of belonging. Someone else who is different.

✱ ✱ ✱ ✱

A few days later, as Leo is brushing his teeth, there is a knock at the door. It's Jai and his brother Matt, weighed down by backpacks.

'Can Leo walk to school with us?' asks Jai.

'Sure,' I say. 'I'll just get him.'

'Jai!' Leo exclaims from the bathroom, spitting into the sink and hurriedly shouldering his backpack. 'Matt!'

I resist kissing him goodbye at the door.

My brother Simon has a baby: a girl, Lilly. She is the first child to be born in my family since Leo, nine years ago. I send them a butterfly mobile, pink and blue with wings woven in a patchwork of patterned fabric. The butterflies are braided on a wire, like an enormous drop earring. It's not quite the right present, more my taste than theirs. I buy it from the hipster baby shop down the street, a place that sells tiny designer clothes and retro ragdolls.

Mum is in England somewhere. 'We're all grown-ups,' she said to me before she left. 'People don't expect each other to change their plans for them.' She says that being overseas will mean she can buy Lilly something special while she's there, a souvenir of her birth.

'So, you'll be in Europe while the grandchild is born?' asked Margaret.

'It's unfortunate,' said Mum, 'but Simon understands. We've been planning this trip for a long time.'

'Go Grandma!' said Margaret, and offered her a broad wink. 'It's *your* time now.'

Nana looked after me every day, all day, for nearly two years while my mum worked. She had grandchildren to stay every school holidays. That's what grandmothers *do*. I understand that Mum has spent the past few decades looking after five children and a husband, then finishing renovating and selling the family home on her own. I understand that she often paid much of the mortgage for a sprawling five-bedroom home (and did all the cooking and housework) by herself, even when Dad was living with us.

I understand she might relish being selfish for once, I guess.

* * * *

Mark was the one who found the specialists to diagnose Leo; I take on finding a child psychologist for his emotional management therapy. I am picky about psychologists. The right one can help impose a pattern on the chaos of your life by guiding you to make connections. Showing you why you make decisions, so you can figure out how to make better ones. It's like holding a piece of paper with an invisible message written in lemon juice over a flame and watching it appear in relief against the heat, seemingly by magic.

That's what I want for Leo.

It's very different from someone offering you a message or solution of their own. It's about making meaning by excavating buried fragments that are the missing pieces of who you are, bringing them to the surface and putting them in the right order.

Average psychologists give temporary comfort, but they don't help solve anything in a lasting way. If you have good family and friends, there's no point paying for a listening ear. You pay for insight, to discover new truths.

'I need my psychologist to be smarter than me,' I tell Mark. 'Otherwise, what's the point?'

He snorts in reply. But I'm not being egotistical, at least I don't think so. I'm being honest.

'This is for Leo,' he reminds me. 'Doesn't that just mean they have to be smarter than Leo?'

I laugh. He has a point; this person needs to fit Leo, not me. But seeing as he's a child, and his parents need to work with him closely to help him succeed, I can't help feeling this person needs to make sense to us, too. To help us see and understand new things.

Like Leo, I don't trust authority figures (teachers, doctors, managers at work) just because they're in a position of authority. I need to trust them because I respect them as individuals who are good at their jobs.

I have references for two child psychologists, both of them experienced in working with Asperger's children. I ring the first one, whose focus is 'child-centred'. I like the sound of this; I have a vague leaning towards hippie-ish models, at least until I examine them closely. This psychologist's model is play-based, which means that she works with the child and lets them lead her to whatever needs working out, through play or drawings or similar.

'What if we come to you with an issue he needs to work on?' I ask. She doesn't work that way, though she *can* keep things in mind and address them if they come up, in the context of their sessions.

'Can you provide us with a kind of framework, with practical solutions?'

Again, it's not really that kind of practice.

The other psychologist is the opposite. She, too, focuses on the child, but she's all about addressing issues and coming up with practical solutions and plans to tackle them. She works both directly with the child and separately with parents to talk through any issues. She has toys in her room, too, but the focus is on talk.

I choose the second psychologist.

* * * *

A week after Lilly's birth, I fly to Adelaide.

My family was still a unit when Leo was born. Mum and Dad were still together; Nick, Liz and Sarah lived at home. They all flew over on the weekend after Leo's birth, along with Simon and Nana. I wanted them to stay with Mark and me—for them all to camp out in our lounge room. Mark, overwhelmed by sheer numbers, arranged a house for them to stay in, a short walk away.

We walked Leo between the houses in the pram; I changed nappies on their kitchen table and they helped Mark bathe him on ours. Babies transform so quickly at that age. They double—then triple—in size, as the weeks evaporate in a haze of lost sleep and new discoveries.

My niece is tiny and wrinkled. She has unimaginably small fingers, fingernails translucent as teardrops. I touch a finger to her curled fist, marvelling as it opens to let me in, a part of her holding a part of me. I am amazed to think that Leo was once so small, so newly made. We are tentatively making her acquaintance; we don't know who she will be. Not even her parents, who know her intimately already, know this. Yet they are involved in her every cry, her every meal, her every excretion, even (and especially) her sleep.

Kate is sore from her caesarean; she moves with difficulty and sleeps in an artfully angled armchair in the lounge room. Lilly sleeps in a bassinet by her side, though she is more often found burrowed into Kate's chest, or lain across Simon's knees. I had forgotten what it is like.

The aftershock that descends just as your life slips out of your control. The tsunami of emotion: love and exhaustion, fear and elation.

I stay with Dad. His house is at the end of Simon's street. It takes five minutes to walk from one house to the other; you only have to cross the road once. It's a three-bedroom house with a swimming pool and an attached granny flat. Dad bought it almost on impulse a few months ago, after he drove past a *For Sale* sign on his way to his tennis club, where he has been a member since I was three years old. The first thing he tells me about the house is that he can walk to the tennis courts in five minutes. (Then he tells me how close it is to Simon.) One room in his house is stacked high with boxes of tennis balls—he has recently become club president.

One of the spare bedrooms has a double bed, with an unclothed mattress and pillows. I find sheets and pillowcases in the cupboard and make the bed. My sister Sarah, who has moved into the granny flat while she studies to be a teacher, helps me ease the quilt into its pink floral cover. I recognise it from my parents' shared bed, years ago. We hold it at either corner and shake it flat.

Dad's new house is littered with hammers and power tools—there is hardware paraphernalia in every room, including my temporary bedroom, where an electric drill sits on a shelf. The kitchen is piled with cardboard boxes, some of them empty, others half-full of rubbish. Outside, under a covered pergola, Dad's weights bench is propped against the pool fence, in pieces. Petals decorate it like confetti. Behind the fence, the pool water is iridescent green.

I want to sit out here in the early spring sunlight, to read on the garden swing rescued from our childhood. But I can't relax amid this chaos. While Dad is at work, I decide to clean up, starting by ferrying the obvious rubbish to the outside bin and razoring the cardboard boxes into slabs that can be filed in the carport. Sarah comes out of her room to help; together, we collect all the tools and hammers, along with buckets of chlorine and planks of Dad's tool bench, and haul them to the back shed. The last thing I do is take a half-moon dining table from a corner of the kitchen and carry it into the spare bedroom. It is now my desk.

* * * *

Lilly is sleeping in the bassinet beside Kate's chair. Girls in leather bras and hotpants are pole dancing behind a rapper on the flat-screen television that dominates the lounge room; no-one pays any attention. I'm eating a chocolate doughnut I've bought from the bakery across the road. It doesn't taste like I remember; I didn't expect it would, but I'm still disappointed. My mobile rings.

'Jo,' says Dad, his voice strange. 'I've just arrived home.'

'Oh,' I say, realising that I've effectively stepped in and rearranged someone's entire home without consulting them. 'You have?'

'Thank you so *much*,' he says. 'It's unbelievable. I've been planning to get around to it, but it just seemed like too much.'

'Sarah helped,' I say. 'We did it together.'

'Well, you two are wonderful. I'm a lucky guy.'

* * * *

Dad's house is not far from my childhood home, the one I lived in until I was a teenager. I follow the creek across the road from Simon's house, the ribbon of trees and unkempt grass that winds along the main road and takes up again on the other side, leading me back through the years. I pass my old primary school, where Simon will send Lilly some day, along a path that changes from dirt to gravel and back again. It doesn't take long before I reach the patch of scrub across the road from the house we grew up in. The park seems so small now—a left behind afterthought from when the land here was cleared for development, back in the 1960s. But in my memory it looms large.

There is a bench directly opposite my childhood home. Dark-green painted metal with a curved mesh seat. It is decorated in crude, anatomically correct penises, spray-painted graffiti tags. The uppermost branches of the eucalypts whisper in the wind as I watch. It reminds me of Enid Blyton's *The Enchanted Wood*, which I once read, over and over, in the house across the road. *A-wish-a-wish-a-wish-a.*

That's the verandah where we were all photographed for our first days at school: me first, in tight plaited pigtails tied with red ribbons. I half expect to hear a dog whistle, calling me home. I can picture Dad now, standing there in his short red shorts, knee-high socks and his worn Life.Be.In.It T-shirt, little fingers inserted either side of his mouth as he blew. Our relatives would laugh, half-embarrassed for us, as we came running out of the trees in response to his call. He would shake his head back at them. 'Look! It does the trick.' It took years before we thought to be embarrassed at being whistled up by our owner.

This is where my brothers and sisters and I acted out our childhoods, where we played and fought and sat and talked. We even ate the weeds that grow here, yellow-flowered soursobs—we'd suck the juice of the bittersweet stems, feeling adventurous for gathering our own food.

This is where I first developed the habit of carrying notebooks with me, of compulsively writing down what I observed. I organised a spy club, the Sherwood Secret Service, with my brothers and the boy down the road. We would meet here once a week and read out our notes.

We moved from here when I was fourteen. I'd had two boyfriends whom I'd never kissed because I was scared I didn't know how to. Each had only lasted a few weeks—probably because I kept coming up with reasons not to kiss them. I'd had a long, impossible crush on a classmate who lived down the road, whom I stalked with fake-accidental phone calls and lots of lurking outside his house. But I was still pretty innocent. I once told a classmate that he needed *a good head job*, in an effort to be breezy and flirtatious. I thought I was telling him he needed a haircut.

Then we moved into a new house in a new housing estate, where my neighbour boasted that she had multiple boyfriends. *She* knew what head jobs were. She read her stepfather's *Playboy* stash while her parents were out. We hung out at the skate ramp at the top of the road, invented our own graffiti tags and scrawled them on our schoolbooks. My aunts and grandmother helped us move house because Mum had just been moved to a psychiatric hospital, where she'd stay for three months.

Dad, looking for a way to cheer us up, took our family van on a high-speed drive around the cleared land at the back of the development: mountains of dirt and precipitous dips where fields and gum trees had recently been. My brothers whooped encouragement in the middle seats; behind them, my sisters cried and begged to go home. Sitting next to Dad in the front seat, I looked out the window at the empty land and said nothing.

This is where I wore gumboots in summer because I couldn't be bothered with sneakers, where I weed behind bushes rather than go home to use the toilet. Where I spent whole days catching tadpoles, or sitting on a rock hoping my crush would come out of his house.

This is where I lived when my whole family was only a dog whistle away.

32. CRICKET WHITES

Jai has played cricket in the same club, with the same team, for years. The boys play football together in autumn and winter, then move from tight shorts and tall socks to cricket whites in the spring. Leo wants to join them.

'They're a great team,' Kerri tells me. 'Number one in the competition. They win the grand final every year.'

This scares me.

'It's very social. The parents have a few drinks as they watch and stay and have a chat afterwards. It's really fun.'

This scares me too.

But of course I say yes, to what I assume will be another bout of tears, tantrums and enforced socialising; early Saturday games replaced by Friday nights that stretch forever. More fierce, edgy, unforgiving competitiveness, where the person hardest on Leo is Leo himself.

He is the smallest boy on the team, a good year younger than the other kids. His cricket shirt billows about his knees and his kneepads rise stiffly towards his thighs, rendering his running wooden and clumsy. In his first game, he throws the bat towards the wickets in a misguided attempt to prevent himself getting out. The boys on his team shout at him. *You can't throw the bat!* But then, they explain why he can't throw the bat (and that it would only work if he threw himself, still attached to the bat, at the wicket). Later in the game, he does exactly that; his team cheers. Leo stands as upright as I've ever seen him, his chin held high, face bright.

The fact that the other boys are older, with an insouciant confidence about them that makes it clear tantrums would be, well, *babyish*, seems to guide his behaviour. And cricket is a much more structured game than football; a stereotypical benchmark for fairness, after all. And he is not as passionate about it as he is about football. Football is a heady, dangerous affair. Cricket is a pleasant relationship.

Mark is thrilled that Leo is playing cricket: he played for years, only stopping after Leo was born. In fact, cricket has been hugely influential in Leo's life, without him knowing it. Mark has one damaged eye, a permanently dilated pupil that sits oddly frozen beside his active good eye. He was hit in the face with a cricket ball during a game, early in our relationship, and was hospitalised. I was visiting from Adelaide for the weekend—I'd recently been retrenched and had been welcomed back to my previous job in my home town, where I was tempted to stay. I was sitting on Mark's hospital bed when he asked me to move in with him. We'd been together for only a few months. I said yes: it seemed like a thrilling adventure, to live with my much older boyfriend in Melbourne, rather than move back in with my parents in Adelaide. Besides, I was quite besotted with his mature charms—weekend trips to wineries, the ritual of the Saturday newspapers, long conversations about books. My previous boyfriend had been a cabinet-maker who lived with his parents; when I lost myself in a book, he'd hover, bored, in the background.

Without cricket, maybe that moment would never have happened. Maybe I would have stayed in Adelaide. Maybe Leo would never have been conceived, let alone born (which was less inevitable an outcome than you might think).

Kerri has offered to take Leo to cricket practice a few suburbs away, on Tuesdays, picking him up from school and dropping him home in the early evening. It would be tricky—and exhausting—for me to take him on public transport. But of course I feel bound to attend the actual games. They start at 5 pm on Fridays, and finish three hours later. Tony says he can't come because he's still at work when the matches start. Which is fair enough—though I think we're both aware that this is a savvy way to dodge the bullet of watching three hours of cricket.

Mark can't attend the second match. Kerri picks us up and drives us under the West Gate Bridge into an industrial suburb, to the ugliest sportsground I think I've ever seen. It backs onto a complex of oil containers, tin cans towering over spindly trees. On the other side of the cricket ground, facing the containers, is a row of houses, some with bikes or basketball rings in the front yards.

Kerri carries two folding chairs to the edge of the grass, where she greets the coach and introduces me to the two mums who've arrived before us. We sit under some trees and watch the boys line up to bat.

'I've got to go,' says Kerri. 'I promised some girls from work that I'd meet them for a couple of drinks. But I'll be back. You don't mind, do you?'

'Of *course* not,' I say, though in fact I mind quite a bit. What can I say, though? She's already being so kind by driving us to the match and taking Leo to practices every week. It's not her job to babysit me or help me make friends, as much as I'd like her to.

More parents arrive. They talk to each other, over my head. Then one of the mums suggests to another that they move to the other side of the ground. In pairs and groups, they pick up their rugs and their eskies, their folding chairs, and gradually form a staggered line to my right, lined up with the containers at their backs. I stay where I am, on my own, too shy to follow them.

And then it starts to rain, before Leo has even touched the ball. It begins lightly, with quick spits so surreptitious I wonder if I'm imagining them. But then it builds into a steady barrage of drops, thick and fast; the boys scatter from the pitch to the skirts where their parents wait.

'Where's Mum?' asks Jai. Matt runs from the other side, where he's been playing with friends. He echoes his brother. I tell them that she's gone to the pub, and Matt rolls his eyes. 'Again!' he says.

'What'll we do?' asks Leo.

I don't know. In the absence of any plan, we run to the playground by the carpark, where we huddle under the slide platform, the three of us close together in the small space available, the rain pelting us through the gaps in the wooden boards overhead, and blown sideways towards us by the wind. I call Kerri's mobile, but there's no answer.

One of the dads calls out to us, asking what we're doing, and where Kerri is. Jai tells him that she's at the pub; I tell him that I've called and left a message for her to pick us up early. The dad calls her too—he gets through, and tells us that she's on her way.

'Will you guys be okay?' he asks, looking at his son, who's watching us from inside their car, then back at us.

'Yeah, fine,' I say. 'I don't think she's far away.'

'Well, I'll wait till she arrives,' he says. 'Just in case.'

I tell him not to worry, and after an obligatory protest, he leaves, duty done.

It feels like hours as we wait, our clothes becoming slick and stiff against our skins, but in reality it's only minutes.

The carpark is empty, the cricket ground deserted, when Kerri pulls up in front of the playground. She sounds the car horn to signal her arrival, though of course there's no need.

'Are you drunk?' asks Matt, as we clamber into the car.

'No!' says Kerri.

'You're *always* drunk,' says Matt.

Kerri hoots, half-amused and half-embarrassed. She turns to me. 'He's always saying that,' she says. 'He thinks you get drunk if you have two beers.' Then she turns to the back seat. 'I only had *one* beer, Matt! How could I be drunk?'

And then the car lurches off through the rain, my car door still open, the folding chairs half in the front seat with me and half sticking out into the carpark.

We take Leo to see the psychologist, Ann. Her office is on St Kilda Road, a short walk from Mark's house. He is pleased by the coincidence. Leo is uncomfortable about seeing a psychologist; he squirms at the idea. In the waiting room, he sprawls on the leather couch, laying his head on its arm. It's as if he is trying to retreat from the situation.

'There's nothing wrong with having a psychologist,' I've told him. 'I have one. Tony has one.' This made little impression. 'Poppa has one. Or at least, he did. Nick has one. Margaret has—'

'So, you're saying everyone has one?'

'Yes! Well, everyone I know.'

'What about kids?'

'I don't know many kids.'

'Did you have one when you were a kid?'

'I wish I did.' I went to a psychologist once, after Mum had her nervous breakdown and while Dad was still recovering from his, when I was in trouble at school. She said I seemed to be doing pretty well, given the circumstances.

'It's just someone to talk to about your problems,' said Tony. 'Someone outside your family who you can tell anything to. And someone who can give you some tips on controlling your temper on the sports field. Won't that be useful?'

'I guess. Yeah.'

Ann is an elegant, jolly woman with white hair and warm eyes. She treats Leo as an equal from the start: not falsely elevating him to adult level, but speaking to him frankly and engaging with his interests. When he lolls on the couch, she pretends not to notice, reading it correctly as nerves rather than rudeness. (Whereas my impulse is to scold him to sit up and be polite.) When he picks up a texta and begins to doodle on her whiteboard, she lets it lead into the conversation. We come out with tentative bonds formed, another appointment, and some solid guidance we can apply at school and on the cricket field.

'That wasn't so bad, was it?' I ask, as we get into the lift and squint at ourselves in its mirrored walls.

'It was okay.'

'She's great,' says Mark.

We have found a useful ally; a wise guide to help us all through the years ahead. Mark and I feel lucky.

I'm sprawled across Leo's old baby quilt on the edge of the oval, eating crackers from a box. Beside us, on the tartan picnic rug—a proper one, backed with waterproof plastic—Mark reads a picture book to Quentin, who sits contentedly on his knee, eating a segment of apple. Kerri sits on her deckchair behind us, stately as a queen, her sunglasses a headband for her long red hair, a beer comfortably in her hand. She's telling me about the big night out she has planned—her sister is taking the boys for the weekend.

And that's when I'm stabbed in the hand—or so it seems. 'FUCK!' I shout, involuntarily. '*Je*-sus.'

The other parents gape at me, some of them glancing sideways at young children. A bee is disappearing from view; a long spike is stuck through my finger. I tweeze it out with my fingernails and leap to my feet, running in circles around the lawn in an effort to distract myself from the pain. As the shock subsides, I come back to the blanket and apologise to the parents, including Mark. One of the mums takes the lid off her esky and gestures for me to put my hand in, batting away my apologies. I wiggle my wedding and engagement rings off my swelling finger and zip them into my purse. Across the field, a sprinkle of small white figures squat and run and stand solemnly against a backdrop of browning grass and rainbow-splashed graffiti.

I recover myself as the pain fades to a dull throb, and accept Quentin's invitation to help him climb a tree. Matt follows us and scales the trunk with the ease of a monkey, watching, laughing, from the branches as I boost Quentin up the trunk.

* * * *

I'm in a bookshop on Brunswick Street, browsing its selection of diaries and calendars, when I hear my name. It's Sarah, a radio producer I've recently started working with. I introduce her to Leo.

'What are you doing today?' she asks him.

'I'm going to the soccer.'

'Who's playing?'

'Australia and Zimbabwe.'

'Oh, wow.'

'It's the Homeless World Cup,' I explain. 'My husband is taking him and I'm going to the pub for the afternoon.' I'm going to a blog meet.

'And my mum's not wearing her wedding ring!' says Leo.

There is a long, quiet moment as Sarah and I think our separate thoughts and Leo returns to browsing a pile of graphic novels. Chief among my thoughts: that Leo has inexplicably implied I'm plotting an afternoon of random adultery.

'A bee stung my finger,' I explain. 'I can't get my rings over it.'

Sarah nods and makes sympathetic noises.

* * * *

Leo wants to join Jai's football team next year. I've said no. His Auskick coaches have told me he has the skills, but perhaps not the emotional maturity, to play competition next year. But after his exemplary performance in the first cricket game, I told him that if he can keep his temper and emotions under control for cricket, I'll consider letting him join the football team.

'So, Mum,' he says, later that weekend. 'Do you think I'll be able to join the footy team?'

'Yes,' I say. 'If you keep going like this. It's looking good.'

'Thank you Mum, THANK you!' He squeals and throws himself at my waist in an enveloping hug.

We step out into the ebbing light to get fish and chips for dinner and a DVD. Walking back towards home, he slips his hand into mine. 'Mum,' he says. 'I haven't got a care in the world right now.'

'Really?'

'Yep. I'm just really happy.'

I squeeze him tight, carefully negotiating the fragrant paper parcel in his arms, translucent grease spots spreading across its surface. 'Well, that makes *me* really happy.'

He thinks. 'I suppose I do have a *couple* of cares. I care about global warming, of course. And wars and people not having enough to eat and running out of water. But everyone cares about that.'

'True. Well, at least everyone *should.*'

'But I don't have any *personal* cares.'

'Oh good. That's great.'

The last Triple R broadcast of the year is not recorded in the studio. It's a public event, staged on the rooftop of an inner-city pub. Nikki comes to pick me up; we're going out for breakfast afterwards. It's weird, travelling to do my segment in a car, with another person, rather than on a train and then a tram, alone. Though I'm largely pleased to have the company, my routine is disturbed. I usually spend that hour going over my notes, skim-reading the book I'm reviewing and practising talking about it in my head. I can't do any of these things while sitting beside Nikki in the front seat. Instead, I watch the early-morning traffic slow our progress across the West Gate Bridge.

'So, are you sad?' asks Nikki. I have told the producer that I won't be coming back to do the show again next year. 'Or relieved?'

'Oh, I'm relieved! So relieved!'

'Really?' she says. 'But you've been doing *great*.'

'Well, of course I'll miss it. So I'm a little sad. But I'm happy to have my Monday nights back. Next Monday, I'm going to watch rubbish TV for hours and eat ice-cream in my pyjamas.'

'But you don't have to prepare so much any more, do you?'

'Oh, Nikki, *of course* I do.' I rarely panic anymore, but I stave off anxiety by careful preparation as much as I do by the knowledge that I've done this—and succeeded, or at least not failed—many times.

She rolls her eyes, not unkindly.

When we arrive on the roof, I'm shocked at how many people have turned up to watch the broadcast. They are sitting on chairs, lining up at the rooftop bar or standing in clumps, shading their eyes from the morning sun. The producer tells me to go to the bar and collect a free coffee, if I want one. (Of course I do.)

'There are so many people,' I can't help saying.

'Oh yeah, the outside broadcast is really popular. Listeners love to see what everyone actually *looks* like.' I have been known to wear a poncho into the studio, or shorts and thongs. Luckily, today I am wearing a summer dress and eye make-up.

Nikki takes an empty seat in the front row and waggles her fingers at me as I stand nervously by the makeshift wooden stage, waiting my turn.

'Don't be so hard on yourself.' Nikki is methodically demolishing a plate of scrambled eggs with fetta; I'm picking at French toast slathered with maple syrup. 'You were really good.'

This is not true. I was *okay*: I didn't lose the ability to speak, didn't visibly shake and technically managed to fulfil the brief of listing my top five books of the year, albeit rushing through them rather lamely.

'I didn't say anything at all intelligent.'

'Well, you didn't say anything stupid either.'

I raise my latte glass across the table. 'I'll drink to that!'

I tell her about my bee sting, in some detail; she tells me about a friend who is returning from aid work in the Sudan. Her friend thinks she has typhoid. Nikki is worried she'll be stopped at the airport and put into quarantine.

'She *thinks* she has typhoid? She doesn't know?'

'There are probably no doctors where she's been.' She shrugs, then frowns at her plate. 'Do you think it's contagious?'

'I think so.' There is a pause while we consider this. 'Is there a cure?'

'I think so.' Nikki rubs at a lipstick stain on her latte glass.

'So,' I say. 'Your friend has typhoid and I have a bee sting.'

'Yep.' We laugh so hard that the crop-haired waitress clearing the table next to us looks up to stare.

Back in the car, I give Nikki a small wrapped present. 'Happy Christmas.'

She looks both pleased and alarmed. We don't usually exchange Christmas gifts; we both think there are too many people to buy for already, without adding to the task by bringing friends into it.

'It's just something small,' I say. 'I just felt like it.' I'm pretty terrible at choosing presents—except for Leo and my mum. It's impossible to figure out what most people will want, or like. But I saw this in a bookshop window near Leo's school and I knew immediately. It's a mug, made to look like the cover of a Penguin Classic. The title is Virginia Woolf's *A Room of One's Own*. I've bought one for Kabita, too: *Wuthering Heights*. My own mug library of sorts is sprouting atop the microwave at home, to Tony's bewilderment. ('Why do you need so many?' he says.)

Nikki smiles when she opens the little cardboard box.

'Thanks for your support this year,' I say.

'Don't be silly,' she says. 'You never ask for help. You should do it more.'

I hate asking for help, but I nod and say that I will.

33. A SURPRISE

I go straight from the airport to a family barbecue. My sister Liz greets me with a hug. She's wearing thick black eyeliner, lashings of mascara, a plunging black top with black leggings and knee-high leather boots. Gold chains of different lengths garland her neck.

'Where are you going?' I ask. 'You look like you're going to a nightclub.'

Liz shrugs. 'I never get to go out anymore,' she says. 'I just wanted to dress up.'

Liz and her boyfriend, Theo, have moved in with Theo's mum, taking the spare bedroom in her housing commission flat on the western side of the city. Liz tells me, casually, that without Foxtel her life wouldn't be worth living; the flat is small, the neighbourhood daunting and they have no money to go out as they're saving to buy a house. So when she's not working, she sits in their bedroom and watches reality television. It sounds miserable to me, but she says it's worth the sacrifice. She and Theo are engaged—or, they've agreed *to get engaged*. Liz has chosen a ring, which Theo has put on lay-by, and the plan is that he'll 'surprise' her with it. Then they'll be officially engaged, and can tell everyone. Until then, it's a secret.

I tag along with Liz and Theo as they go Christmas shopping. We've all practically grown up at Tea Tree Plaza. I caught the bus to school via the interchange in the shopping centre carpark. Most mornings I'd wander into the near-empty centre, its fluorescent lights dimmed, moving past rows of shuttered shops to the bakery where I'd buy an illicit chocolate doughnut for breakfast. On weekends, my friends and I would try on clothes we couldn't afford, walk circuits around the maze of shops looking for people to talk to (or about) and pile our plates high at the Chinese all-you-can-eat buffet in the food court.

Charlie Chan's is one of the few eateries of my childhood that's still there; it's in the same corner, though it's no longer a buffet—and only marginally Chinese. These days, it serves rice-paper rolls and made-to-order Vietnamese pho alongside the trays of fried rice and lemon chicken. I eat there every time I visit, ordering one of the spring rolls I've always loved and a bowl of pho, sprinkled with fresh chilli and bean sprouts.

Over the years, the centre has expanded to swallow up the old council offices and the library, replacing them with a cinema, a video-game arcade and corridors of ever-changing shops. It resembles a house that's acquired extensions over the decades to accommodate a growing family: a patchwork of mismatched styles, reflecting the eras in which they were added, from the 1970s witch's hat atop the roof of Myer, to the featureless block buildings of the most recent additions.

In Big W, Liz pulls a shiny pink box from the shelves and asks me what I think of it as a present for Sarah. It's a boxed set of Kate Moss's signature perfume.

'Sure,' I say. 'I suppose.'

She picks up another box, a more generic perfume.

'Yeah, get that one,' I say. 'She'd really like that one!'

Again, what do I know? But at least it's not by Kate Moss.

We part ways at the check-out, where I notice an old school acquaintance a few rows over. Blonde. Puffy. Pink and white. Hair pulled back in a ponytail. Face round, yet somehow delicate. As if she'[d] been stung and is in the first stages of an allergic reaction. I reme[mber] that she always thought she was above me, always flirted ridicu[lously] with the boys in our group to gain their devotion—from the tal[l-] shouldered one whom my best friend swooned over to the sh[ort,] pimpled one who was firmly in everyone's 'friend' cate[gory.] snap assessment and decide I've survived the years bette[r.] Without really thinking about it, I take off my glasse[s] into my bag. The world blurs and softens at the ed[ges] at my covert competitiveness—with a girl who's not even aware of my existence. After I've paid and left, I put my glasses back on.

If any of those boys we once knew were there with us at that moment, they would have chosen her again, in an instant. I still wouldn't rate.

Later, on Facebook, I discover that she's now married to one of those boys, the one I dated for three weeks. The one who dumped me after I threw his shoes in the bin in an overdramatic imitation of the kind of combative flirting I'd seen on movies and TV. (I don't think I ever quite got that it was the boys who were supposed to do the teasing.) I was secretly relieved; it took away the pressure to kiss him.

I decide to walk back to dad's house in the descending darkness. My shopping is piled in a canvas shopping trolley I've bought to keep at Dad's house; the wheels rattle over the footpaths as I walk, their cement grind competing with the traffic from the main road. But at least the traffic is distant and I'm making this noise myself. I'm relieved to be away from the muzak, the press of bodies and clang of voices, the chill of the air-conditioning. The night air is warm on my bare arms and legs.

The only people I pass on foot are a woman and her small boy on their way into Hungry Jack's. He has a white-blond rat's tail and *Crusty Demons* emblazoned on the bum of his jeans. He stares at me and my shopping cart; his mum yanks at his arm, not turning her head at all. No-one walks around here, except to their cars.

Eucalypts line the main road, eclipsing the powerlines. Their scent is in the air, mixed with diesel. The sky seems bigger than it is at home, the stars glass shards against the darkness. A car slows down as I turn off the main road, outside the public pools, and a kind of unintelligible hooting erupts from the open window. I get out my mobile phone and text my sister Sarah, to tell her I'm on my way. I keep the phone in my ⌐d to Sarah's number, the rest of the way home.

⌐or me in the driveway when I get there, standing ⌐he laughs as I emerge from the dark and

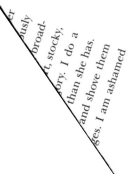

g to keep it here; you can borrow it ⌐ive.

hurt, despite myself—not just at the ⌐ looking at me, her mouth twisted in

Melbourne?' I say. 'Here, you think I'm ⌐al.'

Sarah rolls her eyes.

'Ha,' she says. 'You are odd. You just *are*.'

* * * *

I am sitting on the garden swing overlooking the pool, reading *Madame Bovary*, my legs angled to catch the sun, when Mark calls to update me about Leo's class placement. He has been allocated a teacher who's new to the school, rather than staying in his current class as we'd expected. When we spoke to the deputy earlier this year, in one of our infrequent special-needs meetings, we'd said that it would be best if his new teacher was someone Leo knows, as he always takes at least a term to adjust.

I'm a big fan of Peter, this year's teacher. His laconic style and calm demeanour remind me of Tony. He is country-boy polite, one of the only people I know to address me by my full name, Joanne. This respect extends to his students. He incorporated Leo and Conor's protests about the bay dredging into a class unit and pinned the newspaper reports to the classroom wall. A former rugby player, he has addressed poor behaviour in the schoolyard, particularly around sport, by asking Leo what his favourite football player would do. I have always felt welcome in his classroom, and have been very careful not to abuse the privilege; I try to stay away as much as I can.

To tell the truth, despite my reputation as the parent from hell, I've been a fan of every teacher Leo has had, apart from Kaye last year. But that year was so awful, the mismatch between teacher and student so pronounced, that both Mark and I are determined to have some input from now on. And, thank God, we are backed by a year-old letter of recommendation from Naomi.

Mark tells me that he has spoken to the deputy and asked why we weren't invited to talk about Leo's placement, as we'd been told we would be. He says she told him no such thing was ever promised, that we need to trust that the school knows what they're doing, that all their teachers are good for all of their students. He persuades me to let him have another try at talking to her, in person this time, before I call her.

After he hangs up, I sit with my phone on my lap for a long moment before I throw it at the brick wall opposite. It hits with a gunpowder *thwack* and falls to Dad's uneven lawn. Sarah comes running outside, a spatula in her hand. She looks at me kneeling on the grass, inspecting my scratched but unharmed phone.

'What happened?' she asks. 'What was that noise? And why were you swearing?'

There is good news the following afternoon. Leo can stay in Peter's class for another year.

'Rachel reckons they were probably afraid you were going to go up there and yell at them again,' Mark says. We both laugh, a little longer than the joke probably deserves.

We've been asked not to tell anyone that the class was changed; the deputy has been knocking back all other requests.

Leo arrives in Adelaide wearing the *Tantrum Alert* T-shirt Mark's mother sent him. I hate that T-shirt and perversely, my complaining about it has made him want to wear it even more. I point out that he loves it because I hate it; he doesn't argue.

'*Why* do you hate it?' he asks, for the millionth time. 'Why won't you be seen with me wearing it?'

I point out that if I walk around with him wearing it, it makes it seem as if I think tantrums are funny—and that I don't. 'It makes you look like a brat,' I say. 'And like I find that hilarious.'

'Oh, *Mum*,' he says. 'You shouldn't worry so much about what people *think*.'

'It's not about that,' I say, after a long pause. 'If you like or believe in something, you shouldn't care about what people think. But this is making people think I believe something I *don't*.'

He has no comeback to this. But he doesn't relinquish his enthusiasm for the *Tantrum Alert* T-shirt. I make him take it off as soon as we get home from the airport and put it in my suitcase so he won't wear it again.

* * * *

My birthday is four days after Christmas. Last year, Simon borrowed Toby's house to host a birthday pool party for me. I ask Dad if we can have a barbecue at his house this year, but he comes up with reasons why it's not possible. Chief among them is that he got rid of his barbecue when he moved. Simon offers to wheel his down the road for the afternoon; it is big and top-of-the-range, like everything he owns. Then Dad reveals the real reason. 'I don't know how to have people over,' he says. 'I won't know what to make.'

'We'll take care of the food,' says Sarah. He agrees, but looks so unhappy that we end up moving the event to Simon's house. I don't understand; a few years ago when he lived in the unit, he hosted family barbecues in his tiny courtyard whenever I visited. Sure, the menu was sausages and chops in white bread with tomato sauce, but none of us complained. Similarly, Dad encourages his kids to come over and use the pool as often as we can—and he's always delighted when we arrive— but he tends to slip inside and watch television.

'Is he okay?' I ask Sarah.

'He's always been like that,' she says, and I realise she's right. It's just more obvious without Mum around.

Dad comes to the barbecue; so do Mum and Nana, Ali and her partner, Graeme, my brothers and sisters. Simon calls me on my birthday morning to ask if Toby and his partner, Amanda, can come.

'Of course,' I say.

'Oh, and can Chelsea come?'

'Okay.'

Chelsea has a baby, a few months older than Lilly. The baby is asleep in her pram when they arrive, nappy bunching from her denim skirt. She wears a tiny black AC/DC T-shirt. Behind them, Simon sits Lilly atop his home-made bar, holding her at her tiny torso. He puts her face close to his and blows raspberries, making her giggle.

'She's gorgeous,' I say to Chelsea across the table, gesturing at the pram.

'Yeah, when she's asleep,' she says, with a smile that betrays her. She has always been self-deprecating, quick to put herself down before anyone else can have the chance. She hands me a birthday card. It's awkward, her being at my birthday like this; it highlights the transition we've made from friends to enemies to mere acquaintances. But I'm getting used to it.

I've made a kind of peace with our shared past. I used to think she was the reason that I can never be sure of relationships; that I can never be entirely certain that people really like me, even my closest friends. Even my partner. There is always the thought that they might mysteriously change their minds, like she did when we were in Year Eleven, either for some reason I never sense or for no reason at all. A part of me is always vigilant for clues of ebbing affection. It drives poor Tony crazy; I ask him almost every day whether he loves me. It's a joke and it isn't.

But Chelsea and I were kids. I've come to realise that having your friends mysteriously dump you is a fairly standard rite of female adolescence. I'm sure I've been part of the gang who's done the dumping too, at some point: most girls inhabit both roles during their lives, consciously or not.

I now wonder whether my vigilance is something else entirely. Maybe I'm insecure because I'll miss the cues that my behaviour is wrong or my presence isn't wanted if I'm not actively looking for the signs. And maybe I would be *more* insecure if I hadn't had that close friendship for all those years; if Chelsea hadn't pioneered the attitude that different is good, that the way to find your place in the world is to follow your own path rather than try to conform to the traditional one.

The morning after my birthday, Dad drives me, Leo and Tony to Semaphore, a beach suburb near the city where the three of us are staying in a holiday apartment until New Year's Day. I've made sure there is a swimming pool, but it turns out to be the size of an Oriental rug and is overlaid with a plastic cover. It's too cold to swim anyway. We walk on the beach wearing long pants and hoodies. The wind blows sand into my mouth and bends palm trees against an angry indigo sky. There is an ice-cream shop around the corner and we eat there every day. Leo and I eat the same flavours each time; Tony varies it according to his mood.

I meet Georgia, my blog friend, for lunch at a hotel on the shore overlooking the jetty and the playground.

'You're not blogging anymore?' she says.

'Sort of. Not really. I've just got too much work on, I guess. What's happened to you?'

'Same.' She's been working as an arts editor on an independent newspaper. 'Everyone's disappearing,' she says. 'They've all gone to Facebook.'

This is true. I keep in touch with my online community by email these days; I employ some of them as writers. Georgia lives nearby and she invites me to bring the family over for New Year's Eve. But we have plans.

Leo and Tony go to bed early. I read in bed, bedside lamp on, until it's time for us to get up and get dressed, to walk down the road to the beach and watch the fireworks. My sisters and their partners meet us at the flat just as I'm pulling Leo out of bed and finding his thongs. We've put him to bed fully dressed so we can get him up at the last possible moment.

The street is noisy with people, cars and music. Leo holds my hand and shouts joyfully into the night. Liz and Theo walk ahead, their hands intertwined. Her spike heels click on the pavement. Theo is a solid black bulk beside her, a comforting presence amid the drunken noise. Sarah and George walk behind us, also holding hands. Simon and Kate are home with Lilly. Tony floats between us, still waking up.

'Is Uncle Nick coming?' asks Leo.

'No, hon.'

'Is he out partying?'

Liz looks back at me and we laugh.

'Probably,' she says.

Leo nods sagely. 'That's what I'd expect from him.'

Semaphore Road is crowded with bodies—at sidewalk tables, treading the pavement, swarming onto the road, clustering on the grassy median strip. At the TAB, a ponytailed man leans over his table and strains for the gutter, soupy liquid spilling from his mouth to the cement.

We stop at the amusement park on the foreshore, its neon lights thrusting into the blackness. A school of shifting bodies fills the spaces between the spinning rides and flashing signs. Leo wants to go on the Wipeout, a ride that spins its passengers upside down, but none of us has the stomach for it. A friend of Liz and Theo's is operating the sideshow games; Liz urges Leo to join the line for the inflatable slide without a ticket, smiling seductively over the boundary fence.

'Who's your friend?' I ask.

'Oh, that carnie over there,' she says, waving at a bearded, stocky man in his early forties in a grey hoodie and jeans. I splutter in response.

'Don't tell him I said that! He'd kill me.'

The carnie comes over to talk to Liz and Leo runs to the top of the inflatable slide. He takes several turns, one after the other. He's sliding down the pillowy plastic when the first of the fireworks explodes over the park in a posy of pink lights against the darkness.

We walk into a clearing, away from sideshow alley, and stand, both separate and together, staring up at the sky. Liz is curled into Theo. Sarah leans back against George. And Leo stands with me and Tony, jumping on the spot in his excitement as we savour the last moments of the year together.

Liz rings me the next day to tell us that Theo proposed on the beach, after we'd all gone our separate ways. They are officially engaged.

It is a semi-annual tradition for my family to go out for a Mexican dinner on my birthday at the restaurant where I used to eat twice a week (on half-price nachos nights) when I first left home. This year, we're doing it a little late. The walls are hung with framed sepia photographs of solemn Mexican men and women in traditional dress; giant brass suns and moons adorn one wall of the main dining room. The floors are cool brown tiles, the ceiling thatched straw. Most of the light comes from lamps perched on the walls. The menu is resolutely Tex-Mex: mostly variations on nachos, enchiladas, burritos and chimichangas, with sangria and margaritas served by the jug.

Leo sits next to Nick and begs him for a sip of his Corona.

'I *love* beer,' he says. 'Please, Uncle Nick, *please*?' Nick tips the bottle to Leo's lips, carefully tilting it so that the liquid doesn't reach its neck. He sneaks a sideways look at me, gleefully anticipating my reaction.

'Go for it,' I shrug, sipping at the lemon slush of my margarita.

As expected, Leo pushes the bottle back at Nick in alarm.

'Can I have some of your margarita, Mum?' he says, changing the subject. In its cone-shaped glass, it looks like a slushie. I slide it across the table. He sucks at the straw, his cheeks collapsing inwards like deflated balloons with the effort, then pulls a sour face and shoves it back.

'How is it?' asks Simon.

'Yum,' says Leo, uncertainly. We all laugh.

'Really?' says Nick, ruffling his hair. 'It doesn't look like you think it was yum.'

'No,' he admits. 'Not really.'

Simon's mobile rings. It's Sarah, who decided not to come at the last minute. She asks him to put her on speakerphone so she can talk to us all at once. Then she tells us she has some news. She's with Liz, who has just discovered she is pregnant. I literally jump out of my seat.

'OH MY GOD!' I yell. 'THAT'S AMAZING!'

By this stage, I have drunk a glass of sangria and two margaritas.

'It's all a bit of a shock,' says Sarah. 'That's why we couldn't come tonight. I'm sorry.'

We shout congratulations down the phone.

'Oh my god, that means I'll have THREE Adelaide cousins,' shouts Leo. 'Am I going to have twenty cousins like you guys?'

We assure him this will definitely not happen. He thinks for a moment. 'I'm going to have *two* cousins whose dads have a Wii, now,' he reflects. 'I'm going to be *so* jealous.'

Simon and I separately text Liz messages of congratulations, with commiserations about the timing and reassurances that she'll be a great mum. She sends us the same message—thanks, and that she'll talk to us later.

We split the bill at the counter, where Leo scoops lollies out of the jar by the register. Spilling out onto the street, we theatrically pat our full bellies and trade raucous, fond insults. Leo calls Nick *anus head*. My good sense is overridden by the occasion and the alcohol; instead of telling him off, I slap his back and say, 'Good one!'

In the car on the way home, Leo, Tony and I sit in the back seat behind Simon and Kate. The mood is sober.

'When do you think Lilly will grow out of her cot?' asks Simon.

'I don't know,' says Kate. 'It'll be a while.'

'Do you think we'll be able to pass it on to Liz and Theo?'

'Ah. Well, no. Not at first. Lilly will still be in it.'

We are all quiet.

'We'll be able to pass on lots of other stuff though,' says Kate. 'Clothes and things.'

'I think I still have an old portacot in our back shed,' I say. 'They can have that.'

There is an unspoken undertone to our conversation, one that no-one dares to mention, as if it would amount to rejection of this baby. *This was not the plan.*

* * * *

I wander outside in my pyjamas to test the weather. The sun is bright overhead. Sarah sits under the verandah at the table and chairs overlooking the pool. Tinsel is still threaded over the clothesline. Her knees are drawn up, her bare feet resting on the chair. Instant coffee cools in a squat white mug on the table. She watches me open the pool gates. I pick up the netted scoop and tread the pebbled edge, dipping the net into the water and dredging the debris of the night before to the water's surface—leaves from the neighbour's maple tree, pinprick insects, a dead bee—before tipping them into sad piles on the cement border. The sunlight is warm on my skin; it illuminates the blue of the water, shining as if lit from beneath. At the head of the pool, I drop the skimmer and dive in, my T-shirt billowing at my back as I swim to the end of the pool and back.

When I raise my head, Dad and Sarah are at the pool gate, watching.

'The water's great,' I say.

'That's what people always say when they're in the water,' says Leo, coming up behind them.

'True.'

'You're wearing your pyjamas!' he says as I haul myself out, my boxer shorts weeping onto the cement.

'Yep.'

'Can I do that? Swim in my PJs?'

'Sure,' I tell him. 'But let me clean the pool first.'

I've been accompanied on my swim by crumbling flakes of algae, some of them viscous as drool.

Sarah and I tag-team the cleaning of the pool. The vacuuming is best done slowly: as if you're in a dream and need to push against curiously weighted limbs to move at all. I find it hard to achieve that kind of patience and control. I do things quickly and vigorously by nature. When Dad cleans the pool, the slow deliberation that always infuriated us when we were kids serves him well. He makes it look easy. An image from my teenage years surfaces: Dad painstakingly tying a shoelace as I wait for him to drive me to the bus-stop; I am jumping on the spot with a frustration that only seems to slow him further. Now, Sarah squats beside me as I train the vacuum on the bottom, making a slow aquamarine swathe and sending up clouds of dust. Then I sit on the edge while she leans into the long pole of the vacuum. The sun beats a tattoo on my arms and neck—warning of sunburn, and maybe worse.

It takes us two hours to get the pool clean enough to use. It's not perfect, but it's much improved. Leo jumps in and splashes around in his pyjamas. Then he wriggles out of them. They float to the surface, brightly patterned debris. He watches me, waiting for a rebuke. 'I'm naked!'

'I can see that.'

'Don't you care?'

'Nope.'

By the time Liz arrives, Leo and I are respectably dressed in our bathers, having a water volleyball championship over the inflatable net we got for Christmas. She emerges from the back door in her bikini, her body lithe, her belly almost concave. It's hard to imagine a child growing inside her. She looks so young—but then again, so did I. She is twenty-six. I was twenty-three when I was pregnant with Leo; the same age Mum was when she was pregnant with me.

I tell Leo to go inside; he needs a break from the sun. This is not entirely a lie. Liz eases down the steps of the pool and sits, half in and half out, while I loll in the water. She confirms what I already expected: that this is not good timing. She's not sure if they'll be able to save the money for a house now. Theo, on the other hand, is thrilled. Her lips crease into a sad smile. His family are excited, too. Their idea is that Liz and Theo should keep living with Theo's mum, and that she can help them look after the baby when it's born. Liz says *there is no way* that she can live in that bedroom while pregnant, then with a baby.

'We'll be looking for a house to rent,' she says. 'We'll move out as soon as we can.'

'Well, that's good,' I offer. '*There's* a silver lining.'

We laugh.

'It's not that I don't want this baby,' she says. 'Really. I just didn't want it to happen like this. I wasn't ready.'

'Of course.'

'Well … you know what I mean.'

'Yeah.' I look at the back door, checking for Leo. 'You'll be okay,' I tell her. 'You're just in shock.'

'I know.' She says it as if she doesn't believe it, not yet anyway.

'At least,' I say, 'you're engaged. At least you know you're going to be with Theo for the rest of your life, that you want him to be the father of your children. That's a start.'

34. A CHILD (WAS) BORN

I find out in a St Kilda doctor's office, a month after my twenty-third birthday. It's my first day back at work after a week at home; the stomach pains and nausea that have kept me wrapped in a blanket on my couch have seeped back into my morning of reordering stock and returning emails. The secretary whose desk sits outside my office door insists on driving me to see a doctor, though I tell her I'll be fine. But her kindness wears me down and I agree to let her drop me at her own doctor, a short walk from my apartment.

The doctor is a diminutive, thickly accented European woman of few words. Her glasses are comically large on her face. She leans over me as I lie on a bed spread with butcher's paper. I lift my shirt and unbutton my pants. She prods my stomach and lower abdomen, speaking only to ask me when and where it hurts. She decides to send me for an ultrasound; she doesn't say why.

'You not pregnant?' she asks, looking up from the notes she is writing for the technician.

'No!'

'Any way you could be pregnant?'

'Well, *technically* yes, but …'

She produces a white stick and sends me to the bathroom, just to be sure. While we wait for the results, she makes a phone call. I sit opposite her, watching the wall and listening to the waves of traffic outside the window. I glance down at the stick. A pink line is surfacing in the blank porthole, a message that I seem to have forgotten how to translate. Doesn't a pink line mean pregnant? I must have it wrong. Or maybe the test is defective.

I wave the stick across the desk. 'What does this mean?'

The doctor cups a hand over the mouthpiece. 'Oh,' she says. 'You're pregnant.' And then she ducks her attention back to her conversational partner as I erupt into panicked sobs. She quickly rounds off her call.

She asks me a series of pointed, practical questions. I try to navigate through my tears to answer them. Do I have a partner? Yes. Do I live with him? Yes. Is he likely to stick around? No.

In fact, Mark and I have just agreed to break up. I am moving back to Adelaide, to finish my abandoned arts degree. He is applying for jobs in London. I was planning to quit my job today.

There is no single reason we are breaking up; it's about compatibility. The ten-year age gap is starting to test the limits of our relationship. Differences that were once endearing have become exasperating—embarrassing, even. He likes activities: cricket, sailing, bike rides, group camping trips. My favourite weekend pastime is to sleep until midday, then spend the afternoon reading the newspapers on the couch or our balcony, glancing up occasionally at the strip of sea visible from our windows. His best friend is a textbook editor who plays jazz and is some kind of maths genius; my best friend is a chef who works at the local shopping centre and collects rare recordings by The Cure. Mark and Andy like to tag-team poetry readings after a few red wines; Jason and I like to sit at the window and make up stories about the abandoned mansion across the street.

I call Mark from the doctor's waiting room to ask him to pick me up and take me to the ultrasound. I can barely speak through my sobs and refuse to tell him what is going on. I'm not yet ready to say the words aloud, let alone on the phone. To say them would make them real.

I wait on the Nepean Highway outside the clinic, wailing into the oblivious traffic. Even in my panic, a part of me stands outside myself and is already ashamed. Ashamed of my wanton behaviour, yes, but more than that: ashamed of my grief about a baby, a baby I already know without question that I will keep and love. I am already betraying my child, just minutes after I learn of its existence.

Mark pulls up at the kerb. His face reflects my panic. He'd been concerned on the phone, but my swollen face and roadside keening have intensified his worry.

'What's wrong?' he asks as he opens the passenger door. 'What's happened? Are you okay?' He'll later tell me that he thought I was dying.

I spill the truth through a strangled chain of sobs, feeling a fresh wave of shame, as if this is something I've brought on us by my own stupidity. Of course, it's *our* stupidity. Let's just say (with a full knowledge of how ridiculous this sounds) we had never been particularly careful *not* to get pregnant. In fact we had joked about the possibility, never once thinking it might happen. I thought this was the kind of thing that happened to other people—like lung cancer or car accidents. It was the same blithe expectation that had landed me in Melbourne a year earlier: if you opened yourself up to the world, the world would somehow make sure everything turned out okay.

Mark's immediate response to the news is relief. *Is that all?* In comparison to dying, unexpected pregnancy is really not so bad. His next response, coming seconds later, is a distilled, measured version of my shock. *It will be alright. We'll figure it out.* Whatever I decide, he's happy to go along with my decision. Before we reach the hospital, I tell him I've decided to have the baby. It isn't that I want to have a child, or feel ready to be a mother. But if the child is there, I can't *not* have it. I believe everyone has the right to choose an abortion or not, but I can only choose *not*. And despite the shock of this new knowledge, despite the blinding panic, deep down I still think that everything will somehow work out.

As soon as we get home from the hospital, I call my parents.

'Congratulations,' says Mum, even though she knows that Mark and I have broken up, that I am coming home. My teenage sisters squeal their excitement in the background. I had been expecting them to be ashamed for me, devastated. When they're not, I dare to think that maybe I can do this.

Mark and I have several long, winding conversations about whether I should move back to Adelaide after all. I offer to stay. Mark says he'll have to think about it. Living with me *and* a baby is a big commitment, he says. He's not sure if he's ready to make it. It's fair enough—and will turn out to be true—but I am a terrified girl just two years out from my twenty-first birthday. I need someone to tell me, without hesitation, that they will be there to love and support me. This is something my family can offer and Mark can't. So I move to Adelaide and enrol in my university course. Mark goes to France for a last-ditch holiday, a compromise instead of moving to London.

We don't break up, not exactly. Mark contributes to my rent in Adelaide, enabling me to have a spare room where baby clothes pile up on the single bed my sisters use when they sleep over. They are all gifts, from my sisters and other excited family members. I am not ready to buy a cot.

Mark's mother calls me while he's in France, to check on how I'm doing. Sick and swelling and sweating in the Adelaide summer heat, I silently hate Mark for not taking me with him.

'Isn't it *wonderful* that he's in France?' his mother says. 'Aren't you *so glad* he went?'

'Yes,' I say.

My sister Liz accompanies me to the hospital for my check-up, where I'll find out the sex of my baby. I am sure that it will be a girl—*I have a feeling*, I tell people. The hospital is a half-hour walk from my flat. I count the numbered streets to the back of my inner-city suburb, then cross the main road leading into the CBD and walk through the Botanic Gardens, past the zoo, over the river and across the university sports grounds.

'I can't believe you want to know,' Nikki had said in an email. 'Don't you want it to be a surprise?'

'I've had my surprise,' I told her. 'If the doctors know something about my child, I want to know it, too.'

Of course, it is a boy.

To my horror, this makes me cry. We walk home across the Parklands, just my sister Liz and me, alone in the middle of the manicured lawns that border the city.

'Why are you crying?' she asks. 'What's wrong?' She is just sixteen.

'I don't want to have a boy like our brothers,' I say, and we both gasp at what I have just said. I didn't plan for this to come out of my mouth. I didn't even know what I was thinking until I heard it. This seems to happen a lot these days. 'It's not that I don't love them,' I continue, 'of *course*. I just don't want to go through what Mum did. I don't think I could do it.' Nick's ferocious temper sent my parents on a round of doctors in search of a cause and a cure. Simon left school without finishing Year 10 because they gave up on him from sheer exhaustion. Now, he's occasionally working at a supermarket, or selling vacuum cleaners door-to-door, but he's mostly smoking weed with his friends.

'You won't,' says Liz. 'It'll be different.'

Later, I share these heretic thoughts with my mother, who wryly tells me that I was no picnic either. 'Of course, *your sisters* have never been any trouble,' she says. 'But the rest of you … sometimes I've wished I never had kids.'

'Thanks Mum.'

'Your brothers talked back to me in a way I would never have believed *possible*,' she says. 'I would never have dared to talk to my parents like that. But you were trouble in your own way.'

She means the drinking and the marijuana and the nearly failing high school and the friends she didn't approve of. The wagging school and lying about what I was up to on weekends. I think all of this is just normal teenage behaviour; Mum wouldn't know, as she was never a normal teenager. She thought maths was fun and was a few marks away from being dux of her school. She only got drunk once in her life, and then because someone spiked her orange juice with vodka.

'Boy, girl; it'll make no difference,' Mum says. 'Both can be their own kind of trouble. It'll be up to you. There are things I would have done differently. Maybe I should have been tougher on you all.'

'You were really tough on us!' I say. 'On me, anyway. You were the toughest parent of all my friends.'

She shrugs. 'Maybe,' she says. 'Anyway, you can make your own future.'

At first, I spend weekends in a spare bedroom at my parents' house, then nights during the week, too. I don't want to be alone, but I don't want to be with people either. There's a certain kind of crowded solitude that only families can provide.

Mark and I spend hours on the phone every week, talking about whether I should move back to Melbourne; if we should try to make it work. He is excited about being a father—at thirty-three years old, he feels ready—but is less certain about whether he is ready to settle down with me. He floats an outlandish plan for our son to spend six months in Melbourne, then six months in Adelaide. *No way*, I tell him. I hold out as long as possible for the unreserved commitment I long for. Childishly, secretly, I want a proposal of marriage to somehow undo the wrong sequence of events. (According to the schoolyard rhyme, marriage is supposed to come *before* the baby carriage.) But eventually, I accept *Let's move back in together and see how it goes* as the closest substitute I'll get to a declaration of undying love.

* * * *

The truck full of my possessions that made the eight-hour road trip from Melbourne boomerangs back, this time landing in East St Kilda, in a tiny cottage with a square of lawn behind a high fence. Living with Mark makes me feel legitimate as a mother-to-be in a way that living half in a lonely flat, half with my parents, did not.

I pass the time reading my way through piles of books or walking around the neighbourhood and browsing in shops. We buy a cot. I watch after-school screenings of *Degrassi High* and its local equivalent, *Heartbreak High*, while eating Maggi two-minute noodles. The biggest fight Mark and I have ever had (apart from when I found the job application to London in our fax machine, prompting the decision to break up) was at the supermarket, when I wanted to buy two-minute noodles and he said he didn't want anyone eating that rubbish while living with him. We ended up standing on the street of our bayside suburb, outside the cafes and hairdressers, shouting about whether or not it was any of his business what I ate.

I borrow oversized shirts from Mark and wear the *Sonic Youth* T-shirt I bought in extra-large at a music festival. Using the hundred dollars my grandmother gave me for maternity clothes, I buy a baggy, red knitted jumper and cargo pants with an elasticised drawstring waist. I wait as long as I can before buying maternity clothes—and when I do, at seven months, it's one pair of stretchy pants with a built-in belly that I wear every day. That's it. Maternity clothes are for a grown-up woman, the kind who plans to become a mother and embarks on it as the logical next step in her mapped-out life. Maternity clothes would shift me out of my world as the twentysomething who had to give away her tickets to Hole because of morning sickness, and into the shadowy, adult realm of Mother—signified by the women who use antiseptic hand-wipes after touching things at the supermarket, or scrub the bathroom because the neighbours are coming over. Buying maternity clothes would be giving in to a whole new self I'm not quite ready for.

I go into labour in the middle of the night. Mark and I play Scrabble all day, waiting for it to get intense enough for me to go to hospital. I beat him for the first time: he is distracted by what's ahead while I am grateful for having something to focus on.

I am in the hospital for thirty-six hours. I had expected to swear and shout—I had warned Mark of this. But instead, I just cry.

When Leo is finally born, after what seems an eternity, I fall violently in love. He is so small and helpless and beautiful and he loves me, needs me, more than he does anyone else in the world. Already. Here is that undying love, that grand passion I've been longing for.

I will never again think about having wanted a girl, except to scoff that I am *glad* I have a boy, that girls are *a whole other world of trouble* and I wouldn't know what to do with one.

I feed him and then he sleeps at my side in Mark's arms while I am stitched back together. A nurse comes in and asks if she can have the placenta, for some kind of medical purpose. I say yes, through a descending fog of weariness. I couldn't care less what happens to it, frankly. Then she asks if she can take a sample of blood, also for research purposes. The thought of one more intrusion on my worn-out body overwhelms me. I dissolve into tears and turn my head into the pillow. I hear her walk away. I sleep, the deepest sleep I will have in many months, though I don't know it yet.

We go out for dinner in a laneway cafe—Mark, Leo and I—a few weeks after we get home from the hospital. Mark asks a waiter to photograph us, to mark the occasion. He is so proud: we're not going to change our lives just because we have a baby! We're still the same people.

I don't sleep much, for weeks and months. I get up at night and feed Leo in his tiny bedroom at the back of the house. Often, I fall asleep on the futon couch, holding him in my arms. Mark has banned Leo from the bed: he needs his sleep for work the next day.

I spend hours sitting on the couch, watching television and eating Freddo frogs as I breastfeed. The wrappers form purple piles on the coffee table. I let Leo sleep in my arms as his mouth loosens from my breast; I sit there until my arm is numb with the weight of him. When I put him in the cot, he cries. I study *What to Expect When You're Expecting* as if it's a religious text and try my best to apply the advice on settling a baby. But though it works in the evening, during the day he never sleeps longer than half an hour, unless it's on my lap or in the pram. I develop the habit of going on long walks around the neighbourhood, to the beach at St Kilda or down the length of nearby Chapel Street, detouring to browse in the shops. I breastfeed in cafes, or even sitting on the kerb, mid-walk. I give in to the rhythms of our days—feeding, resting, walking—and give up any real ambitions or to-do lists. During Leo's short naps or while he plays on a rug on the polished boards of our lounge-room floor, I write huffy letters to the editors of my favourite magazines, like *HQ*, or long emails to my family.

Mark and I fight over the state of the house (slovenly) and my approach to cooking meals (haphazard). One morning, he has no clean underwear and this is my fault. I tell him his underwear is his own responsibility. We shout a lot. He frequently asks, *What do you do all day?* I don't really have an answer; I don't know.

We drive to Adelaide for Leo's first Christmas. He is four months old. Four days later, I turn twenty-four. We stay with my family, who take Leo away and change his nappies in the morning and compete to hold him and play with him. We stay with friends of Mark's for New Year's Eve. They have been dating for a few months; they announce their engagement as fireworks spark over the fields of her family property. I go back to our room and cry. We leave early the next day to drive back to Melbourne and argue during the whole eight-hour drive. Why, I ask, doesn't he want to marry me when *they've* been together for just a few months—and we have a child? I know, on some level, that our relationship is fractured; but I believe that marriage would fix it, that committing to a lifelong partnership would allow us to relax our guards, to give more of ourselves without the spectre of abandonment.

He tells me that I'm only young, that he needs to wait and see how I turn out.

We will break up six months later, but this phrase is the beginning of the end. It breaks my heart. I desperately need him to love me without question. He clearly doesn't. The effect is like a concussion: first, there's the body blow that results in surface bruising and obvious pain. It seems to fade with time, but a hairline crack deep below the surface spreads, unseen and untreated. By the time the damage is obvious, it's too late.

Faced with the possibility of his departure, I retreat a little further every day. I teach myself how to live without him—and then I leave, before he can.

Now that I am the age Mark was then, I can see why he wasn't certain about me; how daunting it would be to commit to someone who hasn't sloughed off the cocooned ease of a teenager. I am both impressed and horrified by how honest he was about it.

* * * *

Becoming a mother did change me, almost from the beginning. It made me both vulnerable and strong in a way I had never been before.

When Leo was a week old, I remember walking home from the supermarket with him in the pram. We lived in an area that was known for its artists and students, for its Orthodox Jewish community (there was a kosher take-away shop at the end of our street) and for its prostitutes, drug addicts and homeless people. I was walking down the main street of East St Kilda, under the railway bridge and towards home, when a man began to walk beside us on the footpath, keeping pace with the pram. He had stringy hair and sunken cheeks, limbs that were skin stretched over bone. He wore a T-shirt on an early spring day, standing out from the stream of people wearing coats and scarves, as I was.

He leaned over the pram, his face hungry for something. 'Wow,' he said, looking at Leo, small and perfect: sleeping under the raised hood, blankets folded under his chin. 'He yours?'

'Yeah,' I said. 'He is.' Not everyone opened that way. I was just as often asked if I was his nanny—already.

'Oh, he's beautiful,' he said, and reached a skinny finger inside the pram to stroke Leo's cheek.

'I know.' I was shaking with fear, despite his innocuous words and the look of wonder on his ravaged face. He was leaning over my baby. *He had touched my baby.* I kept up a scared, scrappy conversation all the way to the corner of my street where, to my relief, he continued on with a friendly wave over his shoulder. When I got home, I shut and locked the door and took Leo out of the pram. On the couch, holding him in my arms, I cried tears of relief.

All the while, I knew how completely ridiculous I was being. I knew the fear was all in my own head, that the poor man had meant no harm. But I felt like we had escaped something.

Is this what I'm like now? I wondered. *Is this how I'm going to be from now on?*

In the same week, sitting on the couch during one of those long breastfeeding sessions—feed, sleep, wake up, rest, feed again—I watched the midday movie. (I was now used to watching whatever came on television during those times I was anchored to the couch; reading a book with a baby in my arms was harder than I'd imagined.) It was *Sophie's Choice*. I had always dismissed such stories as stupidly sentimental—I'd seen the beginning of it before, on the couch with

Mum, and wandered off, bored, before long. But now, when *that* scene came up—when Meryl Streep is forced to choose one of her children to send to the gas chambers or lose them both—I sobbed open-mouthed. Holding my baby in my arms, I knew that a moment like this would be worse than death.

I couldn't believe I had ever taken this kind of material so lightly. Stupidly sentimental? This was the most important subject matter in the world.

It happened again, in Adelaide at Christmas, watching the final episode of *MASH* with Mum. A busload of passengers was hiding from a nearby enemy. A baby wouldn't stop crying. Its mother suffocated it to save everyone.

'I can't believe it,' I wailed. 'How could she do that? I could never do that.'

'Well, she had to,' said Mum, affected at the normal level by a re-run of an old television show. 'Otherwise everyone would have died.'

'No,' I insisted. 'Not her own baby. I wouldn't. *I couldn't.*'

'You would have to, Jo,' said Mum. 'Are you telling me you'd let everyone die so your baby might live?'

'Yes!'

'Well, that's pretty selfish.'

The thing is, I don't believe her. Whenever any of her five children are threatened or in serious trouble, she is at the front line, negotiating with whatever authorities stand in our way, lending us money, finding us a place to live, or just being there.

She has taught me that motherhood means having the tenacity of a pit-bull and the endurance of a tortoise. It means being defeated, over and over again, by challenges you could never predict, and continuing to get up and keep going. It means never having the luxury to say you don't want to, or it's too hard.

Motherhood is not about inspirational phrases or vague affirmations. It's tougher, more pragmatic than that, and has a better sense of humour. Being a mother isn't a set of rules and conventions; it's not a job description you learn or a persona you adopt. It's both simpler and more complex than that; it comes from within.

And it doesn't, after all, take the shape of the women on cleaning-product advertisements, or even the other mums in the schoolyard.

It takes the shape of you.

EPILOGUE

Leo is a teenager now; at the time of writing, he had just turned thirteen. His passion for AFL football has switched to disdain after two years of playing competition, with varying degrees of challenge and success. During the World Cup, in the middle of a Malaysian holiday, he changed his allegiance to soccer and Manchester United, regaling our hotel waiter with his statistics and opinions at every meal. Now, he pretends not to remember the rules or even the players of AFL, though we occasionally catch him making a surprisingly informed remark while Tony is immersed in a game.

These days, Leo's obsession is film; his bible is IMDB, the internet movie database. Our breakfast conversations go something like this. Leo: 'Who's your favourite Batman villain?' Me: 'Um ... I'm still waking up.' Leo: 'Heath Ledger's performance as the Joker was one of the best of all time. He won an Oscar, remember! But if Bane and the Joker were in a fight, I think Bane would win. So ...'

It's actually pretty fun. I've introduced him to *Ferris Bueller's Day Off* and *The Breakfast Club*, Mark takes him to the Astor to see *Citizen Kane* and *Lawrence of Arabia* and Tony gets to relive *Die Hard* and *Blade Runner*.

Leo started high school this year.

Like many parents of Asperger's children, I've spent disproportionate time and effort negotiating (a polite term) with school authorities to make sure Leo has had the educational environment he needs to thrive. In 2009, I had to fight for six weeks—have his therapist write letters to the school, file an official complaint with the education department and consult with a lawyer—to convince his school to allow him to change classes. (He had been placed in a class with no friends and a kid who'd bullied him to the point of tears. The school refused to let him change because it was their set-in-stone policy that *no child* was to change classes *for any reason*.)

That year, many other parents of children with special needs had approached the school with similar problems. Instead of addressing those problems, or rethinking their policy, the school decided not to bend the rules for any of us. It was the equivalent of putting their hands over their ears and shouting, 'I can't hear you, I can't hear you!'

We were lucky. At the last minute, two days before the school year began, Leo was allocated a wonderful teacher with a passion for Harry Potter and a special place in her heart for smart kids who are a little bit different. ('I'm eccentric myself,' she told me.) I stayed away from the school as much as possible, only going there when absolutely necessary, creeping along the corridors, hoping not to encounter the principals. Mark, who had supported the fight but not driven it, took over as the one who popped in to the classroom occasionally to check in on how Leo was doing. I may have seemed fearless in my long battles with the school, but in fact I was fuelled by adrenaline and injustice. Once the fight was over, I was spent.

When it came time to choose a high school for Leo, we decided, after much agonising, to send him to the new government school in Mark's neighbourhood. It is small, with only one year level above Leo. The students use iPads. There is one easy-to-navigate building. They welcome parent involvement. And we were impressed by the principal, who is clever and articulate and at the cutting edge of education theory. It all adds up to the perfect environment for an Asperger's child. We count ourselves lucky that Leo is eligible to go there. (Even as my heart breaks at the inevitability that Mark's neighbourhood, where I can't afford to live, will take over as Leo's community, become his home base.)

High school is a big adjustment, like starting Prep all over again. New teachers, new systems, new friends. Homework. A flood of easily triggered, hard-to-control emotions. But all this seems logical, inevitable. At least we've been through it before. This time, we understand what's going on. We have a language in which to couch the issues that arise and a structure for dealing with them. We have a team of experts to draw on, people we trust, people Leo trusts.

I'm starting to recognise that these things come in waves. Crisis, resolution, calm, and all over again. That's life, isn't it? Life with Asperger's is just more intense.

* * * *

I continue to waver about whether or not I am really Asperger's. I have never been officially diagnosed. I still see Naomi, when I need her.

One day, she began a session by telling me, with some bewilderment, that she'd gone over her notes and realised that we had already come to a conclusion about my Asperger's status. 'We decided you were,' she said. 'Years ago.'

'Yes,' I said. 'I know.'

'Then why do you keep going back and analysing it?'

'Because when you said I was Asperger's, you said *you thought* I was,' I explained, a little embarrassed. 'You didn't seem absolutely certain.'

'Ah,' she said, looking at me as if to imply that this was a pretty Asperger's thing to say. 'Do you want to be properly diagnosed then? To remove all doubt?'

'No,' I said. 'At least, I don't think so.'

To be officially diagnosed seems silly to me. Maybe because there would be no purpose to it. It's not like I'd be using the language of Asperger's to discuss disputes with my employers.

Then, at the Melbourne Writers' Festival, I chaired a couple of sessions with John Elder Robison, author of a bestselling memoir about having Asperger's Syndrome and a participant in autism studies at Harvard University. I was sitting in the green room, talking to John's co-panellist Anthony, a creative writing lecturer who had written a book about his severely autistic son. John entered the tiny room and headed straight for us. He looked at me intently, then turned to Anthony.

'So, what have you written about?' he asked.

Anthony told him.

'But you're not autistic,' said John. 'How did you get an autistic son?' Then he gestured at me. 'She is,' he said. 'I could see that as soon as I walked in here. You're from an autism society, aren't you?'

'No,' I said. 'I'm on the festival programming committee. And my son has Asperger's.'

'And you do too,' he said.

'Probably, yes.'

'Oh, definitely,' he said.

Poor Anthony gaped at me in horror. When John turned to ask his publicist if she could order him a burger, Anthony whispered across the table to ask if I was alright. I assured him that I was, that the idea I might be autistic had occurred to me.

'How do you know?' Anthony asked John when he had finished with his order. 'How can you tell?' He looked guiltily at me. 'Sorry,' he said. 'Do you mind?'

I was as fascinated to hear the answer as he was, though I was also not as fine as I had pretended to be. John leaned in and described, in matter-of-fact physiological detail, how the alignment of my features, the way I held my shoulders, the way my mouth was set on my face and the way I looked at his lips and not his eyes when he spoke was like a flashing beacon to him, signalling my hidden identity.

And then it was time to go on stage, where I interviewed John and Anthony as though nothing had happened, as though I hadn't been unmasked in a closely packed room of my peers, in front of a publicist from Random House.

For the rest of the day, I recounted the story to close friends. *Isn't that so funny! What a weird thing to happen! But I'm totally fine!*

At home the next morning, I broke down in tears while drying the dishes. I was about to catch the train back to the festival, for another event with John.

'I feel like a freak,' I sobbed to Tony. 'Now I feel like I don't know how to act, because I know that *I don't know how to act.* And I have to interview him, on stage. And what if he outs me in front of everyone?'

He didn't out me. In fact, we didn't speak of it again.

I told Naomi what had happened.

'So now I *really know* that I must be Asperger's,' I said, pulling a handful of tissues from the box on the couch. 'That's it!'

She scoffed. 'How did he know?'

'He says he can tell by looking at people. He just *knows.*'

'If only that were true!' she laughed. 'I'd be out of a job! I could just send them all to him. Diagnoses done in fifteen minutes. Easy.'

'I did joke to my friend that he should call himself the Autism Whisperer,' I ventured.

Naomi threw back her head and cackled.

I had to admit, away from John's intense, not unkind, presence and his absolute certainty, that it did seem preposterous. She had to concede that his observations about how I hold myself and the position of my mouth on my face were, at least, interesting.

'But you look people in the eye,' she said.

'Really?' I sniffed.

'Yes.'

These days, I've come to a kind of peace with it. I think. I had one incident that clinched it for me. Well, as close as I can be clinched without the certainty of official tests.

Someone sent me a link to a Tony Attwood interview on ABC Radio National. I listened to it on my laptop in my study when I was supposed to be working on this book. I told myself that it was 'research' and not slacking off. Of course, I had heard much of it before.

But then he talked about women with Asperger's—and Asperger's mothers in particular.

'They can be really good mums, but unconventional,' he said. He went on to illustrate his point: you might go into the house and it'll be a mess, but they've been having a wonderful time finger-painting or immersed in some intellectual pursuit with their children.

I had a flash of myself, many years ago, living with Jason in a house where dirty dishes sprouted like mould in the kitchen, newspapers towered by the fireplace and a tent with a tunnel attached was permanently erected in Leo's bedroom. I drew flashcards of everyone we knew, and we'd play a game based on connecting people like dominoes, in a snake-like map of relationships that wound its way across the lounge-room floor. Sprawled side-by-side on our stomachs, we created comic strips on enormous sheets of butcher's paper: Leo told the stories while I wrote them down and illustrated them. 'It's like a childcare centre in here,' Nana once said, half-impressed and half-bewildered, looking around my texta-strewn lounge room and picking Lego pieces from the couch.

'It's like a tigress with her cubs. She's very protective of those children,' continued Attwood on the radio. 'But also that mum may have had her own issues at school with bullying and teasing and becomes very aware of the vulnerabilities of those children and does not want those children to suffer the same as she did.'

And then I turned off the radio and fled to my bedroom where I sobbed into my pillow until Tony came to find me, wondering at the foghorn cries he'd heard from the kitchen. He asked me what was wrong, but I couldn't speak for a long time. He lay beside me and held me tight as my tears and snot soaked into his favourite shirt. Years ago, he might have been really alarmed by my behaviour, he might have urged me to tell him, *now*, what had happened. But after ten years together, he's come to a kind of weary acceptance of my full-volume emotions. He knows this could equally mean disaster or mere self-flagellation. He knows an explanation will come, eventually, if he just waits it out.

I was embarrassed to tell him that I was crying—really crying—because of a radio broadcast. That I recognised myself in Tony Attwood's words, felt that click of identification deep at my core in a way I never had before. I was crying because I suddenly knew, without doubt, that I have Asperger's Syndrome. I am an Asperger's mum.

I was also crying with relief. I have always felt like a not-good-enough mum—because my bathtub is dirty, because I cook frozen fish fingers for Leo's dinner when I'm tired, because I forget to make sure he's had a shower or to check that he's changed his socks, and he's missed excursions because I forgot to sign the permission slip. Tony is the one who tells him not to read at the table and to use his knife and fork in the correct hands while I'm just as likely to pick at the salad with my fingers and bring my own book to the table to keep him company.

I was relieved to hear a professional—a world expert!—say that Asperger's women have all these faults, but they can be terrific mums anyway. I felt somehow absolved.

'Of *course* you're a terrific mum,' said Tony. 'You're the best mum.'

Hours later, I returned to the study and listened to the rest of the broadcast.

'There is often a different sense of priorities,' said Tony Attwood. 'Other people might say you're not doing what is conventional. But people with Asperger's have *never* been conventional.'

* * * *

Leo's thirteenth birthday was last week. He had a sleepover party, with Conor and Steven and his friend Brad, a super-bright, theatre-mad kid who is popular at school and really clicked with Leo. Brad told Leo one day, in an off-the-cuff remark, that normal people are boring and he likes to be friends with people who are different. Leo has cherished that comment ever since, taken it on as his mantra.

I made cupcakes for dessert: vanilla with chocolate icing and crumbled-up chocolate bars on top. Crunchie, orange Lindt, chocolate with almonds. I arranged them on a tray in the middle of the kitchen table with a candle stuck in one for Leo to blow out after we sang 'Happy Birthday'.

Tony wandered in from the lounge room and peered at the tray. 'Hey!' he said. 'These look fantastic.'

'Really?' I said. 'You sound surprised.'

'Yeah, I wasn't so sure at first,' he admitted. 'But they look great. I wish I could eat one.'

I hugged him, pinning him to the spot. 'You don't know how happy you've made me,' I said. 'You *never* like my cupcakes.'

When I was alone in the kitchen again, I took some surreptitious photos, just for the record.

The kids slept in a row on mattresses we laid across the bedroom floor and watched movies on a television we'd borrowed from Margaret. They had dinner of pizza and soft drink. I brought in bowls of chips and coloured popcorn and mini chocolate bars for them to snack on. They had chip fights in the middle of the night and scattered the carpet, the sleeping bags and their bodies with salty crumbs. They talked and played video games and checked in to Facebook on their iPads until well after midnight. In the morning, they hunched red-eyed over their pancakes, which they ate with lemon and sugar and maple syrup, all at once.

It was just like any teenager's sleepover. It was wonderful.

I went to a baby shower on the other side of town, leaving Leo and Conor lying on his bedroom floor watching *Lethal Weapon*. I put some fish fingers and nuggets in the oven and set the timer, leaving Leo with instructions on when to flip them over.

When I got home, he was lying in his bedroom alone, head on his pillow, limbs stretched across the hard carpet. Daylight had mostly leaked into darkness; the television cast a grey light across his body. The movie had changed to *Ocean's Eleven*. I took off my coat and heels and kicked them to a corner of the room, then picked up the other pillow from his bed.

'Are you enjoying it?' I asked, settling beside him.

'Not really. I think I'm too tired to understand what's going on.'

'You need a comedy when you're tired,' I said. 'You want me to find you a comedy?'

'Can I watch *30 Rock*?'

'Yes!'

'What are you doing?' asked Tony, as I dug into our DVD cabinet. When he put his head around the bedroom door half an hour later, we were lying in the now-complete dark, giggling at the screen. He returned with bowls of warm pasta, which he lowered in front of our faces before going back to the lounge room and Sunday night football.

We sat up and began to eat.

ACKNOWLEDGEMENTS

First and foremost, I'd like to thank my son, 'Leo', the best thing in my life. Thank you for being you. A close second is my husband Tony, who has been wonderfully encouraging and supportive, and endured all the times I shut myself away to write this. He gave me the greatest gift you can give a writer—he told me to 'write the truth' and not to worry about him. And he's the best stepfather ever, to boot.

I need to thank my family, too: Jane Case, for your rock-solid support and your shining example of how to be a mother; Phil Case, for leading the way in being true to yourself (and for your ever-empathetic ear); Simon, Nick, Sarah and Liz (another tenacious and inspiring mother), for being the people in the world I always know will love and support me no matter what—my first and best friends. Jean Clausen, for your unconditional love and sense of humour, and your example of ageing with grace and dignity. (And for offering to give me a kidney if I need one!) My sister-in-law Kate Lewis, who's just plain awesome. And my beautiful (inside and out) nieces Lilly and Ella, who I wish I saw more often. My favourite cousin Ali (sorry, my 18 other cousins—love you too) has been a reliable, much-loved friend and confidante for my whole life.

Big thanks to Margaret and Edwina, for being our Melbourne family, and for your love and support for me and Leo since the early days. And of course to my nephew (yes, that's what you are), the lovely and reliably silly 'Jordan' (aka Nurse Kate). Also to Jamie and Bron; Kirsten, Dave and Cormac (good to have you back!); and Kevin and Erin.

Thank you to 'Mark', for giving me the gift of Leo, and for being a terrific father and co-parent (challenging though the latter can be, for both of us!). Your love for and commitment to Leo has never been in doubt.

Rose Michael, my publisher, came to me with the idea for a memoir on Asperger's, after she read a personal essay of mine in the *Age* (published by Sally Heath—thank you, Sally). She has made this project a reality, put up with my neuroses (sorry!), and made me believe that I could do it. Thank you so much. Nadine Davidoff was the editor I've always wanted—and as a working editor myself, I'm annoyingly picky. She saved me from embarrassing myself, helped me see what was missing, finessed the final product into shape—and was always available to talk things through. My agent, Jenny Darling, has been an invaluable source of advice and publishing savvy, and so has Donica Bettanin. And Oslo Davis's illustrations lend a sense of character, mischief and life.

I also need to thank Louise Swinn and Zoe Dattner at Sleepers Publishing, for publishing my short story 'Hell is Other Parents' in *Sleepers Almanac*—it appears in an altered and fragmented form here. That publication meant a lot to me, as did the story's selection by Delia Falconer for *Best Australian Stories* (Black Inc.) later that year. Huge thanks.

To my writing and editing friends who read the manuscript (or pieces of it) and provided valuable feedback and support: Nikki Anderson, Kabita Dhara, Melissa Cranenburgh; Maria Tumarkin and Monica Dux (my unofficial writing mentors); Rebecca Starford and Rochelle Siemienowicz (my current writing group); Pauline Ryan and Kate Goldsworthy (my first writing group). This book would not be what it is without you all—I feel very lucky to have your friendship *and* borrow your expertise. I did not impose the book on Estelle Tang or Anthony Morris, but I did impose my worrying about it, many times. Thanks for listening.

Thank you to my former colleagues at Readings, especially my extraordinary manager Emily Harms (for everything), Chris Gordon (for the laughs), Martin Shaw (for the gossip and advice) and Mark Rubbo (for the job). To my current colleagues at the Wheeler Centre for putting up with me in the middle of book madness, especially my neighbour squared, Jon Tjhia, Jenny Niven, the fabulous Tamara

Zimet and Shannon Hick, my manager Pauline O'Brien, and Michael Williams, who has supported and encouraged my work in many guises over the years, before eventually employing me. And to my first publishing employers, who are responsible for my career (for better or worse): Michael Bollen and Stephanie Johnston of Wakefield Press.

I'd also like to thank my RMIT journalism lecturer Sian Prior, whose inspiring teaching led to the essay that led to this book. And all my blog friends—you know who you are. Just a few names: Clementine Ford, who was the first person to say I should write a book about me and Leo; Penni Russon, whose kind words encouraged me to think of myself as a 'proper writer', Tracy Crisp and Georgia Gowing.

Jason Wright was hard to keep to the fringes of this book: he was family for so many years and great (unique) company in many houses across two states. I don't know what we would have done without Mary and Liam O'Donovan. You both have a gift for friendship, for which I'm grateful.

And finally, a hearty thanks to some of the compassionate and insightful professionals who've helped our family with Leo: Janine Manjiniova (who has also changed my life), Ann Laufer (an invaluable resource), Leo's wonderful classroom teachers throughout primary school (except the one we had the year of his diagnosis), and his Auskick coach Paul, who was exceptionally kind, flexible and creative in his approach.